GEORGE WADE, 1673–1748

GEORGE WADE, 1673–1748

Denise Chantrey

ARTHUR H. STOCKWELL LTD
Torrs Park   Ilfracombe   Devon
Established 1898
www.ahstockwell.co.uk

© *Denise Chantrey, 2009*
First published in Great Britain, 2009
All rights reserved.
*No part of this publication may be reproduced
or transmitted in any form or by any means,
electronic or mechanical, including photocopy,
recording, or any information storage and
retrieval system, without permission
in writing from the copyright holder.*

*British Library Cataloguing-in-Publication Data.
A catalogue record for this book is available
from the British Library.*

*Arthur H. Stockwell Ltd bears no responsibility
for the accuracy of information recorded in this book.*

ISBN 978-0-7223-3917-6
*Printed in Great Britain by
Arthur H. Stockwell Ltd
Torrs Park   Ilfracombe
Devon*

Contents

Acknowledgements		7
Illustrations		9
Introduction		11
Prologue		13
Chapter 1	Early Years	17
Chapter 2	Military Career	25
Chapter 3	General Wade's Letters to Lord Stanhope	40
Chapter 4	The Fifteen	63
Chapter 5	The Bath Scene	78
Chapter 6	The State of the Highlands	88
Chapter 7	Wade Arrives in Scotland	104
Chapter 8	Back to Bath	141
Chapter 9	Wade's Roads in the Highlands	148
Chapter 10	State Visit of Tomochichi	170
Chapter 11	Old Scotia	181
Chapter 12	The War of the Austrian Succession	192
Chapter 13	The Road to Culloden	208
Chapter 14	The December Campaign	228
Chapter 15	Wade in Retirement	241
Chronology		256
Bibliography		258

Acknowledgements

This book is dedicated to the late David Wade, who asked me to carry out research into the life of his ancestor, General George Wade. He encouraged me to write this book, and also helped with the research in London Offices, Ireland, and the Bodleian Library.

Several others have aided me: Bath Central Library, who helped me find information from their rare collection of books; Colin Johnston and his staff at the Bath Record Office, who helped uncover items of interest about Wade's time in Bath; the Chevening Estate, who allowed me to include the letters between Stanhope and Wade; the dean and chapter of Westminster Abbey for permission to include a portrait of the monument in the abbey; the Scottish National Portrait Gallery, Edinburgh, who gave permission to reproduce the portrait of General Wade; John Freeth, who carried out all the photography in Scotland; Prior Park College for allowing me to include photographs of the panels on Wade's monument; and my grandson, Lee Matthew Chantrey, who was always on hand to give advice on computer problems. I would also like to give a special thank you to Alison Bowers, who not only proof-read the book but answered all my many queries, and supported me throughout. In addition, a number of individuals have also advised and assisted me in various ways, among them, Rick Norton (norton@rictor.freeserve.co.uk) 'Tumult in Glasgow'; Major J. L. Raybould, TD, webmaster B&C Norfolk Section Editor, for the Almanza poem; Mark Warner (mark@teachingideas.co.uk) for the illustration of a Roman road; Alastair McIntyre (alastair@electricscotland.com) for General Wade's report to King George. Finally, I thank my immediate family for putting up with the subject of Wade and for listening to my groans over all the problems of writing.

Every effort has been made to acknowledge correctly and contact the source and/or copyright holders of information on the life of General George Wade. I apologise for any unintentional errors or omissions, which will be corrected in future editions of this book.

List of Illustrations

Plan of a Roman Road	113
General Wade in retirement	114
Wade's shield in Bath Abbey	115
Wade's monument in Westminster Abbey	116
Minorca	117
Bath Abbey Church Yard, 1750	118
Wade's London home	119
Map of Spain	120
Louis XIV	121
Map of the cross-posts established by Ralph Allen, 1721–61	122
Duncan Forbes of Culloden	123
Map of the Rebellion, 1745	124
The bridge at Aberfeldy	125
Bernera Barracks	126
Melgrave, East Bridge	127
A Wade bridge just above Laggan	128
A Wade road at Glen Cochill	129
Weem Hotel	130
A sculpture on Wade's monument in Prior Park College, Bath, showing a new road in the Highlands	131
A sculpture on Wade's monument in Prior Park College, Bath, showing the bridge at Aberfeldy	132
Wade's house in the Abbey Church Yard, Bath	133
Ralph Allen	134
Map of Wade's roads in the Highlands	135

Introduction

George Wade would be the last to consider himself a military genius. He was not a Wellington or a Marlborough; but he was brave, wary, generous and methodical. Neither can he be numbered among our great politicians – he was probably too kindly a man to take his place with either class. It is probable that had he sought election as MP for Bath on a democratic basis, as now understood, he would still have been elected. He was a man honoured in Bath and the country at large. He was given an unpleasant job to do in Scotland, yet he did it without offence. He enforced the Disarming Act, yet he incurred no ill will. As Stanhope in his *History of England* says: 'that he became personally popular even whilst faithfully obeying the most distasteful orders is remarkable, and testifies to his judicious and conciliatory nature'. He was King to his 'highwaymen', paying them well and treating them with consideration. He concerned himself with matters officially outside his brief, such as education, and on behalf of architecture did what he could to save Shawfield, the only house designed by Colen Campbell in Scotland, which was sacked in the Malt Tax Riots in Glasgow in 1725. Wade was a man who made and kept many friends who might easily have been his enemies. He was straightforward and honest, and made a point of seeing the other man's point of view. He was a flamboyant character and he loved cards, wine, women, comfort, good furniture and art. He had friends in high places but gambled in low dives. He was vain and often commissioned portraits of himself, which he gave to family and friends.

The Highland roads and bridges are his best memorial. They may have been built for military purposes, but they were ways for folk moving out of the Highlands to learn about the world. In the light of his career the dark days of 1745 are largely forgotten.

Prologue

Branches of the Wade family were settled in the West Country from very early days. Wills and records from the 13th century show Wades holding lands in Chew Magna, Wraxall and Kingston Seymour on the Somerset side of Bristol; also in Thornbury, Rockhampton, Stone, Berkeley and Fylton-le-Hayes.

The Wades of Fylton-le-Hayes bore arms 'azure on a saltire between four fleurs-de-lis': their motto was *Pro Fide et Patria* (For Faith and My Country). Thomas Wade of Fylton and his wife, Margaret Hollister of Almondsbury, bought from Lord Berkeley in 1563 part of the Manor of Brokenborrow in Wiltshire, including the townships of Almondsbury, Hampton, Patchway, Compton and Henbury. From Thomas and Margaret descended three sons: John Wade, who became a colonel in Cromwell's army; Thomas Wade, later a barrister at law; and William Wade, who may have been the merchant instrumental in sending provisions and troops to Ireland during the Civil War.

Colonel John Wade served Oliver Cromwell, fighting with Horton's Brigade in Wales and acting as deputy governor during the siege of Gloucester. He successfully defended the city against the Royalists and was highly commended by the Protector. At other times he was busy providing men and munitions for the army and navy; and as overseer of the Forest of Dean he was active in blowing shot, forging iron and casting guns for the Admiralty.

In the *House of Commons Journal* it is recorded that Colonel John Wade was engaged in providing men for Ireland and sending oats and wheat to the value of £2,000; and in 1651, in recognition of his loyalty to the Lord Protector, Colonel Wade was given lands in Wales as a reward for his service in the Welsh Campaign. During the Commonwealth years he was appointed governor of the Isle of Man.

Also serving in Cromwell's New Model Army was William Wade, who was promoted to the rank of major in 1649 at the garrison in Bristol (*ref: Clarke's MSS*); and for his services to the cause he was given lands in King's County and Westmeath in Ireland. Major William Wade may be the son of William Wade, a merchant who was busy during the Civil War in sending troops and provisions to Ireland, as noted in the *House of Commons Journal* in 1643:

> That a sum of six hundred and fifty pounds to be paid to William Wade and John Parrott, merchants or their assignees for wheat to Ireland.

And in 1649:

> another entry on the humble petition of William Wade was this day read ... ordered that it be referred to the committee for Irish Affairs at the Council of State to examine the true state of the debt of fourteen hundred and ninety pounds viz six hundred and fifty pounds due by Ordinance of the twentieth day of May 1643 for six hundred and forty pounds and the other of two hundred pounds and to give order for the present payment of what shall appear to be due to the petitioner, or his assigns out of the assessment of fifty thousand pounds for Ireland.

The Prebendary Hayes Robinson (a descendant of Jerome Wade of Westmeath in Ireland) and Commander Evans of Nailsea Court in Somerset occasionally amused themselves in an endeavour to find a common ancestor, and they came very near to establishing his existence. The Reverend Robinson presented a portrait of General Wade and today it can be seen at Nailsea Court beside the portraits of Colonel John Wade and his wife Ann.

Commander Evans descends from Colonel John Wade, whose sons, Nathaniel and William were barristers-at-law when they fell foul of the powers in office and were imprisoned in the Newgate Prison, Bristol, implicated in the Rye House Plot. Nathaniel escaped abroad and joined the Duke of Monmouth in Holland, where he acted as Monmouth's agent and went to and fro between Holland and England, frequently in disguise.

George Wade's coat of arms in Bath Abbey is the same coat of arms as that of the Wades of Fylton-le-Hayes in Gloucestershire, who were granted the arms back in the 13th century. It is recorded at Blaisdon that in '1260 the King granted it to his cook Henry-de-

Wade'. The escallops on the shield signify that the bearer had made a pilgrimage to the shrine of St James of Compostella in Spain. They were later placed on a shield to show the bearer had been a crusader or had made a long pilgrimage.

There are those who believe that George Wade descends from Thomas Wade of Plumtreebanks in Yorkshire, whose youngest son was Armigel Wade (1511–68), a diplomat and Member of Parliament. Armigel Wade, or Waad, known as The English Columbus, was an Elizabethan voyager to Newfoundland in 1536. His monument proudly boasts that he was the first Englishman to land on the shores of the New World. He was Secretary of State to the Privy Council to Henry VIII, in which office he was succeeded by his son William Wade, later to be knighted.

Sir William was a distinguished statesman and a Member of Parliament and, like his father, he was a shareholder in the Virginia Company. Later he served as governor of the Tower of London during the Gunpowder Plot. Sir William was undoubtedly responsible for the widespread use of a rhinoceros crest in consequence of his receipt of a gift of a massive rhino horn from the King of Spain.

The coat of arms of the Wades of Plumtreebanks and Kilnsey is azure on a saltire between four fleurs-de-lis, and bears the motto *Pro Fide et Patria* but Dugdale in his *Herald's Visitation of Yorkshire* in 1665 stated the family were not entitled to bear the coat of arms – in other words, 'without authority'.

Until new evidence comes to light, the known facts are that George Wade and his brothers, Jerome and William, are the sons of Major William Wade who fought with Cromwell during the Civil War period and received lands in Ireland in lieu of wages. After the Restoration, Major Wade went to Tangiers, either trading as a merchant or in the newly formed Tangier Regiment.

Chapter 1

Early Years

Horse, Foot and Dragoons, from lost Flanders they call,
With Hessians and Danes, and the Devil and all,
The Hunters and Rangers, led by Oglethorpe,
And the Church at the Arse of the Bishop of York.

And, pray, who so fit to lead forth this Parade,
As the Babe of Tangier, my old Grandmother Wade?
Whose Cunning's so quick, but whose Motion's so slow,
That the Rebels march'd on, whilst he stuck in the Snow.

This broadside ballad published in 1746, after Culloden, mocking General Wade for his failure to turn back Charles Edward Stuart, the Young Pretender, is the only reference to his birthplace.

George Wade was born in Tangiers, North Africa, in the year 1673, the third son of William Wade, a major of dragoons in Cromwell's New Model Army, who had been given lands in Westmeath and King's County in Ireland. George had two older brothers: Jerome, who inherited his father's estates in Ireland; and William, mentioned in the alumni list of Westminster School. An entry in the alumni lists of Westminster School gives the following information:

> William Wade, son of William Wade, a Major of Dragoons in Cromwell's army, by a daughter of the Rev. Henry Stonestreet, Rector of South Heighton, Sussex, and brother of Field Marshal George Wade. Elected head of Trinity College, Cambridge in 1690, admitted pensioner June 28th, 1690 aged 18yrs and later one of the Canons at Windsor Castle; he died in Bath in 1732

The Alumni Association of Trinity College also gave information relating to the name of the father, added that William Wade was born in Tangiers, North Africa, in 1672, and confirmed the name of the father in an email dated August 2005:

> The Master and seniors, in their wisdom, ruled that from 1675 onwards, certain information including the father's name had to be given by men entering Trinity College. The admissions book gives William Wade, son of William Wade. Although the entry was not written by Wade himself, it is contemporary.

To date, no entry has been found in a parish register for the baptism of Jerome, William or George Wade, and until proven otherwise the above entry in Trinity College remains the only written evidence relating to William Wade as their father.

For the Tangiers connection we need to go back to 1661, twelve years before the birth of George Wade. When Charles II married Catherine of Braganza, she brought as part of her dowry the ports of Bombay and Tangiers and a huge and most welcome cash settlement. Tangiers at that time was a Portuguese possession – one they were only too anxious to give as part of Catherine's dowry. The port was expensive to run and continually under attack from the Moors, added to which the anchorage was unsafe for shipping. The British Government anticipated that it would be of great value as an operational base from which Barbary Coast piracy might be controlled, to the benefit of the Levant Company traders. It was hoped to encourage merchants to trade in corn, hides, oil, copper and such luxuries as gold and feathers.

As soon as the King's marriage treaty was signed, Admiral Montagu, the Earl of Sandwich, was sent to take possession of the port and await the arrival of the English garrison. It may have been at this time that the Wade family went to Tangiers, as merchants or in the military. Major William Wade may have enlisted in the newly formed Tangier Regiment under Henry Mordaunt, the Earl of Peterborough.

The army mustered on a cold October day on Putney Heath, and after inspection they set off to march down to Dover – a journey which took about eight days. The newly formed regiment were kitted out in their uniforms, undertaking training in musketry and drill in preparation for the warm reception they were to meet from the Moors.

In 1661, nineteen ships sailed from Dover for Tangiers, and

the regiment duly arrived in the port on January 29th. On board one vessel was John Churchill, later to distinguish himself at Blenheim and be honoured with the title of Duke of Marlborough. At first the accommodation was very crowded; but once the Portuguese moved out, life became a little easier. Mordaunt invited the Portuguese to enrol as soldiers, but they refused, and after some bitter exchanges they carried off everything of value and set sail for home.

During Mordaunt's time as governor he made a peace agreement with Abd Allah al-Ghailan (known to the English as Guyland or Gayland), the leader of the Moors, and for six months trade was established; it was not to last for long. The first task the regiments undertook was to reinforce the defences and walls against attack, and to build a fortified harbour, known as the Mole. King Charles offered Sir Christopher Wren a commission to survey and direct the works and fortifications of the citadel, but Wren turned it down on the grounds of ill health; the contract went to the great engineer, Henry Sheres. Mordaunt dispatched troops to castles around Tangiers, where they were better placed to ward off the attacks by the Moors.

In 1663 the Earl of Teviot became governor of Tangiers. The Earl was a professional soldier, and during his leadership, redoubts were constructed beyond the walls, which were further strengthened by a number of forts. Unfortunately the Earl was killed when once again the Moors attacked the port. Eventually the port settled down to an uneasy peace.

Many who visited Tangiers during its twenty-one years of British occupancy found it a charming place. After the grey skies of England it was delightful to find a clear blue sky and a sun that suggested perpetual warmth. The town was rich in trees and gardens, filling the narrow, dirty streets with aromatic scents and blossoms. There was hardly a house, wrote one traveller:

> without a little garden full of sweet herbs, and pleasant trees, especially the vines which run up pillars, made of stone and espaliers made of great reeds, all their walks and backsides and the spare places covered and shaded with vines, mightily laden with excellent grapes of divers sorts, sizes and shapes.

Food was plentiful and the inhabitants dined on cold roast beef;

Westphalia polony pudding; and all kinds of poultry, including well-fatted ducks. From the surrounding fields there was a generous choice of vegetables, including peas, beans, artichokes and wild asparagus, with apricots, peaches and calabashes. They could enjoy local Parmesan cheese, musk melon, all manner of salads, and Spanish onions 'thick as a man's thigh' all washed down with fine wines. The meadows outside the town permeated the port with rosemary, thyme, marjoram and pennyroyal.

Social distinctions were strongly marked: the Governor and principal officers of the garrison and their families formed the upper circle, followed by the municipal dignitaries; merchants; ministers; a doctor; and John Eccles, the gunner and writing master, who was in charge of the military school.

Was it here during his formative years that George Wade's interest in all things military began?

The Chapel of Sant Iago was converted for the use of the English garrison, and rededicated to the memory of King Charles the Martyr (Charles I).

The warm climate and two-week journey from Falmouth to Tangiers was a pleasant excursion for courtiers and their ladies. The ever present threat of attacks by the Berber pirates did not deter the visitors, and may even have added to the excitement of this foreign port. There were the usual amusements: balls, banquets, cards and music. There were pretty walks and gardens, and a popular resort, called Whitehall, where the officers and their ladies refreshed and diverted themselves. For George Wade and his brothers growing up in the garrison, Tangiers must have offered a range of excitement.

The Earl of Middleton succeeded as governor in 1668; in that year Tangiers was declared a free city and, with this development, Middleton faced new problems. Jewish and European settlers from Morocco, Spain and France had arrived in the four years Tangiers was without a governor following the death of the Earl of Teviot.

This turbulent civilian population compounded Middleton's difficulties and, with the continuing threat from the ferocious forces of the Emperor of Morocco, Middleton requested reinforcements. His request went unanswered. Middleton in despair became alcoholic, and died in 1675 after falling from his horse. It was a tragic end for a leader who was well loved by those under his command.

Three more governors were to control Tangiers before its

closure in 1684. It had become a liability – remote, poorly defended and surrounded by hostile Arab forces. It was reckoned that maintaining Tangiers cost the government some £70,000 a year. In 1683 the King resolved, in the interest of economy, to withdraw the English presence from Tangiers, and Samuel Pepys, former treasurer of the Tangier Committee in London, was sent by royal command to settle finances and to supervise the evacuation of the port.

Sailing with Pepys on the *Grafton* from Spithead was Dr Trumbull, a brilliant young civilian learned in law; Dr Lawrence, the physician; Will Hewer, the current treasurer of the Tangier Committee; Henry Sheres, the celebrated engineer, who had completed the Mole at Tangiers and was now sent to dismantle the port; and Dr Thomas Ken, the churchman. They were only a few days out to sea when the ship ran into severe weather conditions in the Atlantic. The fleet, driven far off its course to the north, ran through driving rain towards the coast of Ireland. Pepys, suffering from nausea, gave up the unequal struggle and went to bed. Poor Will Hewer lay prostrate in his cabin with seasickness. The following day the weather improved considerably and the fleet made steady progress towards Tangiers. They arrived on September 13th. The coast had been described a few years before in an unpolished verse by a naval chaplain who, like Pepys, was also a secret diarist:

> No sooner from our top-mast we see
> The Turkish hills, the coasts of Barbary,
> But Spain salutes us and her shores discloses,
> And lofty hills against the Turk opposes.

On going ashore, Pepys was dismayed at what he found in the port – corruption, a moral decline and the virtual collapse of discipline. It was evident that the port must be swiftly abandoned. The committee requested all those with property and commercial interests in Tangiers to present their requirements to Samuel Pepys in the Town House.

By 25th October this work was done, and he took a well-earned break by travelling to Seville for a few days. On his return, the business continued of winding down the port, dismantling the Mole, closing down the garrison and arranging passage home for the regiments and the merchants, their wives and children. Most of the ships were back in England by February 1684. The Port of Tangiers was eventually sold off to the East India Company.

On their return home, there was a need to find new schools for the young Wades. William was found a place at Westminster School, but his brother, George, was not listed amongst the boys who attended there. It is possible that he continued his education under the tutelage of his schoolmaster, John Eccles; another possibility is that he attended St Paul's School in London, which gave instruction in military history. John Churchill, later the Duke of Marlborough, and Pepys himself spent some of their schooldays there.

In 1685 James II succeeded to the throne on the death of his brother, Charles II. This sparked a new Protestant rebellion, and in June of that year the Duke of Monmouth landed at Lyme in Dorset. Monmouth was the firstborn illegitimate son of Charles II and Lucy Walter. Had he been born on the right side of the blanket he would already have been king. There were then, and there are still, believers in a marriage between Charles and Lucy Walter.

Among Monmouth's officers, Nathaniel Wade, second in command and acting commanding officer of the Red Regiment, stands out for ability and courage. His father had been a colonel in Cromwell's army. Monmouth led his men against the Royalist forces, but his amateur soldiers, who were mainly drawn from the peasant class in the West Country, were no match for the Royalists and they were easily crushed by John Churchill, the King's commander at Sedgemoor. The rebels were brought before the Lord Chief Justice, George, Baron Jeffreys of Wem and four other senior judges at the autumn assizes on the Western Circuit. Four thousand were brought to justice and sentenced according to their involvement in the rebellion. Public hangings took place in the towns and villages throughout Somerset. Burning entrails, and corpses quartered, boiled in salt and dipped in pitch for long-term exhibition, were among the proceedings taken to strike terror into the West Country. The alternative to hanging was transportation to the West Indies as an indentured servant for a term of ten years. In 1690, however, there was a change of government, and free pardons were given. The Duke of Monmouth was not so fortunate – he was taken to London and executed in the July of that year.

Nathaniel Wade, whose narrative is the best contemporary account of the rebellion, made a list of those officers whom

Monmouth commissioned on board ship. Wade 'remembered' those the King could not arrest: a few killed at Sedgemoor; a few, like Colonel Holmes, already tried and hanged; a few, like Colonel Manley and Colonel Venner, already safe abroad. When Wade, badly wounded, was brought to Windsor Castle, his life depended on a disclosure of information. He was able to smuggle out a letter with his washing, begging for the names of men known to have been killed or safely abroad. The names reached him tucked in the pleats of his 'good Holland shirt', and when submitted to the King, who came in person to see him, provoked the comment "Your friends, Mr Wade, seem to be among the dead." Nathaniel received a royal pardon and returned to his home in Bristol.

He became a great partisan of James II; and it was through his means that the King illegally removed from office some of the town council, and substituted others of different political opinions. Seyer, in his history of Bristol, states:

> The contriver of all this mischief, a crafty and intriguing man, Nathaniel Wade, was rewarded with the office of Town Clerk. In 1681 he was practising as a barrister in Bristol and in 1711 he was Steward of the Sheriff's Court.

Nathaniel died at Nailsea Court in 1718, but he was never able to rid himself of the name 'that traitor Wade'.

The roll call of the rebels can be found in Volume 79 of the Somerset Record Society.

Slowly and insidiously James II moved Catholics into places of high office; the country was growing ever more uneasy and, when a son was born to James and Mary in 1688, alarm bells started ringing. Mary had suffered many miscarriages, and it was believed in some quarters that the boy was brought into the Queen's bedroom in a warming pan. The Anglican leaders refused to accept that James Edward was in truth the King's son and they started negotiating with those who were in touch with William of Orange to offer the throne to him and his wife, Mary, who was the daughter of James II. William accepted. He sailed for England, and landed at Torbay on November 5th.

The King was not a coward, but rebellion unnerved him, especially when some of his trained officers started to desert. Among the first to go was John Churchill, the King's friend and commander of the Royal Army. His terrible memories of how his father had met his end resulted in James II fleeing the country, and on Christmas Day 1688 he arrived in France.

The exiled king was determined to win back his throne, however. In March 1689 he landed in Ireland and, with support from the French, he summoned a Parliament in Dublin two months later, in which he put forward plans to repeal the hated Act of Settlement (whereby Irish Catholics hoped to recover lands appropriated over the past century by English Protestants). However, little could be done until he had achieved control over the whole country.

William III was urged to take action before it was too late, but he was eager to fight France in the Netherlands and regarded Ireland as a minor irritant. He authorised the dispatch of an expedition to Ireland in 1689, but it was not until June of the following year that he himself took control. There followed some very bitter exchanges between the Jacobites and Williamites, ending with a decisive encounter between the two kings at the Battle of the Boyne in July 1690. James II was defeated, gave up the struggle and retired to France.

It is believed in the Wade family that George Wade first saw action at the Battle of Augrim in 1691, but this has been discounted as at that time he was with the Earl of Bath's Regiment in the Channel Islands. In 1690 a sharp battle was fought at Tyrellspass, County Westmeath, between the Jacobites and Williamites, and it resulted in a bloody defeat for the Jacobites. Tyrellspass was subsequently heavily garrisoned by the Williamites, who regarded it, and Mullingar, as the two most strategic locations in their control of the Irish Midlands. George Wade may have witnessed the battle scenes taking place near his home and been prompted to enter the army; in December 1690 he enlisted as ensign in Sir Richard Trevanion's Regiment of the 10th Foot. However, there was a General Wade at the Battle of Augrim, who may have been related to the family, and this may be the source of confusion. In time the family were able to regain their lost lands and return home to Tyrellspass.

Chapter 2

Military Career

George Wade was appointed ensign in Richard Trevanion's Company in the Earl of Bath's Regiment in London on December 25th 1690. Before sailing for Europe, the regiment did a spell of duty in the Channel Islands, but in the spring of 1691 it transferred to Flanders as William III concentrated his troops to confront Louis XIV in the Low Countries. The background to this war is that by 1680 France threatened to dominate and rule the whole of Europe. France at that time was not only the largest nation in terms of population and land area, but also had the most powerful army. The commander of the British Army was William of Orange, who engaged in battle at Steenkerke, a village in the Belgian province of Hainaut, against Marshal Duke François of Luxembourg. After an unsuccessful attempt throughout June and July of 1692, in August William of Orange attacked the main French force, which was in an established entrenched position.

The British and Dutch after an initial success were beaten back by French counter-attacks, and William was forced to order a withdrawal under cover. Wade's regiment participated in the bloody action at Steenkerke and helped to cover the retreat of the Anglo-Dutch Army. At the age of nineteen Wade earned fresh laurels at this battle and was promoted lieutenant on February 10th 1692. Wade further distinguished himself at the Battle of Neerwinden, seven miles south-west of St Truiden in Belgium.

Further promotions followed: on April 19th 1694 Wade was promoted captain lieutenant, and on June 13th captain of the elite grenadier company under the command of William of Orange, who achieved his greatest success in the April of 1695 when he captured the fortress of Namur. The grenadiers were hand-picked men, from the line of companies of every battalion, organised into a special unit which took the place of honour on the right of the battalion line. They were selected on the grounds of being above average height, courageous, strong, robust and 'well in *jambre*' (strong in leg). The military dictionary of 1702 describes a grenadier as a soldier armed with a good sword, a hatchet, a firelock (type of musket) sling and a pouch of three hand grenades. Height and strength were considered essential qualities for these elite shock troops. They wore rimless hats, which exaggerated their height. The addition of hatchets and hand grenades to the musket, bayonet and sword reflects the special tasks these chosen troops were expected to perform.

Besides being an example in coolness, discipline and courage to the rest of the battalion in the linear firefight, the grenadier was called upon to form the nucleus of every 'forlorn-hope' storming party and every last-ditch stand. The grenades then in use were small shells, or hollow balls – some made of iron, some of tin and others of wood or even pasteboard, but most commonly of iron, because the splinters would cause greatest injury. The grenades would be thrown by hand into places where men were crowded, and particularly into enemy trenches. The grenadier carried three of these bombs in a leather pouch. The word grenade comes from the Old French *pome grenate*; the pomegranate is named after the physical resemblance of the fruit to the early grenades.

In May 1697 peace negotiations opened and in the following September the Treaty of Ryswick brought the war to a close. Both sides agreed to return their conquests, and Louis XIV announced his acceptance of William III as King of England and Anne as his successor and his abandonment of the Jacobite cause. In the February of 1702 William was out riding from Kensington Palace to Hampton Court when his horse stumbled on a molehill and threw him, breaking his collarbone. He died the following month, aged fifty-one. On his death, Anne, the daughter of James II, ascended the throne.

The peace of Ryswick was short-lived and England once again prepared for war in Europe – a war provoked by the death in 1700 of the childless Charles II of Spain. Louis XIV accepted the throne on behalf of his grandson, Philip V of Anjou, in defiance of a treaty that stated it should go to Archduke Charles of Austria, and 1701 saw the start of the War of the Spanish Succession. France, Spain and Bavaria opposed the Grand Alliance of England,

Austria, the Netherlands, Portugal and Denmark.

At the outset of the war, John Churchill was appointed captain general of the British forces and supreme commander of the allied forces. Wade, now captain of the elite grenadier company, was once again heavily engaged fighting at Nijmegen, and he was present at the sieges of Kaiserwerth, Venloo and Roermond. In the autumn of 1702 he served at the siege of Liège. It is recorded that Wade's grenadiers greatly distinguished themselves in storming and holding the citadel, one of the strongest fortifications in Flanders. In March 1703 Wade was appointed major, and later that year at the siege of Huy, on October 25th he was promoted lieutenant colonel of his regiment. The 10th served with great distinction in the Flanders campaigns at Steenkerke and Namur, and no regiment was under more continuous fire.

It is almost certain that Wade was present at the storming of the Schellenberg. The infantry selected to storm the fortified heights at the Schellenberg in July 1704 were largely English and Dutch, and were predominantly companies of grenadiers.

The purpose of the war was to relieve the Franco-Bavarian pressure against Vienna; Churchill marched his army up the Rhine, and then moved eastwards preparing to cross the Danube. He set out with 6,000 hand-picked troops over the muddy roads that led to the Schellenberg. In advance went a detachment of engineers whose job it was to make sure that the artillery would not be delayed by bad roads or defective bridges. After some hours of toilsome marching, the town of Donauwörth came in sight and, beyond, the fast-flowing Danube; above them rose the Schellenberg Heights. Riding ahead, Churchill arrived about nine o'clock that morning. There followed hours of impatient waiting for the rest of the army to catch up and for the artillery to establish itself. Ahead lay the fortified camp on the hilltop manned by a garrison of 14,000 good French and Bavarian troops. To storm it would require a major and costly assault which could only be carried out by well-trained troops of exceptional quality.

What concerned Churchill was whether his soldiers, weary after a fifteen-mile tramp over bad roads, could succeed. It was estimated that two hours would be needed in which to fight and win the battle. By five o'clock in the afternoon they were prepared, and, within ninety minutes more, Churchill was victorious. Despite the brevity of the battle, it claimed the lives of 1,400 soldiers while 4,000 were wounded. Seven allied generals were killed, and nine wounded. The brunt of the action was borne by the English foot. Most gallantly did they mount the well-defended hill; three times they were arrested and repulsed, but in the third attack, supported by the Imperialists, who were led by Prince Louis in person, they prevailed.

The Bavarians disbanded and fled in disorder. Many made their way to the Donauwörth Bridge, where two or three thousand of their number managed to cross, but the bridge broke under their weight and hundreds were drowned. Donauwörth, the town below the hill, was now Churchill's and his troops poured into its streets and searched its gabled houses for Bavarian fugitives or plunder.

When the storming of the Schellenberg became known, the whole of Europe was electrified by the news that a new military factor had entered the field – a spirited and well-trained army, well equipped and led by an able and ruthless general. Churchill had won his first major battle in the war and the British troops basked in the glory: they were now regarded with an unaccustomed respect. By this hard-fought action Churchill had cheered and inspired his men: he had gained for them a strong position, destroyed a greater part of the Bavarian Division, and scattered the rest across the Danube. Before leaving Churchill's army for the campaign in Spain, Wade may have served once more at the Battle of Blenheim, which was fought on August 13th 1704.

This battle, so well documented by military historians, will only be briefly referred to here. The battle was forced on the Franco-Bavarian Army by the allies to break the strategic stalemate on the Danube Front. Two thirds of the Franco-Bavarian Army was destroyed, and the threat to Vienna removed, when the Allies overran Bavaria. The casualties were heavy, with the Allied Army losing up to 12,000 killed and wounded. And on the victor of Blenheim, John Churchill, a grateful queen and government bestowed the title of Duke of Marlborough.

Having established his reputation during a decade of fighting in Flanders, Wade volunteered for service in Portugal as a British contingent was about to be dispatched under the Earl of Galway. On January 7th 1704 the regiments were at Portsmouth awaiting a favourable wind to carry them to the Portuguese mainland. Archduke Charles (later Holy Roman Emperor Charles VI) landed at Portsmouth from Holland to join them; and on January 17th 188 ships, including transports and troops, set sail. Eighteen days later most of them were back again at Spithead owing to the stormy weather, and it was not until February 4th that they finally departed. The regiments sailing for Portugal were those of General Meinhard (the Duke of Schomberg), Harvey's Horse, the 2nd Dragoon Guards, the Royal Dragoons, Lord Portmore's Regiment, Stewart's 9th Foot, Stanhope's 11th Foot, Barrymore's 13th Foot, Blood's 17th Foot, Duncannon's 33rd Foot, and Brudnell's and Mountjoy's regiments.

It is essential at this point to mention the two key players in the ensuing battles which took place in Spain from 1704 until the signing of the peace treaty. They were James FitzJames, the Duke of Berwick, who commanded the Franco-Spanish Army, and Henri de Massue, Marquis de Ruvigny, the Earl of Galway, who commanded an international force of British, Dutch, German and Portuguese troops.

James FitzJames, Duke of Berwick, was the son of James, Duke of York (afterwards King James II) and Arabella Churchill, the sister of John Churchill, Duke of Marlborough. After a fine career in Europe under Charles, Duke of Lorraine, he returned home and was appointed colonel of the 8th Foot and Lord Lieutenant of Hampshire; and on March 19th 1687 he was created Duke of Berwick, Earl of Teignmouth, and Baron Bosworth in the peerage of England. He later served in Hungary in another campaign under the Duke of Lorraine. On his return to England his father, James II, appointed him governor of Portsmouth and on February 4th he was promoted colonel of the Royal Horse Guards, the Blues. Finding it impossible to hold Portsmouth, he fled to France to join his father, the King, now in exile. He proposed that James should return with French troops, and accompanied the French Army under Saint-Ruth to Ireland.

FitzJames served at the siege of Derry and commanded a detached force against the men of Inniskillen. He was present at the Battle of the Boyne and was appointed commander-in-chief of the King's forces in Ireland. On his return to France he became a naturalised Frenchman in order to be eligible for the rank of marshal of France and to take command of the Franco-Spanish Army for the campaign in Spain.

Henri de Massue, Marquis de Ruvigny, the Earl of Galway, was a Huguenot. He entered the English service as a major general of horse and in so doing he forfeited his fine estates in Champagne and Picardy. He was at the Battle of Augrim in November 1691, and, in recognition of his services at Augrim and later Flanders in 1693, the title of Earl of Galway was bestowed upon him. By 1704 Galway was resting at his residence, Rookley, near Winchester, growing old, troubled with gout and anxious to retire from active employment. This was not to be – the government had need of his services. In June 1704 he was given command of the forces in Portugal and, with the rank of general, he took over from the Duke of Schomberg.

By March 8th an Anglo-Dutch fleet brought the Habsburg pretender, Charles III of Spain, to Lisbon. The Anglo-Portuguese made preparations to invade Castile with an army under Pedro II of Portugal; Lord Galway led the British and Freiherr von Fagel the Dutch contingent, and early in 1704 Spain declared war on Portugal. Galway arrived at Lisbon on August 10th and in the following months he was busily occupied in preparation for a new frontier campaign in the spring, and in furnishing the Prince of Hesse with additional forces for the defence of Gibraltar.

The campaign opened with the invasion of Estremadura. Galway's plan for an immediate attack on Badajoz was rejected, but in the spring the capture of Albuquerque and Valencia was accomplished. In the autumn Galway was back in Badajoz and on October 2nd the siege began under his direction. While he was superintending the erection of a battery, his right hand was shattered by a shot from the fortress and he was compelled to retire.

Galway was now anxious to take advantage of Hesse's attempt to recapture Barcelona and decided to advance straight to Madrid. The scheme, though a bold one, was approved by Marlborough and the English ministers, but the Portuguese put forward so many obstacles that it was only by taking a firm stand that he accomplished his purpose. Now so weak that he had to be lifted on to his horse, Galway drove the Duke of Berwick from the Guadiana to the Henares, took from him 8,000 Spanish troops with 100 pieces of ammunition and provisions, and reduced the fortress of Alcantara and Ciudad Rodrigo.

In May the Franco-Spanish Army under Marshal Berwick invaded the Portuguese province of Beira and captured the fortress of Castel-Branco on the direct route to Lisbon. Berwick managed to cross the Tagus at Vila Velha to capture Marvão and Portalegre. In June, frustrated by the terrain and bad climate, the Franco-

Spanish Army retired from Portugal. Back in Spain Berwick prepared his army to face Galway on August 24th at Malaga. It was after this battle that Wade received the staff appointment of adjutant general in Portugal. March 10th 1705 saw the Allied Army at the Battle of Marbella, and in May a siege of the frontier town of Valencia d'Alcantara ended when it was carried by storm on May 8th. At this siege Robert Duncannon, colonel of the regiment (afterwards the 33rd Foot) was killed, and the colonelcy was bestowed on Wade.

On April 10th 1706 Wade was wounded at the siege of Alcantara but continued to serve on Galway's staff. He accompanied the allied forces to Madrid, where the regiment entered in triumph on June 27th. For the next few weeks the regiment maintained their position, giving time for Galway and his army to recover from their injuries. There were some who rested and feasted too well – the food, wine and the temptations of the female population of Spain all taking their toll. Galway watched in despair as his army rapidly succumbed to these attractions and hundreds of his men became ill. They had survived the last round of battles and sieges, and they had seen their comrades killed; now they celebrated that they were still alive. There were more battles to face in the months ahead; soon thousands would lose their lives in the disastrous Battle of Almanza. Galway, finding the capital was demoralising his troops, decided to move them to Guadalajara, where he was in a better position to establish communications with the British forces in Valencia.

The 'retreat was made in so good order', wrote Lord Galway, 'that the enemy, superior as they were in number, never durst venture to attack us after the warm reception twenty two of their Squadrons met with two Battalions under the command of Colonel Wade in the town of Villa Nova'.

Wade earned fresh laurels at the Battle of Almanza, where he commanded as brigadier general.

In April, after long delays, Galway and das Minas began their forward movement, and having first destroyed some of the enemy's outlying magazines they attacked the castle of Vilena; but they speedily changed their purpose, raised the siege and pressed on. By that time Berwick had already received the greater part of his reinforcements, although the Duke of Orleans, who had made a circuit through Madrid to pay his respects to the King and Queen, had not yet arrived. It could not fail to be noticed that both the pretenders to the crown had quitted their armies only a few weeks or months before and were in comfort in their palaces instead of leading the battle in which their fate would be decided. Lord Peterborough was heard to exclaim, "What fools we are to fight for such as these!"

The Earl of Galway with an international force including Dutch, German, Portuguese and British troops faced the Duke of Berwick, commanding the Franco-Spanish Army. The allied forces engaged were twenty-five infantry battalions, seventeen cavalry squadrons and thirty guns – in total a force of 15,000 maximum against Berwick's army of 25,000. In spite of this disparity in numbers, Galway was determined to raise the siege of Vilena and to advance against Berwick.

On the night of April 24th the Allies camped at Caudete, and at daybreak they marched in four columns towards Almanza, some eight miles distant. At noon they arrived on the plain, and after a short halt they formed up in line, weary from their long march, facing Berwick's army, who were fresh and ready. The 5,000 recruits Galway had requested from the British Government had failed to arrive. The Duke of Berwick's army also formed up into two lines. Galway took his position on the left wing and began the onslaught that same day, towards three in the afternoon. He fought as always with great bravery but was disabled by a sabre cut above his eye and was forced to quit the field. Tyrawley took his place.

On the left was Carpenter's Brigade of Horse, the 3rd Light Dragoons. Essex's 4th Light Dragoons and Guiscard's Dragoons joined Killigrew's Brigade, comprising Harvey's Horse, the 2nd Dragoon Guards and Pearce's Dragoons. Killigrew's Dragoons (the 8th Hussars) were opposed to the Spanish horse under Popoli. Carpenter's Brigade was at first driven back by the Spanish cavalry, who were fired at by Wade's infantry brigade; then Killigrew's, including Pearce's Dragoons, charged and drove the enemy back with considerable slaughter. Berwick now sent St Gille's French horse to the attack. The Portuguese horse fled the field after the first exchange of shots, leaving the British contingent and a few Portuguese squadrons under das Minas outflanked. At this juncture Berwick sent nine French battalions from his second line, and at the same time a powerful array of fresh squadrons made a final charge on the shattered English and Dutch troops.

The allied left wing, undaunted but greatly fatigued, were obliged to give way. After fierce hand-to-hand fighting Galway's entire army was routed. The commanding officers of Essex's, Killigrew's, Carpenter's and Peterborough's Dragoons were killed, while Pearce was wounded at the head of his regiment and six British colonels died fighting at the head of their regiments. Battalions dwindled until there was only a cluster of men fighting around their colours. The battle scenes were horrific. Wade, who had witnessed the scene so many times on so many battlefields throughout Europe, watched helplessly as his friends and comrades lay dying.

The Allied Army, reduced from 15,000 to 3,500, retired from the field in good order and proceeded to Ontiniente, some twenty-two miles distant. The Allies had lost 4,000 killed and wounded and 8,000 had been captured, along with two Portuguese guns, baggage, twenty-four pieces of artillery, 120 banners and a number of regimental colours and standards. The French loss was estimated at 6,000 killed and wounded, and so severely had they been handled that Berwick did not make a move for five days after the battle. The Duke of Berwick, who always felt he was English, avoided fighting Englishmen wherever possible, instructed his men to give the English quarter and invited the captured officers to a large banquet which he held in their honour two days later.

The battle was lost for the want of more troops, and through the desertion of the Portuguese regiments, which left the Allied Army in the worst possible position. They fought bravely to the last, and Berwick applauded their courage. Berwick was the victor but he took no pleasure in seeing his countrymen defeated. There was some magnificent fighting at Almanza but the odds were stacked against the Allied Army. The British infantry, not realising the Portuguese had fled, fought their ground desperately for a while but they were eventually driven back slowly step by step. It was the only recorded battle in which an English general at the head of a French army defeated an English army commanded by a Frenchman.

The Duke of Berwick and the Franco-Spanish Army had won a decisive battle, described by Frederick the Great as 'the most scientific battle of the war of the Spanish Succession'. One survivor wrote a ballad about that terrible day, and it was quoted in full in a broadside published in 1726.

The following report confirms that the army were indeed undermanned at Almanza:

> The House of Lords Journal Vol. 19. January 31st, 1711, reported the number of effective men in Spain at the time of the Battle of Almanza; what was on the establishment in Spain at that time and what was needed – that it appears to their Lordships, by the papers given in by my Lord Gallway's Secretary that the establishment for Spain was 29,395 men. The effective men in Spain at the time of the Battle of Almanza was 13,759.

Galway left the scene and marched with what was left of his exhausted and tattered army for Alcira on the Xucar and stopped there for six days. Wade emerged from the disaster with an enhanced reputation: he commanded the 3rd Brigade of British infantry, which had encountered fierce fighting and suffered accordingly. Wade evaded capture and with 1,500 stragglers, chiefly infantry, joined Galway some days later. Galway retired into Catalonia in order to make up another army, and within five months of his defeat at the hands of Berwick he was able to take the field with 14,000 well-equipped troops. Although unable to avert the fall of Lerida, in the October of 1707, his energy had saved the situation. With the ending of the Almanza Campaign the allied forces went into winter quarters at Reus and nearby Tarragona, with a strong garrison at Tortosa further south-west. On January 1st 1708 Wade was promoted to brigadier general in the British Army and returned home with dispatches.

On his return to Spain in the spring of 1708 he found that Galway wished to be relieved of his command so that he could return home. He was now suffering from his infirmities and injuries, and he was feeling the effects of all the years spent on battlefields. He had lost his hand, a severe wound to the side of his face had left him blind in one eye, and in addition he was suffering from gout. It was quoted at the time, 'No Irishman proved a bolder hero than our French General.' Galway's wish to retire was refused, however: the government posted him to the consul in Lisbon to carry out diplomatic duties.

It was decided that Lord Stanhope should succeed Galway as commander-in-chief of the British forces, and in March 1708 he arrived in Spain to take command of the army in Catalonia. His appointment was both military and diplomatic and in April that year Stanhope went with Marlborough to The Hague to consult with Prince Eugene on the war. The want of a port in which the British Fleet could winter had been much felt, and on July 15th

Marlborough wrote to Stanhope: 'I conjure you, if possible to take Port Mahon'. In September that year Stanhope acted on this suggestion and with skill and vigour he sailed from Barcelona to Minorca.

The chief town and port of Minorca is located on the island's south-eastern coast. Port Mahon is not only strategically located 225 miles south of Toulon, 100 miles south-east of Barcelona, and 150 miles north of the main sea route between Gibraltar and Naples; it also has one of the finest natural harbours in the Mediterranean. The harbour entrance was guarded by a powerful fortress (San Felipe). In the late 17th century Minorca was a poor island amidst hazardous seas. Redbeard, Mustapha, Piali and the Berber pirates had looted it many times. Life on the island was organised around its scant resources and in accordance with its medieval code of laws; it was remote from the Spanish court and from the rest of Europe alike. This was all to change radically in the 18th century.

In Europe two great blocks of power fought to gain control and divide up the wealth of the world: on the one hand, Britain, Holland and the Holy Roman Empire; and on the other, France and Spain. This struggle and the increasing problems in the American colonies made political and commercial control of the Mediterranean highly important, and re-emphasised the need for Britain to put a fleet there permanently with a good port where it could winter and take on supplies. General Stanhope was commanded to take control of Minorca, and Wade's record as a competent and courageous officer led to his selection as second in command.

The army sailed from Barcelona in September 1708 and entered Port Mahon on September 14th with a battering train, forty-two great guns and a force of 25,000 men, including the marines from the fleet, who would serve on shore. The objective of the expedition was to reduce the fortress of San Felipe, defended by 100 cannon, with its garrison of 1,000 men.

Stanhope's first difficulty was the landing of his siege guns. The ground was very hilly and rocky, and it may well have been here that Wade had his first experience of road-making, for Minorca, like the Highlands of Scotland, was then without roads. Sir John Cope, Stanhope's aide-de-camp, left an account of how the troops made a very good road for the cannon. Twelve days were required for the toilsome transport of no more than two miles through the most rugged country before the cannon could be brought into position.

Wade led one of the storming parties, captured the outer defences, and negotiated the fort's capitulation the next day. On the fall of the outer works, the citadel surrendered, the fortress was reduced, and the whole island at once submitted and became a British dependency. When the army marched into the fortress they found it to contain more than 100 pieces of cannon, 3,000 barrels of powder, and all other supplies that La Jonquière would have needed had he resolved to continue his defence of the island. There were two other walled towns on the opposite coasts of the island – Fornells and Ciudadela – but they were not strong enough to withstand the assault and immediately surrendered.

The entire conquest cost the allies fewer than fifty men; but, sadly, among them was the general's brother, Captain Philip Stanhope, an officer of much promise who was serving on shore with his marines. Stanhope felt very strongly the importance of retaining Minorca as a station for the British fleet.

In the November Wade was granted the honour of returning home with the news of the reduction of Minorca, and in 1709 he received a flattering letter from Charles III, the allies' candidate for the Spanish throne, along with a commission of major general in the Carlist army for his bravery.

Port Mahon became one of the busiest ports in the Mediterranean. The people of the island improved their standard of living while managing to retain their own identity. In 1802, however, almost a century later, France and Britain accepted the need for a truce, and the Peace of Amiens was signed. Under this agreement, Spain, with the aid of Napoleon Bonaparte, recovered Minorca once and for all.

Fort Marlborough can still be seen today. It is situated at the mouth of the Port Mahon harbour on the cove of Sant Esteve (Es Castell). The fort was built by the British between 1710 and 1726, and it was named after the most outstanding general of the time. Descendants of his French enemies still remember Marlborough as 'Mambru' in a popular children's song.

To visit the museum at Fort Marlborough today is a most interesting journey back into the 18th century. Visitors can see a film of what life was like in the fort, watch the soldiers going about their duties and take a forty-five-minute walk through the underground galleries, the countermines and the halls hewn out of rock. Then, after skirting the moat, visitors reach the upper enclosure from where the old part of Port Mahon can be seen: the fortress of Isabel II, the remains of the castle of San Felipe and the Stuart (Penjat) Tower. The route is signposted and can be walked without a guide.

In 1708 the allies went on to capture Sardinia, and Berwick was recalled to Flanders in the wake of the Battle of Oudenarde. In 1709 Galway was recalled from Lisbon and promoted commander-in-chief of the English forces in Portugal, once again facing the enemy at the battle on the Caya. He displayed great personal bravery when his horse was shot from under him, and narrowly escaped capture.

The campaign is chiefly remarkable for Stanhope's great successes at Almeria and Saragossa, and his subsequent advance to Madrid from Catalonia and Aragon. Several English colours and standards taken in the Battle of Almanza were found hung up in the chapel of Nuestra Senora de Atocha and restored to the English general. At the Portuguese frontier, however, where the regiment was engaged, Galway was hampered by the Portuguese Government. They refused to allow him to advance and the campaign was ended. The General was obliged to retreat into Aragon at the end of the year. Relieved of his command, Galway left Portugal for England that year to enjoy his remaining years in retirement at his home, near Winchester.

Wade returned to England to negotiate for more troops, transports and equipment. From his letters to Lord Stanhope it is clear he was concerned about the military authorities and the government, who did not fully appreciate the problems the Allied Army was facing in the Spanish Campaign.

Almanza, April 1707

The French and Spaniards under the Duke of Berwick defeated the Confederates under the Marquis das Minas and the Earl of Galway at Almanza on April 25th 1707. This heartrending ballad was written by a soldier who was present on that terrible day and witnessed the slaughter of his comrades.

Down by the crystal river side,
   I fell a weeping;
To see my brother soldier dear,
   Upon the ground lie bleeding.

It was from the Castle of Vino,
   We marched on Easter Sunday;
And the battle of Almanza,
   Was fought on Easter Monday.

Full twenty miles we marched that day
   Without one drop of water;
Till we poor souls were almost spent,
   Before the bloody slaughter.

Over the plain we marched along,
   All in the line of battle;
To beat of drums and colours fly
   And thundering cannons' rattle.

Brave Gallaway, our General,
   Cried, 'Fight on! while you may;
Fight on! brave-hearted Englishmen,
   You're one to five today.

'Hold back! nor make the first attack
   'Tis what they do desire:
But when you see my sword I draw,
   Let each platoon give fire.'

We had not marched some paces three,
   Before the small shot flew like thunder
Hoping that we should get the day,
   And likewise all the plunder.

But the Dutch fell on with sword in hand
   And that was their desire;
Thirty-five squadrons of Portuguese,
   They ran and never gave fire.

The Duke of Berwick, as I have been told,
He gave it out in orders,
That if the army should be broke,
To give the English quarter.

'Be kind unto my countrymen,
For that is my desire;
With the Portuguese do as you please,
For they will soon retire.'

Now to conclude and make an end
Of this my dismal story
One hundred thousand fighting men
Have died for England's glory.

But let no brave soldier be dismayed
For losing of a battle;
We have more forces coming on
Will make Jack Frenchman rattle.

Chapter 3

General Wade's Letters to Lord Stanhope

Wade, newly appointed brigadier in the British Army was sent back to London to oversee shipments of troops, food and clothing for the forthcoming campaign in Spain. His task was made all the more difficult by the government's failure to appreciate the urgency of the dangers facing Stanhope and Galway and their ongoing situation as described in Chapter 2. Wade set out all the problems he was faced with, in negotiating troops, clothes, corn for the horses and the equipment needed for the army. His growing concern was apparent over the corruption by some of those in charge of the stores and the overcharging on the clothing needed to kit out the regiments and the need to find money to pay the soldiers. The following letter to Lord Stanhope was sent from London on January 21st 1709:

> This morning Brigadier Wightman told me Ensign Marquee of his Regiment was come from Falmouth where he was put offshore [ashore] by a French privateer who had taken him a Runner coming from Barcelona, and that according to the instructions you had given him he had thrown the letters overboard before they were boarded, but the privateer, after having stript him of what was valuable and knowing him to be but an Ensign thought him not worth keeping. I am extremely concerned for the loss of the letters (since I have not had any from you since in London:) especially if there was the estimate relating to Port Mahon in his pacquett, which will be wanting very soon to be laid before Parliament: you will find by the votes the enquiries after what manner the 500000 was expended as likewise of the effective troops in the Service of Spain and Portugal the last year, this was introduced by Mr. Harley and Sir Simon Harcourt with great hopes to bring matters to a ferment and strike at the ministry, but I make no question but you have by sending over your accounts, baffled

their designe, They have not thought fit to make that Account which is to be laid before the House in the same form you have sent it over, but the particulars are taken out of your papers with some additional changes that were not come to your knowledge when you sent me away, but I have taken care to keep the original papers that you signed in my own hands, in order to produce them to the house, or otherwise for your or the Governments justification as occasion may require.

My Lord Treasurer has been informed that Mr. Timperling has been tampering with the stores and has been instrumental in stirring up the disaffected party to these enquiries. I am apt enough to believe it may be true for he is? with my Lord Peterborough and others of that stamp, besides he has often asked me to procure him the sight of your account of the money expended for the King of Spain, which I never would grant, for I hear he has told some who have spoken with him on that matter that the Parliament have last year 40000 for the King's household but that it was applied to other purposes. I need not enlarge on these proceedings of his, since you know him so much better than my selfe.

He had prevailed with my Lord Treasurer to listen to some proposals he made to him to give him money to buy cloaths for 4500 foot and 1500 horse for the King of Spain's troops, but his Lordship has now rejected his propositions, but as I know the want of cloaths both for the Spanish and German Troops, I represented it to his Lordship and he told him also of the great abuses in the extravagant prices of cloathing sent to Spain the last year. He told me he was very sensible that those employed in sending over that clothing had too great a regard to their private interest, but to prevent it for the cloaths that were now wanting he would depend on my care, and ordered me to bespeak such a quantity as was necessary with all expedition, except of such species as were allready in the Queen's Stores at Barcelona.

I have in obedience to his Lordships commands, bespoke coats, waistcoats, and breeches for seven thousand five hundred foot, and the same for 2500 horse with the addition of a cloak to each suit of horse clothing, the greatest part of them will be white faced with red, blew, green and yellow. And the waistcoats of the same collours if the weather will permit their being dyed without losing time; for I am promised they shall all be finished by the end of February, at which time I hope there will be a convoy ready to go, and if they have tollerable passage they may be with you before the Campagne. I have not yet fixed the prices, but I hope to convince you that the only advantage I shall propose to my selfe will be to gain his Lordships and your good esteem. I should not have thought of sending so many over, if the Commissary the Marshall intended to employ for his troops was assigned, but if any delays are made it will be impossible to have them ready in time.

The Regiments that are expected hither from Ostend have been delayed by frost and I am told they have not above 800 private men left, but since the Recruit Bill is likely to pass with some good amendments I hope they will be completed soon after their arrival, and that some of them will fall to our share but as yet the Regiments on the Spanish and Portuguese Establishments are not named. Lapell and Mundens who are ordered from Ireland are not yet sailed from thence, so that I can't yet tell you what you are to depend on the purpose you know.

I have lately had a letter from my Lord Galway with his opinion to keep the same two Regiments in Gibraltar, because he says they being acquainted with the passages on the Mountains and the duty of the Garrison, makes them more usefull there than two others, but he has this represented to him (I suppose) by the Colonels of the Regiments quartered there who are unwilling to move from such warm quarters. Yesterday Sir Simon Harcourt's election came on, the House sat till three in the morning in hot debate, both party's using their utmost efforts, but at last the Whigs got the better and threw him out by a superiority of sixty, this being a considerable victory and will give us great hopes the latter part of the session will be better than was at first expected – I am Sir – Brigadier George Wade dated at London January 21st. 1709

Wade, frustrated by the lack of interest shown by Parliament in matters concerning the army in Spain and the fear of losing the battle in Catalonia for the want of extra manpower, sets out his concerns to Stanhope in a letter dated February 15th 1709:

I was in hopes by Colonel Desbords to have received the honour of your commands, not having received any from you since I left Barcelona. You will find by the enclosed establishment that there is 49000 less in the extraordinarys of the war and King of Spain troops than was given last year. I often urged to my Lord Treasurer the necessity of augmenting rather than diminishing the extraordinary's which not withstanding your frugal management, was hardly sufficient the last year, but the demand for Spain and Portugal amounting to so much, it seems he was resolved to make an abatement before it was laid before the House, and no article would bear a retrenchment of so considerable a sum except that. I was not present when Mr Walpole carried the estimate to the Treasury for his Lordships perusal, in order to lay it before the house, and I believe it was designed I should not be there for I had attended several days before when it was to have been settled but it was always put off to another time.

I find their thoughts are rather employed to prevent clamour in Parliament than in a just consideration of what we may suffer for the want of succour and supplies. You will likewise see by the enclosed that the Regiments are on the Establishment that were there last year, the reason is yet a secret to me, for Mr. Walpole told me once that none should be placed there but those that were designed for thither, those that were expected from Ostend are still there, and in so bad a condition that it will be impossible they should be fit to be sent in time to do us any service. Mr. Walpole told me he would write to you at large as to the particulars in the establishment, and how you are to employ the pay of the Commander in Chief, which he says was a project of his for your service, but I have ventured to assure him you would have been much better pleased to have continued on the same foot you were before, provided they had not retrenched so necessary an expense as the extraordinary's of the war,

This entirely puts a stop to our acting offensively if we were in a condition to do it. I was the last week ordered by the Council to attend the Board of Ordnance to consider what part of the demand for the service of the Artillery was most useful, the whole amount to above £100.000 that Mich [? Michael] Richards sent over, at last we reduced it to £82.000. But Mr. Erle has told me that he believes it will entirely be laid aside, for my Lord Treasurer will not allow any more demands to be laid before the House, and I believe they will hardly be prevailed on to furnish it out of what is given for the service of the Ordnance.

I cannot forbear telling you that their zeal that was at first shown for our affairs in Catalonia seems to cool, or at least their resolutions of putting many things that were promised in practice is delayed till my Lord Marlborough comes over, but I intend in a day or two (as well as I can) to represent the state of our affairs in writing by way of memorial, I cant tell you how pleasing it will be but I am sure they ought to know the worst, and indeed if anything will force them to save us from the blows that threaten us it will be representing the true state of our affairs and the terrour they will have of the next session of Parliament if Catalonia should be lost for want of having your demand complied with. I hope the clothing for the foreign troops will be ready to sail with the first convoy. 6000 suits of them will be sent to Portsmouth next by land, and I hope will come to you before you take the field
Brigadier George Wade

Lord Stanhope's letter to Wade, dated February 21st 1709 from Barcelona:

> I cannot sufficiently thank you for that all you have done and said at London. I wish you may not at last be disappointed of the Regiments you are made to hope for in case you should succeed. I send you here enclosed the best instructions which I am able to give at this distance. But because my Lord Galway hopes to make a considerable impression into Andaluzia which I think is of the greater consequence to us to the end, and that undertaking may not be starved for the want of a few men. I leave it entirely to my Lord Galway to make use of you and the troops you may have if he should be engaged in Andaluzia and should judge it necessary to be reinforced by you. I expect in a few weeks Sir Edward Whitaker from Italy with three thousand Germans which with the troops we left at Majorca, I will try to relieve Alicante. If I succeed in that attempt I shall be so much nearer to the scene where I propose you should act and if you should give me any encouragement would soon join you. I must particularly recommend to you one thing, . . . which way so ever you and the troops avoid you do not suffer there to be any delay in sending hither the Corn Ships which will be safe with a small convoy now that we are so strong in the Mediterranean.

Wade received another letter from Stanhope, dated March 6th 1709 from Barcelona:

> I have little more to add to the enclosed duplicate of what I have writ by way of Lisbon to you, more than that I will try to send to Gibraltar some persons acquainted with the Country of Granada to be assisting to you; by the best information I can get, Almeria is situated near the Country called Alpjianna [?Alpujarra] which is a very fruitful valley about three times larger than the Campo of Tarragona, and surrounded by mountains impracticable over which there are not two passes, which if you possess you may keep an enemy from coming into it.
>
> And if you should find encouragement to advance to Granada which is eighteen leagues distant from Almeria the same passes will secure your retreat into the Aplujaria [?Alpujarra] which as it is represented to me you may maintain with a small force? Especially if the Country be inclined as they tell us. But of this you will be the best judge upon the spot. I am taking measures to send some Emissary hither to prepare them if this undertaking is to be made – I am ever with great friendship Stanhope.

In a letter to Lord Stanhope from London on March 9th 1709, Wade once again endeavoured to put before Parliament the seriousness of the situation developing in Spain and the desperate need for more troops, ammunition, food and clothing, without which they faced utter defeat:

> I have solicited for the draft out of the Regiments in England to recruit the Regiments of foot in Catalonia, Mahon and Alicante which I believe might want 800 men. I could get no answer but that it was the Duke of Marlborough's repeated orders that no more drafts should be made. But that they should be raised in the same manner as the recruits for the service in Flanders were, although I was assured this was impracticable, as well in point of time, as for the want of officers, yet I was willing to convince them of it by using my utmost endeavours. The Board of General Officers appointed the County's for the several Regiments to receive such men as should be delivered over by the commission that were under the description of the Act of Parliament; Hampshire, Surrey and Sussex were allotted for the Regiments as being the nearest to the place of embarkation except for Sir Charles Hotham's who pretended he could by his interest get the 300 he wanted in Yorkshire. All the Officers I could find here belonging to the Regiment were eight of my Lord Mordaunts and I have employed twelve more who were dismissed as Serving Officers. They have all been in the Country for this week past and not one volunteer raised. This day the Commissioners meet to impress those who are under the description of the Act, and I shall be able to Judge in a day or two if we are likely to have any or not. I am pretty well assured that neither their numbers nor condition will be such as will be in any way serviceable to us in this Campaign.
>
> I have at last received my final answer that we are to expect no Regiments from hence except those who are to relieve the Garrison of Gibraltar – I wish no new projects prevent us of those for both the Lord Treasurers and Sunderland, when I first came over promised four more, and I suppose you have assurances of it by the Courier, but since the project of sending 5 Regiments to the West Indies has been on foot, they have changed their minds. I have not spared to let them know what they are to expect, if you are not better supported. They seem convinced that although the Emperor recruit, and the 3000 men from Naples should arrive before the beginning of the Campaign that our Army would not be stronger than when we came into winter quarters last year, as I made it clear to them by the losses we have sustained at Denia, Alicante and Tortosa, besides the Garrison at Port Mahon, and

what have died and deserted since that time.

But their whole dependence is on the enemy's drawing a great part of the French forces from Spain, and on that uncertainty they place our security. The Duke of Marlborough is just arrived at St. James and I hope in a day or two to have the opportunity of putting him in mind of our present circumstances, and when they all know the storm that threatens us, tis they and not you are to be answerable for the event. The stores I mentioned to you in my last are ordered to be sent. I believe their coming sooner or later will make no great difference since we are no way in circumstance to make a siege. They talk of agreeing for 3000 Germans for Lombardy which the Emperor has offered to lend, but they don't care to engage for them, till they are assured the Emperor will re-emplace them to the Duke of Savoy. I am sorry to hear by the French news that our attempts to relieve Alicante have been unsuccessful.

The clothing is all ready and will be sent next week to Portsmouth but I believe there will be no convoy till that which goes with the Regiment to Gibraltar which cant sail in less than a month, for if they send Lapell and Mundens, who are just landed from Ireland it will be near that time before they arrive at Plymouth. I intend with Colonel Debourgay and Captain Hare to begin my journey by way of Italy at the end of next week, and am under no small concern that I have not had the honour of your Command since my arrival in England; if my negotiations have not had the success you desired I hope you are convinced it has not been for the want of soliciting for I have disobliged some people by speaking my sentiments too freely. I am – George Wade.

Later that same day, Wade sat down to write a coded letter to Stanhope giving details of a meeting with the cabinet:

Sir – Since I had the honour to write to you I had orders to attend the Cabinet Council who were pleased to communicate to me a letter from 263.20.6 in which there was a proposition for an attempt on Cadiz 55.4.8. They are pleased to order me to consider the said proposition, and make my report of it, which accordingly I did, of which I shall give you an account more at large by Col. Debourgay who sets out from hence next week 7.7.6.7. (Spain) is ordered to continue here till answers of the 263.20.6 comes, and if some objections are removed and the thing resolved on, I am immediately to be sent to you and inform you of the resolutions taken 4.3.3.4. (Her M) seems well pleased with the design. I wish our circumstances may be such that you 7.2.1 may be spared from the place where you 7.2.1 are as likewise some of the 27.5.4 (English) now with 7.2.1 in my next place has further particulars.

Stanhope's letter to Wade from Barcelona, dated March, mentions that former letters have been lodged at Barcelona and lay there a great while waiting an opportunity:

> Since my last to you I have returns from some people I had employed to get me advices and intelligence of the situation and dispositions of the people about Granada, but confess they are not so satisfactory as I wished, and as I was a great while made to hope: therefore I see little likelihood of your being able to do anything; and would have you make the best of your way hither (where we shall probably want troops) unless my Lord Galway should be engaged in Andalusia and require you to join him in which case you are to do 'as he shall direct', first having regard to send away the corn ships and recruits if you have any without the least loss of time – I am ever Dear Wade – Stanhope

Wade wrote to Stanhope on April 5th informing him that the enterprise on Cadiz was no longer viable – at least for the time being. The government was now intent on making a diversion in Granada. This long letter to Stanhope shows the enormous task undertaken by Wade and the setbacks he encountered at every turn. Wade was still negotiating in London when he desired to be with his troops in Spain.

> I did myself the honour to write to you about three weeks ago of a proposition by my Lord Gallway for an enterprise on Cadiz, which at first was favourably received here, but the consideration of the great expense of fitting out Bomb Vessels, and sufficient Squadrons, has since altered their intentions and the courier arriving with your letters of the 6th, and the 21st, of March has fixed their resolution to follow the first project of making a diversion in Granada.
>
> This day it was debated in Council and upon examination it was found the three Regiments of foot could be spared out of the Garrisons in Britain for this service (besides Lapells and Mundens) who are on their march to Plymouth in order to embark to relieve the two Regiments at Gibraltar. I urged that they would be too few considering the men were unseasoned and that you would be obliged to send one of the Regiments to relieve the Regiment of Colonel Harrison at Port Mahon, since you were disappointed of

the marines you desired for that purpose, upon which it was proposed to send a battalion of the Scotch Guards which are in Garrison at Edinburgh, and to replace them by sending a Regiment less than was intended to Ireland, and this my Lord Wharton who was in Council did all he could to obstruct it.

They ordered that Whiteman's Regiment designed for Ireland to march and relieve the Scotch Guards, who are to march to Hull which was appointed for the place of embarkation of the Regiments that are quartered thereabouts, so that with Lapells and Mundens we shall have six Regiments.

The other four are the Scotch Guards, Portmores, Lord Mark Kerr's and Colonel Churchill's, who has lately bought of Colonel Johnson. All these I look upon to be the best Regiments now in Britain and if they are not complete at the time of embarkation I hope (since the Duke of Marlborough is abroad) with Mr. Walpole's assistance to get them completed by draughts from the Regiments who stay at home.

I cannot yet be able to judge the time we shall be ready to sail, you know how little convoys are to be depended upon, and how slow embarkations go on here, but the orders for the march of the Regiments to the places of embarkation being sent away this night we may hope to be ready to sail by the latter end of May. O.S. As for Lapells and Mundens the transports being ready at Plymouth I hope they will sail with the first convoy; they may continue with Elliots and Watkins Regiments at Gibraltar till I come over with the other four. If my Lord Gallway does not think it necessary to employ this Brigade in his army (as you are pleased to order they shall be at his disposal) I shall according to your instructions proceed to Granada with the Regiments, and to the utmost of my ability observe your orders, but I cannot forbear being of the opinion that unless this expedition is countenanced with your presence as well as with some more troops, and the necessary materials to put such a body in motion we may not only fail of success, but hazard the loss of troops and the ships . . . the town of Almeria is not well fortified as to be taken with cannon.

I find they are unwilling here to be at much expense, especially since it is yet uncertain how these Regiments may be employed, so that all I shall desire from hence is the good quantity of provisions, some of the powder and ball destined for the service of Spain, and some small arms to deliver to the peasants that are willing and ready to make use of them for the King's service and if there is a necessity for cannon, if stake and block carriages or two with some harness, the men of war may supply the rest if the Commodore pleases; but if you have any prospect of making impressions further in the Country 5 or 6 field pieces with their attendance I believe might be spared out of our English train to come with you from Catalonia.

Since the discouragement you have lately had from letters writ hence I believe you will be doubtful whether you may rely on these six Regiments being sent; which made me ask my Lord Sunderland if I might write to you to depend on it, that you might take your measures accordingly, he told me I might write to you as a thing certain, and though he had not time to write to you himself by this opportunity of Colonel Debourgay, he would when Mr. Moyser went, which will be in 8 or 10 days.

Several of the Corn Ships which sailed about three weeks ago from Portsmouth have been driven back, and are still in Port waiting a wind. The greatest part of what you demand is embarked. The Commissioners of the transports who were the persons employed to buy it and send it away, have for the week past promised to give me an account in writing of the quantities and in what ships embarked, which I intended if they had kept their word to have sent you.

I heartily congratulate with you for the justice her Majesty has done to your merit, it is as yet left secret till the commission has passed forms, and it is sent away, for you know the rusty old ones will clamour. You will be the best judge if it may not be necessary for me to have the King of Spain's Commission as Major General, especially if I were to land before you joined us with the troops in Catalonia. I assure you Sir, I do not propose it from any vanity as I have no desire of title but as everything must be transacted in the King's name it would give me a better authority and repute to act in whatever may offer for his Majesty's service, if you think this might be of use, you may get it sent to Gibraltar, I believe before I pass that way.

All the recruits we could raise by virtue of Parliament is about 140 men for my Lord Mordaunt, Harrison's and my Regiment: and indeed I did not expect so many considering the great disadvantage we were under for the want of Officers and Sergeants. The 140 for the other Regiments are on their march to Portsmouth and will I believe sail with the convoy.

Colonel Debourgay has been detained here waiting for letters from the Ministry and if he is not with you before the beginning of the Campaign it is not his fault, however I hope you will send him with your further instructions if you do not come yourself, for he would be very useful in the beginning of an enterprise of this kind, which is commonly attended with the greatest difficulties in the first motions. I shall use my utmost diligence in forwarding everything as much as I can, for I am impatient to have the honour of being more immediately under your Command and of having frequent occasions of showing my sense of the great obligation you have laid on me. George Wade.

Seven days later, Wade was able to report to Stanhope that the transports had at last sailed from Portsmouth with the corn and clothing:

> Since Colonel Debourgay went away the transports sailed from Portsmouth with the corn and clothing. The Commissioners of the transports have sent me the enclosed account of the several quantities and the ships on which it is on board, those marked at Plymouth were to fall in with the fleet as they pass by; and I hope have already joined them. I have nothing further to acquaint you concerning the troops than Lapell's and Munden's Regiments I believe will not sail till the 4 goes. 10 that I shall take and the six Regiments under the said convoy. My Lord Portmore having on pretence that his Regiment is commanded by Officers in Seconds, desired it may remain in Britain.
>
> Colonel Dormers is ordered to go with me in his place and to be made compleat out of Portmores, so that all the Regiments I shall take with me I hope will be completed to a man. What I fear will retard us here, is that the Scotch Guards are not to move till Wightman's arrive at Edinburgh to relieve them; the Council to sit tomorrow to consider further of this matter. I am ordered to attend, and shall by the next opportunity give you a further recount of what is done.

Still facing problems with the government and with the impending arrival of the Duke of Marlborough, Wade intended to put before him the true state of affairs in Spain and the threat to the allied forces for the want of ammunition and troops. It was also hoped that the troops preparing to leave for Newfoundland would be designated to serve in Spain and Portugal.

May 3rd 1708 London to Lord Stanhope.

> Since Colonel Debourgay went away I have used all my endeavours to hasten the embarkation of the six Regiments; but I need not tell you, if you were to make the same preparations in Catalonia it would have been done in a quarter of the time, for the Commissioners of the transports, victualling office, and others

on whose care everything depends will not be first out of their road, of which I have complained often but can have no effectual redress; the Transports are still in the river and will not sail to the north till the end of the week at the soonest.

The Scotch guards are embarked at Edinburgh, Lord Mark Kerr's at Berwick, and Churchill's and Dormer's at Hull, so that if no accident happens the soonest we can hope to have them at Portsmouth will be in the beginning of June. I am sure you heartily wish there maybe an occasion of sending them at all, and if the Dutch persist in their resolutions of making peace without having due regard to our just demands as is reported, I believe it will not be long before it is concluded.

We are of the opinion here that Monsieur Bernard's breaking was not so much a necessity as a contrivance of the French to bring the States to comply with their proposals, for by this bankrupt the Dutch have lost 17 millions of livers [sic] in which most of the States are concerned, and tis certain the French have given them great hopes of making good the said sum, or the greatest part of it, if they will agree to some of their unreasonable propositions.

Since the account we received yesterday of the surrender of Allicante I am afraid the force of the enemy will be so increased in Catalonia that you will have occasion for these six Regiments for your reinforcement, however, I have made a demand (tho very frugally) as I was directed of some Ordnance Stores which with the assistance may be given from the men of war, might be of some use, should you continue your project for our landing at Almeria, and likewise as many necessaries for a hospital of 500 sick as will last six months. The charge of both which will not be lost if according to your instructions I should either land in Portugal, or proceed to join you in Catalonia as I earnestly desire. I have in my demand 300 pair of pistols which will be wanted for any small body of Cavalry that might be raised in Granada if we should land; but have omitted saddles, knowing there are so many in the stores at Barcelona which, with proper officers you may send from there, if the necessity of our affairs in Catalonia does not occasion your altering the instructions by which I am to act.

Major General Mackartney is not exchanged so that Whetham has his orders to proceed with the Regiments to Newfoundland; if by further delays that expedition is retarded a month longer; the season will be too far spent for the undertaking so that I hope we may have the service of those troops in Spain and Portugal before the end of the campaign. Sir Charles Hotham is disappointed by your having his Regiment for he has been in great hopes it would be taken that he might keep his recruits for a foundation to raise his Regiment again in England, tho indeed I cannot say he has raised any, for he will give no returns. The recruits for Sibourg's Regiment being about 100 were left behind by the carelessness of one of the Commissioners of the transports and I am afraid we shall lose most of them before another opportunity offers.

Lord Stanhope at long last received the overdue letters from Wade at Barcelona on June 9th 1709.

Dear Wade,
I am to thank you for your letters of the 1st and 19th of March and the 5th, and 12th of April. All of which I received together by the ships which brought Colonel Debourgay, who arrived three days since. I am extremely obliged to you for all pains you have taken, and for the hopes you give me in your letters that we may have six Regiments. Our project of Granada is laid under nor indeed did I ever depend upon it, but upon the hopes we might have preserved Alicante, and that from thence we might have supported it, but our attempt to relieve that place proving impracticable. We have not done a little to save the Garrison, and the troops which I carried thither have been back here above a month, and are now at camp with the Marshall. If therefore you should prevail to get the six Regiments which indeed I never expected, and still doubtful about, we must employ them another way, and I do verily believe that we may make good use of them tho they should not come before the beginning of September. I therefore recommend to you to use your best endeavours to bring them up thither. We have a Navy report here of an action which has been to our disadvantage in Portugal, which if true the army will be in no condition to act offensively this year: nor is it likely that the enemy will press on this side, but immediately draw away all they can to strengthen themselves. On this side at the latter end of the summer especially if the peace should be made, and the French troops be sent out of Spain; have all reasons in the world to believe the Duke of Anjou and the Catalans will not give up the game this year even tho the peace should be concluded between us and France; what you mention about a Commission from the King of Spain, I would immediately have sent it you if you had been to proceed on my first design, so soon as you arrive here you may depend not only upon having that, but whatsoever else it may be in my power to procure for you being truly sensible how much I owe to your friendship, and the Public to your zeal.
I am ever with the greatest truth – Lord Stanhope.

Wade remained in London, but hoped to sail for Lisbon in two days, weather permitting. Wade was further incensed by the incompetent, lazy commissioners and voiced his concerns in yet another letter to Stanhope on June 10th 1709:

> I did myself the honour to write to you last Tuesday by the courier which my Lord Lind sent to you with his letters. I now enclose an account of the Ordinance Stores which will sail with the Regiments. The first proportion is in the ship by themselves which I demanded when I received your instructions to proceed according to your first, and the last proportion is what we believe may be useful for the service we may now undertake, the rest are what was granted of the demand you made by me when I first came over. There is likewise to sail with us two bomb vessels equipped with all materials and a third will be got ready if it can be done without retarding the convoy. I have likewise acquainted their Lordships that you have two more at Port Mahon which may be brought with you, so that having an account of the stores that goes with us will be better able to gauge what may be useful to be supplied from Catalonia. It was impossible for us from hence to provide a little field train which would certainly be of great use, especially if we should have the good fortune to succeed in either prospect.
>
> And I hope (if your affairs admit of your coming) you will have transports sufficient to embark some field pieces with you and mules to draw them as likewise a small body of them and with some of the saddles out of the stores at Barcelona to augment their number. I am detained here two days longer to take with me the letters and bills of Mr. Morris for the subsistence of the troops and as soon as I arrive at Lisbon will employ him in collecting such species as may be found there proper for our use, which he will have time to provide before I return from the Frontiers, and for this reason I believe I shall re-embark at Lisbon and not yet the place where I told you in my last, for a ship may be sent in there to receive me without the convoys coming into port.
>
> I must likewise acquaint you that I believe the convoy will be retarded here 10 or 12 days longer by the idleness of the Commissioners and Victuallers. But I hope another advantage will attend it which is to compleat the Regiments by drafts from those who stay in England for which I have earnestly solicited this day and hope it will be done. There will likewise be marines enough to form a Battalion of 400 men.
>
> I hear there has been great solicitations to put in a Lieut. Colonel to mine, to the prejudice of D'Harcourt, who for his long services and suffering I am obliged to recommend to you for the

Commission, my Duke of Marlborough having consented to it by letters that came by the last mails from Holland. I likewise recommend to you Colonel Harnage for Major and having supernumerary officers until I have the honour to see you, in the meantime I have put a stop to their taking commissions here which I find they too readily grant, although her Majesty has given you the full power of doing it for the forces under your command.

Colonel Harcourt is in an ill state of health but I hope will be in a condition to follow me to Lisbon in a month at the farthest. I forgot to tell you Wills was made Major General this last winter. My Lord Treasurer has been pleased to promise me a thousand pounds from the Queen. I have likewise received great favour from him and Lord Lind which I must acknowledge to proceed from the favour of your recommendations. We have likewise 2000 suits of soldiers cloth on board that were made to send to the West Indies but will go with us.

With the greatest respect imaginable your most obliged humble servant – George Wade

Stanhope sent a short note to Wade from Barcelona, dated June 28th 1709:

I don't know where this will find you, whether with the troops or under what orders, but if you should be going to Lisbon and are at liberty to follow directions from me, you will see by the enclosed paper what we think is best to be done. Enclosed you have a confirmation as you had desired from the King of Spain. I heartily wish you success in Cadiz, but whether you have or no shall be very glad to see you here with as many Regiments as you can bring up for I am persuaded that we shall not want Employment for any even tho the peace with France should be concluded before you come. – Stanhope

After many long and weary months, negotiating in London and disheartened by all the delays, Wade at long last arrived in Lisbon, from where he sent his next report to Stanhope, dated July 24th 1709:

Tis about a month since I left London and a week since my arrival with orders to confer with my Lord Gallway and receive his commands for the troops that are coming from England with Major General Wills, of which I have for you an account by the courier that was dispatched to you by my Lord Sunderland and further particulars in a letter I sent by post the day before I left London, both of which I hope come into your hands, to which I have only to add that upon presentation to the Council that the 7 Battalions wanted about 600 of their complement they were pleased to order my Lord Rochfort's Regiment of Dragoons to leave their horses in Ireland and embark with the three Regiments Admiral Baker is to take on board at Cork, and believing you would reduce the two Regiments that were at Alicante into one of the recruits of Sibourg. Sir Charles Hotham's amounting to about 160 men was ordered to be given to Boles and Hawley's Regiments in order to complete them.

You will find by the letter you now receive from my Lord Gallway that by our own mismanagement and the vigilance of the enemy it is impossible to attempt anything on Cadiz, and considering the present posture of your affairs in Catalonia gives him hopes you will be in a condition to act offensively. He has laid aside the thoughts he had of employing those forces at Vigo and resolved to send them all to your assistance.

Our last letters from England of the 28th June O.L. says that they are still at Spithead waiting for a wind; I wish that may be the true reason of their stay. I wonder I have not heard from Wills, who promised from time to time to give me an account of the proceedings. I hope he has been more punctual in his correspondences with you; in the mean time I am embarking four months subsistence for the said troops on board a ship that lies in this river in order to join them on their first appearance, and my Lord Gallway has ordered Mr Morris to procure as much money as he can get together for the use of the troops in Catalonia. Sir John Jenning arrived with his squadron yesterday, by whom I had the favour of yours of the 28th June, with your instructions and a commission of Major General from the King of Spain. I am truly sensible of this and the many favors you have been pleased to bestow on me, having no other means of showing my gratitude than by using my utmost application whenever you are pleased to honour me with your Command.

Our affairs here seem to be in a very bad posture, the misfortunes of this Campaign one would have thought would have roused them from their lethargy, but instead of using means to put the Army in a condition to take the field the men famish for want of bread and their horses perish for want of corn. My Lord Galway to prevent this bought considerably quantity of the latter from the merchants in Lisbon and gave the Portuguese credit for it out of the subsidies that should become due, but they thought fit to dispose of it as soon as it came into their hands without sending a grain to the Army, by these methods their Cavalry are reduced to such a condition that they have not 500 horses fit to take the field, so that the enemy will have little else to do in the latter Campaign than to plunder the Province of Alentego [?Alentejo] For his Lordship is of the opinion that there will be no Campaign on our side; in my last to you from London I sent you an account of the Ordnance Stores that are coming with Admiral Baker, you will be pleased to consider what part of them shall be left at Barcelona if your orders should come to us to proceed farther with the troops. Captain Otway, who comes to you with recommendations from the Duke of Somerset, will deliver you this.

Wade was busy during his month-long stay in Lisbon, and on September 8th he sat down to write his report to Stanhope, mentioning his concern over the slow passage of his last letters:

I am concerned to hear the Dutch ships which carried my Lord Gallway and the letters I did myself the Honour to write to you, had so ill a passage as not to get to Barcelona before you sailed from thence, being pretty well assured that the letters you received by the last courier from Britain would as on the like occasions engage you in design, whatever difficulties you might meet with to obstruct the execution of it.

I indeed wonder how it was possible for you to embark so many horse and train of artillery in so short a time; before I left England they were in great concern lest Admiral Baker with the Squadron and troops should lie too long at Gibraltar before you would be able to join him from Catalonia. I hope this will convince them that the measures they take in their embarkations at home are quite different from your manner of proceeding since so many months have been spent and we have no assurances of their being yet gone to Ireland to take in the four Regiments that are to come from thence.

The last account we have of them is from Torbay from whence I have letters of the 12th August A.S. that they were there wind bound after having sailed twice towards Landsend and driven back by contrary winds, so that in Admiral Jennings opinion that it is possible they may be here in two or three weeks, yet, at this season of the year it is more probable they may in as many months.

We are in some doubt here whether the letters you may have received by the Dutch ships have not occasioned your return to Catalonia, tho if the transports in which your horses are embarked are homeward bound, I hope it will be an argument with you to proceed hither where they may be landed and disposed of (if you think fit) at a good advantage to the Regiments of Horse on the

Queen's pay that my Lord Galway is now forming. His Lordship has received answers to the letters he wrote to England telling them it was his opinion that since it appeared impracticable to employ the troops that were come from thence as was intended, that they might be of use if they were sent to you in Catalonia and her Majesty has consented they should proceed hither.

The same letters say that there are 2 Battalions of foot added to the 7 which I suppose are a Battalion of the Scotch Guards of Dormers, which when I left England were in expectation of being sent to Flanders. For want of Holland mails we are uncertain what they are doing there. The last news say the Citadel of Tournay was to be surrendered to us the 5th day of September N.S. if not relieved by Marshal Villiars before that time. That some Battalions of Squadrons were left there to blockade the place and all acts of hostilities were to cease between them and the Citadel, and that the Duke of Marlborough was marched with the Army and encamped within two leagues of the enemy.

Their manner of defending that place and the little loss we have had in making ourselves masters of it looks as if the Preliminaries were agreed on and that the war with France would end the Campaign. Another reason that induces me to believe it is the news we have received that the enemy have abandoned Newfoundland after having demolished the fortification of Fort St John and selling back to our Colony there the boats and other implements of fishery they took from them when they first surprised the place.

My Lord Gallway has prepared an apartment in his house for your reception believing you will find it necessary since you may arrive there at the beginning of the next session of Parliament, so that the expectations I am in of having the honour of seeing you here has prevented my waiting on you at Gibraltar as intended when I first heard you were coming hither. The Marquee de Montemore and Count Garrock pass to England with Sir Jennings who intends to sail three days hence.

In his letter to Stanhope, dated September at Lisbon, Wade congratulated Stanhope on his safe arrival at Gibraltar and reported his concern once again over the inadequate number of troops available for the ensuing conflict in Spain:

> I heartily congratulate your safe arrival at Gibraltar, and although you have met with a disappointment in the undertaking that brought you thither, I believe it will occasion such a diversion of the enemies troops on these frontiers as will save the Province of Alemtye

[?Alentejo] which as well as the whole Kingdom lies at their mercy, as I suppose my Lord Gallway has more particularly informed you. The last Paquett from England informed us that Admiral Baker passed by Falmouth 17 days ago on his way to Ireland with a fair wind which they say continued for 4 days, if it proves so when they sail from Cork we have reason to hope they may be with us in a few days. There is embark on board the 'Torbay' who tell me they have been working at the Preliminaries to find an expedient for the 37th Article, the proposal on our side was that the French should deliver into our hands three of the Spanish Garrisons that may be of most use to us in procuring us the full possession of that Kingdom. But they say it is not in their power, and have offered instead of them three towns in Brabant that we shall name, which were not included in the Preliminaries. But this not being sufficient for the purposes of the Allies is rejected. The treaty for the surrender of the Citadel at Tourney being rejected by the French King they continue to make a vigorous defence.

I have not received a letter from Wills since I left London; I believe you find the Regiments he brings with him very defective as to numbers since they wanted of their complement before embarkations. I believe it will be your opinion as soon as they come to reduce some twenty six thousand Morgan's for the service of the troops in Catalonia besides twenty thousand that went with the Dutch ships, which I suppose you have an account of, and I shall continue to press Mr. Morris to procure as much as possible to bring with me in the 'Winchelsea' which is the ship I hear is ordered to come into this river to take me on board when Admiral Baker approaches this coast. The draughts in Speci, from this Kingdom has occasioned so great a scarcity that I believe it will be very difficult if not impossible to supply Catalonia with money another year, which makes me wish the more that the scene of the war where you are to serve remove to some place where you might with less difficulty be supplied with both men and money, but that I fear cannot be done till the peace is concluded with France. George Wade

Wade continued to fret about the state of the regiments and the frauds he believed were being carried out in Lisbon, but he was heartened to learn that the Duke of Marlborough gained a decisive victory in Flanders. The following letter from Wade to Lord Stanhope was dated October 9th at Lisbon:

I take the liberty to congratulate with you on the Victory gained by the Duke of Marlborough in Flanders the particulars as far as we know of them you will find in the printed account. Here are some private letters which add that Lt. General Withers and Wood are killed, and a Holland Gazette gives an account of some Battalions that surrendered to Prince Eugene the day after the battle. All agree that the Victory is complete, and that we shall have peace with France on our own terms.

About ten days ago there arrived a small vessel from Cork who was 12 days in her passage hither, he says Admiral Baker sailed the morning before he left with ten Regiments on board. Those that came from Britain had suffered very much by sickness but that the three ft and Lord Rochfort's Dragoons from Ireland were completed to a man. Another vessel arrived here yesterday who left the fleet in the Bay of Biscay off Cape Finester nine days before, steering to the Westward, the winds being Southerly, since which we have had Northerly winds for several days on this coast, so that I wonder very much that they are not arrived here.

I have had several wrangles with Mr. Morris about the money affair, which has yet proved but 34000 Moydas, which sum is very inconsiderable since the greatest part of it will be employed in paying the 10 Regiments that are coming, who are cleared on the English Establishment. But he says he will provide 20000 more in a month's time if you will prevail on the Admiral to leave or send a ship to carry it to Catalonia.

I am fully convinced there is knavery in the management of the money, and that they create difficulties in sending the money to have the difference of the exchange between this place and Barcelona which you know is very considerable. My Lord Gallway having given you ample account of the state of affairs here I omit to trouble you with a repetition; I have an account from England that all the Officers belonging to our Regiments in Catalonia that were prisoners in France are released, and that they are loitering in London, I have but two out of eighteen who have thought fit to leave that place, tho I have assured them that till they arrive at their Regiments they will not be accounted as officers, nor enter into pay till they come to their posts, till which time the officers who serve in their places and receive the pay cannot be dismissed.

I am as much tired of this place as I believe you are of Gibraltar, and with the utmost impatience wish for an opportunity personally to have the honour to assure you that I am, with all imaginable sincerity and respect – Major General Wade at Lisbon Oct. 9th, 1709

Another letter from Wade followed on quickly, dated October 10th, with the good news that he was about to depart from Lisbon for Barcelona:

> The Lord Rochfort is just arrived here in the 'Chatham' and brought me the enclosed letter, and I have another from Wills. The whole fleet lying now off the Rock of Lisbon and I believe are by this time joined by Sir George Bing who they saw 8 leagues from the Rock with 35 sail which we suppose to be the transports. I shall embark with the money this afternoon or tomorrow morning. Colonel Windon is here and tells me the troops are in very good health and their loss has been very inconsiderable so that what I wrote to you is not true. My Lord Gallway is at church it being our day of thanksgiving for the victory, and the courier being on his departure with the letters we wrote yesterday.
>
> By this opportunity I have nothing to add but my impatience to be with you will make me hasten my departure without losing a minute. The Count Stampa will embark with me and we have told him we think it impossible to undertake what was intended – Major General Wade at noon on October 10th, 1709

Wade's second last letter to Stanhope from Barcelona was dated November 2nd 1709:

> Being detained at sea by calms and contrary winds it was 3 of the clock this afternoon before we landed here, after waiting on the 'Mary Perlas' I delivered your letter to the King who was extremely pleased at your arrival with the troops, and ordered me to acquaint you that he is very well satisfied with the disposition you have made and will give the necessary orders for the reception of the Horse and Dragoons in the islands, as likewise of the foot in the town of Campo de Taragona. The news of your arrival was no less agreeable to Marshal Stahrenberg whom as soon I heard was here I waited on and delivered your letter of which I presume you will have an answer by this courier with the disposition he has made of the Quarters.
>
> The enclosed letter from the Duke of Marlborough I got from Mr. Mead who has sent on board for the money, so that the 'Chatham' will return sometime tomorrow. Be pleased to give my humble respects to the Admiral and let him know I have no other account of the fleet than that Sir Edward Whitaker went from thence about a fortnight since with 4 Men of War to Port Mahon, that of the six that went to the Coast of Africa two are expected back with the transports and the corn that is ready, and that the other 4 have orders to continue cruising on that coast and to send Convoys from time to time. Corn shall be brought and supplied, and that two other Men of War are gone to Genoa for the money we expect from thence

> We have no account of Mr. Craggs but hope he will come with those ships. I hear of no news from Flanders of a later date than of the Gazette you have seen which (if you have them with you) I believe would be acceptable here. I shall continue hence to solicit the dispatch of the orders for Sardinia and Majorca, which they promise shall be ready sometime tomorrow; if this courier returns I hope to have the honour to receive your Commands, if I do not to the contrary, I intend to be with you 3 days hence – George Wade

After the long weary months negotiating in London and Lisbon, Wade was at last returning to take command of an infantry brigade under Lord Stanhope. There was to be one last letter to Stanhope with an enclosure from Marlborough. Wade throughout the campaign in Spain became thoroughly disillusioned with the government, who failed to understand the needs of the soldiers, for their corruption over money matters in some quarters and the lack of funds for the purchasing of clothes, food, and grain to feed the horses.

Wade, now acting second in command, advanced on Madrid with 24,000 men and defeated 22,000 Spanish troops under the command of Villaderia; and Stanhope defeated the Franco-Spanish force at Lerida in the summer of 1710. At some point during the summer the Portuguese Army advancing on Madrid was frightened off by the French Army and forced to retire back to Portugal. Wade participated in the overwhelming victory over the forces of Philip V at Saragossa on August 10th when a Franco-Spanish army advanced on Madrid. Five thousand prisoners were taken and thirty-six guns captured.

The tables were turned in the December of that year when Vendôme ambushed Stanhope's rearguard at Brihuega on the road from Madrid to Barcelona. The entire rearguard were taken prisoner or killed. Stanhope, one of the captured, was not to see his homeland for three years. Towards the end of hostilities in 1711, Charles III relinquished his claim to the throne of Spain and left Barcelona to become Emperor Charles VI. With the suspension of arms, Portugal signed the peace treaty with France and the Duke of Berwick took Gerona. Catalonia followed in November and the Allied Army at last withdrew from Spain.

Wade returned home and was promoted to major general of the forces in Ireland in October 1714. It is doubtful whether he took up this command as he was returned to Parliament for Hindon in

Wiltshire in January 1715 on the death of Reynolds Calthorpe, Esq. Wade was now an established military name with a comfortable fortune to back it, partly from the spoils of war, and partly from the pickings that went to the colonel of a regiment from its outfitting.

The long months spent negotiating with the government may have prompted in Wade a desire to enter Parliament, where he would be in a stronger position to fight for improved conditions for those who served their country in times of war. In those days, seats in Parliament could be bought and Hindon attracted a variety of candidates without local connections. Hindon in the 18th century had a population of around 793, with a total of 190 houses. What prosperity Hindon had was due to its markets and fairs, and to its position on and near main roads. It boasted fourteen inns and public houses, servicing the coach trade that Hindon attracted.

Wade was duly elected to serve the said constituency as a member for the Whig party. The Whigs thought of themselves as champions of the country's interest and fully supported the establishment of the Hanoverian settlement. The name 'Whig' was originally a nickname given to the insurgent Presbyterians of Scotland, and 'Tory' was a nickname given to outlawed Roman Catholics in Ireland.

In politics the Tories upheld the divine right of kings and the doctrine of non-resistance while the Whigs were inclined to consider the king only as 'an official' who was responsible to the people for what he did and could be dethroned if he ruled unconstitutionally. Within a few months of Wade taking his seat in Parliament, the country was plunged into yet another rebellion on the death of Queen Anne.

Chapter 4

The Fifteen

> See how they pull down meetings,
> To plunder, rob, and steal;
> To raise the mob in riots,
> And teach them to rebel.
>
> At Oxford, Bath, and Bristol,
> The rogues design'd to rise;
> But George's care and vigilance
> There's nothing can surprise.
>
> Base Ormonde's fled and left them
> And Perkin dare not come,
> And Gibbets are preparing
> For those we've caught at home.

This Whig song, denouncing the disaffected, appeared in the Annals of Bristol in the 18th century.

In July 1714 Queen Anne fell ill and it was thought she was not likely to recover. On July 30th a furious row erupted at a council meeting on whether the succession should go to the Stuart line or to the House of Hanover. The Whigs, favouring Hanover, were best prepared and their leaders urged the dying queen to appoint their candidate, the Duke of Shrewsbury, as her minister. A procession of councillors made their way to the Queen to obtain her consent to this appointment. As she obediently handed over the white wand of office in favour of Lord Shrewsbury she managed to say, "For God's sake use it for the good of my people." Early on the morning of August 1st 1714 Queen Anne died. She had survived her husband, and her seventeen children had all died in childhood. Anne had suffered from failing health for a number of years and had lost the affection of her dearest friend, Sarah Churchill; but she had lived long enough to deprive Bolingbroke of any chance of putting another Catholic monarch on the throne and to ensure the relatively smooth accession of George I of Hanover. On Anne's death the Jacobite hopes of putting James III on the throne of England seemed to fade, and the plans of the Jacobite ministry had, in the meantime, been defeated by the energetic activity of the Whig nobles.

The Elector of Hanover, George Ludwig of Brunswick-Luneburg, second cousin to the late queen and also a former suitor, was proclaimed King George I to little apparent opposition, and crowned with great ceremony on October 20th 1714 in Westminster Abbey.

In all areas, however, concealed or overt Jacobite unrest was about to erupt. Right up until the last the Jacobites had hoped that Anne would change her mind and remember the promise she gave to her father. James II, the Queen's half-brother, had clung to his Catholic faith and in so doing lost the crown. As might be expected, the new monarch threw himself entirely into the hands of the Whigs. To them in great measure he owed his throne; he could not help looking upon the Tories as the personal enemies of his family.

The uprising of 1715 to overthrow the House of Hanover was planned to occur simultaneously in London, in Scotland, and in the west. The uprising in Scotland was to be a feint; the most important move was to be in the west. The Bath Jacobites openly said that the rebellion was due there; support was available from Somerset, Gloucester and the ports of Plymouth and Bristol. The imminence of a rebellion and the probability of a new dynasty weighed heavily over the whole country. The uprising faced by George I in the first year of his reign was known as 'The Fifteen'.

The Pretender instigated a rebellion in Scotland, where support for the Jacobites was stronger than in England. John Erskine, the 6th Earl of Mar, was an embittered Scottish nobleman. He proclaimed James Stuart, the Old Pretender, king at Braemar on September 8th 1715. The uprising was, however, a dismal failure, and Lord Mar, known as 'Bobbing John' for his changes of allegiance, fled to France with the Old Pretender in 1716.

On April 23rd, the anniversary of the birth of Queen Anne, the London mob began to assemble towards evening at the conduit on Snow Hill, in London, where they hung a flag and a hoop; and, having been given money to purchase wine, they collected around a large bonfire. From there they moved off in parties in different directions, patrolling the streets during the whole night, shouting, "God bless the Queen and the High Church, Bolingbroke and Sachervell!" (a passionate high churchman and a enemy of dissent), attacking houses, breaking windows, robbing passengers, and levying contributions everywhere. Many of the mob were armed with dangerous weapons and several people were severely wounded. Unrest continued for several nights.

On the night of April 29th, the Duke of Ormonde's birthday, the streets of London were the scene of new riots.

A month later, on the night of Saturday May 28th, the anniversary of the Restoration, the mob rioted in different parts of London, and dangerously wounded some constables. They burnt effigies of the chief dissenting ministers, shouted "High Church and Ormonde!" and publicly drank the Pretender's health in Ludgate Street and elsewhere. A riot of a similar character occurred in Oxford, where the Quaker chapel was attacked. Within a few days the same spirit had spread to several of the largest provincial towns.

In Manchester, early in June, the mob had become absolute masters for several days; they destroyed all the dissenters' chapels, threw open the prison, and drank the Pretender's health. A troop of soldiers was sent to Manchester, and the Mayor of Leeds, who was accused of connivance, was brought to London in the custody of the King's messenger. Similar outbreaks of violence occurred at Wolverhampton, Warrington, Shrewsbury, Stafford, Newcastle-under-Lyne, Lichfield and West Bromwich. When the mob was pulling down the meeting-house at Wolverhampton, one of their leaders mounted on the roof, flourished his hat and shouted, "Down with King George and the Duke of Marlborough!" The Pretender's health was even drunk in some of the Oxford colleges. In the town of Chippenham in Wiltshire there was a series of violent attacks on houses and ill-treatment of the residents over several nights. Up and down the country, reports were coming in of civil disobedience.

The authorities in Berkshire, fearing an outbreak, presented the following address from the county to the King, introduced by the Duke of St Albans. The *Daily Courant* on Tuesday October 11th 1715 printed the text:

To the King's most Excellent Majesty the humble address of the Lord Lieutenant, High-Sheriff, Deputy-Lieutenants, Justices of the Peace, Grand Jury, Gentlemen, and other Freeholders of the County of Berkshire.

It is with equal indignation and Surprise, that we find some of our Fellow Subjects infatuated to that degree as by Rebellious Riots and Tumults to disturb your Majesty's Government, notwithstanding it is that only which under God can secure to us our Religious Laws and Liberties, (the most valuable things Mankind can enjoy,) which by our late Glorious Deliverer King William of Immortal Memory, were rescued from the utmost danger, and which nothing but our own folly or villainy can again render unsafe or precarious under your Majesty's Administration. The Mask is now thrown off, and by the wicked Artifices of restless and designing Men, a Popish Pretender is preparing chains fit only for those by whose encouragement he makes the Attempt: For what true Briton and Protestant had not rather dye in the Defence of your Majesty's Person and Government, than live to endure the Tyranny of a Popish Usurpation. But when we consider your Majesty's consummate wisdom, the Vigilance of an able Ministry, the Bravery of your Troops, once more Commanded by faithful Officers that often have led them into Victory, and above all the Providence of the Almighty hath almost in a miraculous manner appeared on our behalf to save this Church and Nation, we think we may justly promise ourselves a happy event.

As for our part, we lay hold of this Opportunity, in the most solemn manner, to make a new Tender to your Majesty of that Allegiance, which by the Laws of the Land, and the Oaths we have taken is our Duty to pay to your sacred Majesty our Lawful and Rightful King; and at the same time to assure your Majesty, that we will with the greatest vigour and cheerfulness put the Laws in Execution, and with our Lives and Fortunes assist your Majesty in Defence of your sacred Person and Government against the Pretender and all other your enemies whatsoever. And we humbly beseech Almighty God to grant your Majesty a long and peaceable Reign, and that we may never want an Inheritor of your Majesty's Royal Blood and Virtues to Reign over us till time shall be no more.

The main theatre of the rebellion in the south-west of England was focused on headquarters at Bath and objectives at Bristol and Plymouth ports where help might arrive. The expected landing of troops from France never materialised, allegedly owing to Bolingbroke, the Secretary of State in the previous Tory government, having drunkenly revealed the plans to a Whig spy, Madame de Tencin. This has been denied by at least one historian, but Bolingbroke seems to have been an acknowledged connoisseur of wine and women, and had been seen to flirt openly with the beautiful Claudine de Tencin at the court of Louis XIV. Madame de Tencin was a noted political schemer, and operated a literary 'salon', whose guests included Bolingbroke and Lord Chesterfield. Rumour had it that the secrets Madame de Tencin heard found their way to French ministers. At all events, Bolingbroke later left London for Paris in fear of impeachment, and, with charges of treason hanging over him, threw himself into the cause of the Pretender and back into the arms of Madame de Tencin.

Bath, one gathers, was largely Jacobite in sympathy; a city so much in the Beaufort sphere might be expected to lean that way. In the preparations made for a revolt in the South-West, the hopes of the Pretender's friends in Gloucestershire and Somerset rested chiefly on the Duke of Beaufort, the Lord Lieutenant of Bristol, who, though he had renounced the Roman Catholic faith of his ancestors, was an enthusiastic supporter of the exiled family. Fortunately for his house, the Duke fell ill and died a few weeks before the Queen, leaving as heir to his vast fortunes a young son. Had the Duke lived, the situation in and near Bath might well in 1715 have been more of a threat to the Hanoverians; even so, Bath was intended for a key role in the uprising to enthrone the Prince, whose birth (so some claimed) had been aided by his mother's patronage of the waters.

The Jacobite feeling in Bath was reinforced by many of its visitors, such as Clifton and Beaumont, who came to Bath pretending to tour the county to examine natural curiosities and works of art. The government was duly disturbed by the gathering of papists, Nonjurors, and others of the disaffected that converged in the summer of 1715 on the city. Sir William Wyndham, lately made a freeman of Bath, was greeted on his arrival in town by the vigorous peals of the abbey bells.

Lady Carew, upset at the long ringing of the bells in favour of the Pretender, summoned the abbey ringers and asked them to peal in honour of the Hanoverians. This they refused to do, stating that there was 'mixed company at Bath, and that some would take offence at prayers for King George'. Lady Carew stood her ground and threatened to publish their refusal. The bellmen reconsidered, and duly rang the bells in favour of King George.

The western Jacobites then accepted for their leader James Butler, Duke of Ormonde, then in London but who at the time was the Lord Lieutenant of Somerset.

Before leaving London the Duke of Ormonde set about making plans for seizing Bristol, Exeter and Plymouth and even provided horses on the road to secure his rapid progress. Owing to Ormonde's popularity and reputation for energy, the leading Jacobites anticipated greater results from his action in the west than from the revolt in the north. Lord Stanhope knew, however, Ormonde planned to seize Bristol and the other cities. Ormonde was probably aware of this, and although personally a brave man, at the last moment his courage failed him and he crossed to France and openly joined the Pretender. He was impeached in June 1715, his political career in ruins. Twice in 1715 he attempted to land on the Devon coast and raise a revolt, but on both occasions he failed to gain any support, and was forced to return to France. This left Lord Lansdowne and Sir William Wyndham in charge of Jacobite affairs in England.

There was an outbreak of disorder in the country villages in Somerset, where zealots on both sides lost self-control. On May 28th, King George's birthday, the loyal citizens hung out their banners, but the Jacobites carried thyme and rue in their coat breasts to denote their grief. Stuart supporters jauntily decorated their houses with branches of oak, and their persons with oak leaves, and one favoured song was 'The King Shall Enjoy His Own Again'. On the Pretender's birthday in June 1715, his supporters, male and female, bedecked themselves with white ribbons.

The *Flying Post* printed the following item from Beckington in Somerset on August 25th 1715:

> On Friday June 13th, which they call the Pretenders birthday, the bells were rung, and his health was drunk by the name of King James III at Philip's Norton in the Country. They threatened to come and pull down the Meeting house here in Beckington, but were dissuaded by some of their friends who told them they would meet with a warm reception if they attempted. In the July it was reported that a rebellious mob did attempt the Meeting House in Bath, but they were interrupted by the Magistrates and ran away. The Mayor has offered 20'1 to anyone who can discover the actors. The bells were rung at Woolverton on the same occasion. Two of our rioters on the day of the Coronation, of whom I formerly gave

you an account, are bound over to the Assizes, for scandalous and seditious words against the King, too vile to be repeated; yet the Parson of the Parish was pleased to appear on their behalf; and gave them a very good character to the Justice, tho' one of them is known to be as scandalous a Fellow as any in the Country.

On August 24th 1715, a resident of Beckington in Somerset wrote the following letter to the *Flying Post*:

> Sir we are now a little quieter and safer from the High Church Mob, than we have been for many weeks. They resolved as soon as they had certain Intelligence that the Pretender was landed, to have murdered me and plundered my house, with some others. The clerk of the Parish went about drunkening almost every day to cry up the Mob and making them believe he was either landed, or would land in a few days, which made some of them set up resolutions that they would not strike a stroke of work till he was come. This hopeful clerk being a Captain Mobber, he had the impudence to wager about a Fortnight ago with Richard Brewer that when the Pretender was landed, he would be set upon the Throne. About the same time the Parson of the Parish made an agreement with John Yew, my next door neighbour to pay the said Yew one shilling per week 'till the Pretender did land' and the Parson was to have a guinea of the said Yew, when he was landed. The Clerk being bound over for two of his brother mobbers had spoken vile words against the King and Government. Fearing the Pretender will not be here soon enough to rescue them from the approaching Assizes, he and the two rogues are gone since Sunday morning.

That an insurrection in Somerset was imminent was not in doubt – some newly raised dragoons were forced to guard their horses upon notice that a party was coming to seize them. During September the leading Jacobites in the west assembled in Bath under the pretence of drinking the waters, bringing with them a number of horses and a quantity of arms. In Bristol the situation became so serious that the government ordered the Lord Lieutenant, Lord Berkeley, to take measures for the security of the city. Early in October the authorities received intelligence of a plot hatched by the Somerset Jacobites to seize the city, whereupon the militia, headed by Nathaniel Wade, the town clerk, took measures to close the city gates and to mount cannon at Redcliff and Temple. Several members of the Loyal Society, patronised by Edward Colston and others, but described by their opponents as 'a set of rakehells' who kept up a drunken club to carry on treasonable designs, were arrested.

The *Flying Post* reported in the late summer of 1715 the political state of the country and the condition of the West Country from Frome in Somerset:

> Last Saturday we proclaimed our Glorious King George, we would have done it sooner but our officers the Bailiffs and the rest of the leading Gentlemen were at Wells Assizes. Yet notwithstanding they had not an hour to prepare. His Majesty was proclaimed by a Noble Company of Gentlemen who carried loyalty to their hearts, and joy in countenances. No Pretender No Popery was the cry; besides God Save King George. In short we all appeared unanimous in the solemnity, all party distinctions being laid aside and the night concluded with bonfires and all other public marks of joy

A correspondent from Bath wrote to the *Flying Post* on October 8th 1715:

> Sir, This place has all summer been a nest of Tories and Papists, and the factious part of the inhabitants caress them as much for their hatred of the Protestant succession as for the money they pay for their lodgings. Yesterday morning I saw Windsor's Regiment of Horse enter the Town at the sight of whom the Papists and Tories skulked like a parcel of disappointed traytors; three of the rogues of this place were taken and many others are scampered for it. That there was a damnable plot you need not now question since this very moment has been discovered in our Carrier's Warehouse arms sufficient for 200 men.

The situation was now so serious in the west that the government decided to send down Major General Wade, commander-in-chief of the Western Division. With two regiments under his command, Wade entered the city of Bath and garrisoned his troops in the Abbey Church House. It is said that a young postal clerk, Ralph Allen, tipped off Wade about the rebels and their whereabouts, but there must have been many residents in Bath who noticed an unusual number of Jacobites and their followers assembling in the city.

It did not take long to discover eleven chests of firearms, a hogshead full of basket-hilt swords, and another of cartouches, plus three pieces of cannon, one mortar, and moulds to cast more cannons, some being hidden underground and in Slippery Lane. There was also the discovery of 200 horses located outside the city. After a thorough search of the city, arrests were made and the ringleaders captured; they included Sir William Wyndham, Member of Parliament for Somerset, suspected of being the ringleader in the plot when compromising papers from Lord Lansdowne were found in his pocket along with a list of persons favouring the Pretender.

Wyndham subsequently escaped, but finding it impossible to leave the country, gave himself up, and eventually when the unrest died down he was pardoned. On October 18th, Brigadier Bowles' Regiment apprehended eight persons at Bath, including Sir George Brown, Colonel Lansdown, captains Doyle and Sinclair, and Messrs McCarthy, Dunn, McDonnel and William Hibbert. The prisoners were escorted to the Tower of London. Hibbert was a member of a family celebrated through several generations for their skill as engravers. One Charles Hibbert who was hanged in 1819 for forging banknotes was a descendant.

On October 5th at the quarter sessions held at Marlborough:

> John Napper, a clothier of Trowbridge, stood trial for villainous words highly reflecting on his sacred Majesty King George. He pleaded guilty to the indictment, upon which a motion was made by some gentlemen on the bench who considered the heinous nature of the crime, to fine him 500 pounds, to imprison him for a year, and set him in the pillory at three market towns, as an example to like criminals for the future. However, as he promised to mend his ways, he got off with a small fine and the obligation to make a public recantation.

With further outbreaks of hostilities in Bristol, Colonel Erle sent for General Wade to bring over some troops to help quell the rioters. The 18th-century Annals of Bristol gave the following account:

> Hordes of colliers and labourers, hired for the purpose and primed with liquor by some fanatical Tories, had burst into the city, where they were joined by a great number of the lower class. A report had spread that the dissenters had prepared effigies of Sachervell, with the intention of burning them at the bonfires; this provoked

an attack on the meeting house in Tucker Street, and several private houses. After committing much destruction in the city, the sufferers being dissenters or prominent Hanoverians, the rabble adjourned to Queen Square where they smashed the windows of the custom house, and forced the terrified ladies within to seek safety in flight.

The Bristol Corporation, angry and indignant, requested the government to issue a special commission for the trial of the rioters, and three judges were accordingly sent down in November 1715. A great crowd assembled on the arrival of the judges, and their entry into the city was converted into a political demonstration in which seditious slogans were much in evidence. An ultra-Tory merchant named Hart even ventured to exhibit Jacobite sympathies in the court but was suppressed by Colonel Erle, who charged him to his face with being an instigator of the riot. The prisoners were of the lowest class and they were dealt with very leniently, the ringleaders having absconded, to the joy of the Jacobites.

Once peace was restored in the city it was time to celebrate and to entertain those who had come to their aid. The cost to the corporation amounted to several hundred pounds, which was chiefly for the entertainment of the troops. Amongst the expenses incurred was the sum of £114. 12s. for entertaining Lord Berkeley, who also presented a butt of sherry; £107. 10s. was given to each captain of the ten companies of the militia, as payment to their sergeants and drummers. There was a sum of £111. 5s. 6d. for batteries and persons to attend them; and for entertaining General Wade a further sum of £20. 3s. 6d., including 1s. 8d. for a barrel of oysters and 38s. 5d. for a Westphalia ham. Added to this total was the sum of £42. 8s. for candles at the Guildhall to maintain a guard. For some weeks to follow, the gates of Bristol were locked nightly at eight o'clock. So confident had the western rebels been of victory that a report spread throughout Paris that on October 29th Bristol had actually fallen into their hands. This curious fact came to light in 1889, on the publication of some letters of the celebrated Duchess of Orleans.

Back in Bath the magistrates received a stern letter from Lord Stanhope, one of the Secretaries of State, rebuking them for allowing such a concentration of rebels to flourish under their noses. The following reply to Lord Stanhope was printed in the *Daily Courant* in London on October 8th 1715:

The Right Honourable Mr. Secretary Stanhope having written a letter to the Magistrates of this town, dated the 1st instant, they have returned an answer, a true copy of which is as follows.

Honoured Sir – In answer to your letter of the 1st of October, we beg leave to assure you we are much concerned at the concourse of Papists, Nonjurors, and other disaffected persons to the present Government of late in the Town. And that any occasion has been given here, or in this part of the Kingdom, which have the honour to serve his Majesty.

We are most thankfully sensible of his Majesty's regard for us in sending Major General Wade with such a force as may be sufficient to prevent the increase of any disorders already begun and fomented in these parts, and to secure our peace for the future; and we hope that by our ready and sincere concurring to support him, our affection to his Majesty's person and Government will be unquestionable and that further apprehensions of danger, or any violation of the public peace, will be prevented.

Our zealous and hearty endeavours for the future shall not be wanting to discountenance any measures that may in the least cast a reflection on his Majesty's happy reign over us: And as we readily embrace every occasion to declare ourselves determined to support the Church by the Law Established, so we shall by our dutiful behaviour towards King GEORGE, the Glorious Defender and Head of it, endeavour to deserve his protection and favour – We are – With all Duty and Respect Your Honour's Most Obedient faithful Humble Servant.

General Wade returned to Bath for the celebrations ordered by the corporation to show their respect for King George. The London *Flying Post* reported the event taking place in Bath on October 29th 1715:

The Loyal Inhabitants of this City expected ere now that their Zeal for his Sacred Majesty King George, and his Illustrious House, shewn on the Day of his Coronation, in their just Celebration of it, would have been transmitted to you by some more able Hand in order to be made publick, and by their example, not only to animate and encourage our true friends, but to deter and shame our Enemies, by so laudable an Undertaking; which I shall communicate in as few words as possibly I can.

The Day was ushered in with the ringing of Bells in all the Churches, which continued for three hours without intermission; about ten o'clock, the Mayor (who had adjourned his being sworn on the usual Day the better to grace the Solemnity of this) with the rest of the Corporation, met at the Guildhall, and proceeded to the Abbey Church in the following manner –

First marched the several companies of Tradesmen, with their Banners displayed; then about a hundred Woolcombers; belonging to a worthy, loyal neighbouring Clothier, all dressed in their best attire, with neat long caps and sashes of Wool, of various beautiful colours; then 50 boys and girls, neatly dressed belonging to the Charity School of this place with a banner both between them, with a Portraiture and Motto suitable to the Day; then came divers Trumpets, Kettle Drums, and other instrumental music, and in magnificent Habits laced with silver, then two Serjeants with large gilt Maces, after which came the Worthy Governor of the City, his Excellency Major General Wade, between the old Mayor and the Mayor elect; after them the Bench of Aldermen, all clothed in Scarlet, and the other members of the Corporation in their proper Formalities.

They were attended by Brigadier Gore, General Meredith, Sir John Rayney, Sir Robert Rich, Colonel Pocock, Colonel Merrik, and Colonel Shute and a numerous train of Officers and Gentlemen in rich apparel with Cockades in their hats. After prayers and a sermon suitable to the Day, all the Congregation proceeded to the Walks behind the Church, where was Lord Windsor's Regiment of Horse, drawn up in Arms in great order; three pieces of Cannon were thrice discharged, with three Vollies of small arms of the whole Regiment, with Trumpets sounding; Drums beating and the ringing of bells, and all other real demonstrations of Joy; The Spectators who were very numerous throwing up their hats and crying Long Live King George, the Prince and Princess and their Royal Issue. At night a magnificent Ball and Collation was prepared at the Town House at the Charge of the General and Officers, and never were such illuminations and bonfires seen in this place; nor was there the least disorder happened, but everything appeared with a face of joy and satisfaction.

It did not take long for the Bath Corporation to realise that by befriending General Wade their fortunes would take an upward turn. He was a man with numerous connections, both political and military. Wade's assignment was a happy stroke for everyone: for the King, whose enemies he routed; later for Bath, to whose welfare he became permanently devoted; for the General himself, who found valued friends; and for Ralph Allen, whose fortune he helped to establish. The following year the Mayor and corporation met to find a way of thanking him for his help in their late troubled times. It was agreed on August 27th 1716 that Major General Wade should be made an honorary freeman of the City of Bath, and in due course he returned to Bath to accept the honour and the event was duly entered into the record books. From that day onwards Wade came to care deeply about the city and the citizens who had taken him to their hearts.

In 1716 there was a threat of another invasion. The King of Sweden, Charles XII, with the promise of 12,000 good Swedish troops, was suspected of aiding and abetting the Jacobites. The British Government received word of it and was forced to take measures to baffle its enemies. General Wade, an expert in counter-insurgency and now charged with maintaining the internal security of the country, was ordered to arrest Count Gyllenberg, the Swedish Ambassador, then resident in London, and take possession of his papers. Accompanied by Colonel Blackney, who had previously reconnoitred the Count's house, Wade proceeded to gain admittance. After the usual courtesies, the General acquainted the Count with the nature of his commission – that he was to put a guard on his person and secure his papers, laying hold at the same time of such as were on the table, and demanding those that were in his escritoire. The Count was indignant at such a breach of international rules and denounced it as a gross outrage, to which Wade stressed the nature of his instructions and his inability to modify them. Finding his visitor inflexible, Gyllenberg desired that he might send for the Spanish Ambassador to consult with him on the grave issue raised. Wade declined to accede to the request, explaining that he had positive orders not to let him speak with anyone and, turning to the Count's lady, respectfully asked for the keys to the escritoire. She haughtily refused the request, declaring that it contained nothing but linen and plate. "Then it must be broken open," was the reply. The escritoire was forced, and inside was found a great many papers and much correspondence, all of which were impounded. Leaving a strong guard upon the residence, Wade conveyed his prisoner to the Tower of London.

There was sufficient evidence in the documents to prove that Charles XII and his ministers knew of the conspiracy. Baron Gortz, his favourite minister, was compromised, and the British Government contrived to have him kidnapped in Guelderland and brought back to England, where he also was lodged in the Tower.

After about a year, the Ambassador and Baron Gortz were released, the King having pardoned them. At the same time, Mr Jackson, the British resident, who had been detained by way of reprisal in Stockholm, was set at liberty. For helping to uncover the conspiracy, George I bestowed on Wade the colonelcy of the 3rd Dragoon Guards. When there was a threat of another invasion in 1719 it was decided to send an expedition under Sir Richard Temple to Vigo with Wade acting as his second in command.

Cardinal Alberoni of Spain, a major figure on the European political stage, sent for the Duke of Ormonde, the disgraced captain general in the British Army, to come to Madrid and discuss the proposed invasion of England. It was agreed to send twenty-nine ships carrying 5,000 soldiers, and another force of 30,000, to the forces of the Duke of Ormonde, who was to take command of a full-scale landing of troops in the West of England. It was then expected that there would be no difficulty in raising an army to support the Stuart cause, to attempt an attack on London. At the same time the senior Jacobite, General James Keith, the Earl Marischal, was to land in the Western Isles and raise the Jacobite clans.

A storm wrecked the fleet carrying Ormonde's army, and only a few hundred Spaniards under the Earl Marischal reached the Isle of Lewis and crossed to Kintail in August 1719. Very few Highlanders joined them, and they were soon rounded up in the valley of Glen Shiel. The ships, badly damaged by the storm, limped back to Spanish ports.

The government, forewarned of the danger, took prompt measures: the troops in the west were reinforced and a powerful fleet was fitted out to cruise the Channel. Sir Richard Temple, with General Wade, sailed to the shipyards of Santona on the northern coast of Spain, where they captured the port of Ribadeo. They landed with 5,000 troops and went on to occupy Vigo and Pontavedra. Vigo surrendered and Pontavedra capitulated and was taken by Wade, who captured and destroyed the arsenal after removing the most valuable guns, stores and ammunition, which were sent on board the fleet. The whole attack was supported by the fleet and, by October 14th, bombardment from land and sea forced the town's surrender. The expedition was completely successful, the only real peril to the troops being from an abundance of wine found in the houses abandoned by the inhabitants. The army remained in Vigo for about four weeks. A defenceless Galicia suffered severe damage to property and crops, and no attempt was made by the English officers to prevent looting. The conflict came to an end in 1720 when Spain was forced to join the Quadruple Alliance and take part in the peace talks, the outcome of which, it was hoped, would bring about the long-awaited peace in the Mediterranean.

Throughout 1720 there were more plots to restore the Stuarts, and Bath was once again implicated. Thomas Carte, the historian, was a lecturer at the abbey; he was an arch-conspirator, and for years acted as an emissary between the English Jacobites and the court of the Pretender in France. Wade arrived in Bath to arrest the traitor, but Carte eluded arrest by jumping from a window in full canonicals and sought refuge in one of his hiding places. He was accused of high treason and fled to France, where he adopted the name of Philips. On his return to England in 1728, he commenced his *Life of James Duke of Ormonde*, published in 1735.

Chapter 5

The Bath Scene

The years Wade spent abroad on one campaign after another left very little time for his family. It was now time to set about finding a permanent residence in London and Bath. The architect chosen to design the house in London was Richard Boyle, 3rd Earl of Burlington, known to art historians as the Architect Earl. He was Lord Lieutenant of the West Riding from 1715 (the year of the Jacobite Rebellion) to 1753. He took the lieutenancy at the age of twenty. His father, Richard, and a great-grandfather, also Richard, preceded him in office. Burlington's status as a major landowner in Ireland (he was also 4th Earl of Cork) and Yorkshire was recognised by George I, who appointed him Lord Treasurer of Ireland and Lord Lieutenant of the East and West Ridings, Yorkshire. He also owned the estate of Marston Grange, in Frome, Somerset. Richard Boyle was celebrated for his architectural tastes and his friendship with artists and men of letters. His earliest project in 1716 was to alter and partly reconstruct Burlington House, Piccadilly, which had been built by his great-grandfather, the 1st Earl of Burlington. He spent great sums in contributing to public works, and was known to prefer that the expense of erecting buildings should fall on him rather than that his country should be deprived of beautiful edifices. In this way, he caused some fine buildings to be finished, both in London and the provinces.

In 1723 Burlington adapted a palazzo facade drawn by Andrea Palladio for the London home of General Wade in Old Burlington Street (which was engraved in *Vitruvius Britannicus* iii). It must also be noted that Wade's name appears among the subscribers to the leading architectural books of the day, including Leoni's edition of Palladio's *Four Books of Architecture* and Campbell's lavishly illustrated *Vitruvius Britannicus*. Wade's London home appears in *Vitruvius Britannicus* iii (as do the homes of a number of Burlington's associates). Wade was a subscriber to the publication of John Gay's poems in 1720, and he was also one of the governors of the Royal Academy of Music. George Vertue, the famous engraver and antiquarian, mentions Wade owning a fine illuminated prayer book, once the property of Queen Margaret of Scotland; this he presented to Lord Burlington. Was it a gesture of thanks to Burlington for building his house?

What were the attractions of this small city that prompted Wade to give up his seat as the Member of Parliament for Hindon in Wiltshire and put himself up for election in Bath? He was duly elected in 1722 to serve with John Codrington.

Bath at that time was a walled city, entered by four gates, and even as late as 1728 the city comprised some 400 to 500 old houses crowded into a small area – no more than fifteen streets, sixteen lanes, five open areas, four terrace walks, and a few private ones. The streets, though less narrow than those of nearby Bristol, were often muddied. The poor state of its lodging houses, and bad lighting of the streets, left much to be desired. One visitor described the city as standing in a hole, and built on a quagmire. Apart from the healing waters, there was very little to recommend it. It relied on its cloth trade and was home to no more than 2,000 to 3,000 people.

The climate is distinctly mild, due to Bath's fortunate location, surrounded by hills which protect it from the extremity of cold and wind. Few places in the British Isles enjoy such mild winters, and high winds in autumn are usually fresh rather than cold. The climate has long encouraged cultivation of crops such as grapes: in the early 18th century, Bath's vineyards were noted for their Black Cluster and muscadine grapes, trained on standards in the foreign manner. In 1719, sixty-nine hogsheads of wine were shipped from Bristol at a price of ten guineas a hogshead. Unfortunately, the crops failed around the year 1730 owing to climatic changes.

By the time Wade came to Bath it was already host to the rich and famous. Royalty, senior military figures, statesmen, aristocrats, country squires, all manner of tricksters and card sharps flocked there. Royalty put an early stamp of approval on the city by their visits: it was undoubtedly continuing royal patronage which transformed Bath from a mere watering place into the unique resort of the fashionable world. The visits of Anne of

Denmark, queen of James VI of Scotland and James I of England, for whom the Queen's Bath was named, were followed in 1677 by the arrival of Charles II, who brought with him his queen, Catherine of Braganza, in the vain hope that a course of the waters would enable her to conceive a healthy child. He seems to have enjoyed his stay enough to make later visits, accompanied on these occasions not by the Queen, but once by the Duchess of Cleveland (better known by her earlier title of Lady Castlemaine). In 1687 James II visited Bath with his second wife, Mary of Modena. In the following year, and again four years later, his daughter, Princess Anne, who suffered from gout, came to take the waters, accompanied by her husband, Prince George of Denmark. In 1702, the year in which she succeeded to the throne, she made a third visit, and then a fourth in the following year. They all came to consult the growing number of apothecaries and doctors. Occasionally, however, visitors expressed a dislike for the place. The Duchess of Marlborough disliked the city and only came because it 'did her dear Marlborough some good'.

During Wade's time in Bath he was to become much more than its representative in Parliament. He became its fast friend; he lived there and loved it, and identified himself with its local institutions. The city had indeed found a generous benefactor, and Wade rewarded the people for their friendship and loyalty. There were those who remembered him back in 1715 riding in the parade resplendent in the red coat of an officer. He was described as of handsome appearance, tall, burly and, as the artist van Diest described him, with dark blue-grey eyes, light-brown eyebrows and fresh complexion. He was also rich, affable, open-minded and practical; there was a bluff good nature about him. He was vain and loved to have his portrait painted; and there are numerous portraits of him in the major galleries, apart from those in private hands.

Wade's love of 'deep play' in low gambling houses was well known, but he seems to have played with the caution which characterised his military tactics; he had nothing of the infatuation of the addict. Deep play was continuous gaming over prolonged periods of time for very high stakes.

Cash and land securities changed hands, and the game led to the downfall of many; by 1721 deep players were bidding large sums at Bath's faro tables and in other popular games, such as ombre, piquet and bassett – an old Venetian game where fortunes could be squandered all too readily. Faro (or pharaoh) appears to have been the most popular of the three at Bath. It required a special table painted with a suit of thirteen cards, on which bets were placed and against which the banker drew cards, one at a time, from a dealing box, with the odds constantly changing according to the order of the cards. In 1739 faro and its variant bassett, together with the ace of hearts, a game witnessed at Harrison's rooms in 1725 were banned by Parliament. The game still operated illegally much later in the century.

Wade's love of women was also renowned, leading Walpole to write, 'I would trust Wade with my life, but not where women are concerned.' No doubt he set a few female hearts a-flutter during his time in Bath, as his great nephew, the grandson of his brother, William, was to do many years later. Captain William Wade, known as the Bath Adonis, was for many years the master of ceremonies at Bath.

Four men have been credited with making Bath the beautiful city we know today: they are Beau Nash, the extrovert impresario; Ralph Allen, the postal pioneer and wealthy quarry-owner; John Wood, the architect; and General Wade.

As early as 1704, Captain William Webster was appointed the master of ceremonies in Bath. Webster set about organising a series of balls at the town hall at half a guinea a head, and proceeded to provide facilities for gaming. The effect of this was immediate, and the spirit of gaming daily increased, causing a great disturbance amongst not only the visitors but the inhabitants of the city. Bath was becoming a lawless place, but this was soon to change on the arrival of a man who was to put Bath firmly on the map.

The facilities for play drew large numbers of visitors, enthusiastic to try their luck at the gaming tables; in 1704 a party of young men came down from London and among them was Richard Nash, ex-military officer, ex-lawyer, who appeared to make his money from gambling. Nash came to win a few pounds at hazard, and achieved a fortune and great celebrity for the next fifty years. Nash soon formed a friendship with Captain Webster; and, after Webster was killed in 1705 in a duel in the Grove, the corporation offered the post of master of ceremonies to Nash. They had chosen well: he seized the opportunity and lost no time in making Bath attractive to visitors, having observed that, apart from gambling, there were few enjoyments to be had there. There were pleasant walks, and a stroll in the Kingsmead, to sample the little cake houses and to try the fruit syllabubs, was always looked upon with pleasure; there was a bowling green but very little else in the way of amusements. For five months of the year Bath was crowded, and for the other seven, quietly forgotten. Had it not been for the natural springs pumping out warm mineral water it is doubtful that anyone of importance would have been remotely interested in visiting.

Richard Nash was to change all this. He made the amusements self-supporting. He engaged a band from London to play in public places, and charged a subscription of one guinea to the visitors during the season. Nash further collected subscriptions to the amount of £1,800 to improve the roads and lighting. Not content with that, he persuaded Thomas Harrison to build a room for dancing on the east side of the Grove with access to the bowling green, which then became known as Harrison's Walks. He laid down strict rules of behaviour at social functions: for example, gentlemen were not allowed to wear riding boots or swords, and duelling was banned; members of the aristocracy were firmly told that rudeness to fellow guests of a lower station would not be tolerated; and the ladies were informed that their apparel and behaviour was to be beyond reproach.

Nash, it was said, did as much as any other person in the 18th century to civilise the neglected manners of the people. He was a truly remarkable man. With the attractions now provided, the popularity of Bath rose by leaps and bounds: it was no longer a mere health resort, but the first pleasure ground in England and the ideal place outside London to socialise with the nobility and the upper classes. Richard Nash, now known as Beau Nash, had become its king.

The second pioneer of major change to arrive in Bath was Ralph Allen, who at home in Cornwall had assisted his grandmother, the postmistress at St Columb. According to the official history of the Post Office of that period, there were only two cross-posts in 1710, as distinct from branch routes on the main London road. They connected Exeter and Chester, Bath and Oxford. At the time of the 1710 developments Allen was a youth of sixteen years, and by 1714 he was a postal clerk in the Bath office. Although only a young man, he saw the possibilities for developing the cross-posts as a valuable public service. It was believed at the time, in 1715, that Allen gave General Wade valuable information on the uprising in the West.

As the sub-postmaster, Allen may have looked into suspicious correspondence – something deputies were allowed to do upon written warrant from the Secretary of State. He may also have learned of the rebel movements from his friends and relatives in Cornwall, where it was believed the common people were ripe for rebellion. In St Columb, six or seven people publicly proclaimed the Pretender; two were captured, and a reward of £100 was offered by the government for the others. Allen was a go-ahead young man who felt that with the right backing he could transform the postal service. He put forward his ideas to General Wade, who was garrisoned in Bath with his regiment. Wade listened to Allen's proposals and examined his scheme, discussing its possibilities and risks and ultimately giving Allen not only his warm approval, but the promise of his influence and financial backing. He undertook to find others to back Allen's scheme.

Wade knew from experience the need to have in place a well-run and honest postal system. He put forward Allen's plan through his connections with the son of Mr Erskine-Hill, the postmaster general. He was Allen's bondsman to the Treasury when proposals were put before Charles, the first Earl Cornwallis and James Craggs, a dependant of Marlborough and Lord Sunderland. They granted Allen a farm (i.e. a monopoly investment), partly based on the surveyor's report that Allen kept strict accounts of all the by-letters from his first years of employment in the postal business. The need for cross-country posts had been met in 1660 with the institution of the by-post system – the carriage of mails along the byways. Sheffield, Derby and Lincoln were typical of the towns which had previously been isolated and were now provided with connections to the nearest point on the trunk postal routes. By the end of the 17th century, smaller towns, like Stratford-on-Avon, Shrewsbury, and Coventry, were included in the growing network of by-posts.

Wade agreed to stand bondsman to the government. The contract was signed on April 12th 1720 and was to extend for seven years. Allen was to pay an annual fee of £6,000 – £2,000 a year more than the actual revenue when he took over, indicative of his faith in the way it could be developed. As it happened, he lost money on the first contract, but in this preparatory period he steadily went on organising routes. The contract was periodically renewed for the rest of his long life. From that time, his management of the postal system went from strength to strength, making a handsome estimated profit for himself and no doubt for his patron, General Wade. Ralph Allen was truly a man of vision. Wade was quick to recognise the capabilities and integrity he found in him and in return Allen was for ever indebted to the man above all others who helped in laying the foundation of his fortune.

Mr Erskine-Hill in *The Social Milieu of Alexander Pope* not only attributes Allen's early political views to Wade's influence, but also his love of Palladian architecture; this resulted in Ralph Allen's beautiful mansion, Prior Park. Allen supported John Wood in his schemes for transforming Bath into a classical city. If this is so, our debt to Wade is enormous and it can be truly said that Wade, along with Beau Nash, Ralph Allen and John Wood created the 18th-century city. It was believed at the time that Allen married General Wade's daughter, Jane Erle, and that she died within a year of marriage. This is impossible, as Jane Erle, who was Wade's illegitimate daughter, was still alive in 1748 when she was mentioned in his will.

For a vivid portrait of Allen, it is worthwhile studying the character Squire Allworthy in Fielding's *Tom Jones*, which depicts him. By then he was a wealthy quarry-owner, friend of royalty, and man of letters, Mayor of Bath, and postmaster of the city when it was one of the most important provincial mail centres in the country.

The third pioneer of change was John Wood, an architect, born in Bath in 1705, the son of Thomas Wood, a local builder. Wood was a pupil at the Blue Coat School and later left Bath to take up an apprenticeship in London. He returned in 1727 fired with a dream of building houses in the classical style, true to the orders of Roman architecture – with Doric pillars at the foot, Ionic in the middle and Corinthian at the top, with a forum and a circus in the Palladian style. Wood at that time was a young man without the means to carry out his scheme to turn Bath into a Roman city.

James Brydges, the Duke of Chandos, was staying in the city for the treatment of a 'twitching upon his nerves' and, in order to be close to the Cross Bath, he took up lodgings with Mrs Anne Phillips. Chandos found her lodgings objectionable. They were, he wrote, 'old rotten lodgings' and he resolved to do something about it. In the expanding market, he intended to make money into the bargain. He negotiated with Mrs Phillips to buy the site and the architect chosen to design Chandos Buildings was John Wood. A partnership was forged between the Duke of Chandos, England's biggest financial tycoon, and John Wood, an unknown and struggling surveyor. The dream became reality and today tourists from all over the world come to Bath – a World Heritage City – to admire the beauty of its buildings in the honey-coloured freestone mined in Ralph Allen's quarries.

The fourth man, now relatively unknown, was General Wade, intelligent and cultivated and with an enthusiasm for the new Palladian architecture, the orderliness of which accorded well with his Whig politics. This was reflected in the construction of three houses and the Scottish bridges, roads and garrisons for which he became best known.

It is worth detailing a few of the numerous gifts Wade gave to the city during his lifetime. The first mention of a gift was to Bath Abbey of a stone christening font bearing the date 1710. In 1725 he donated a magnificent altarpiece, which was composed of a rich marble structure by Samuel Tufnell surrounding a painting described as *The Wise Men's Offerings* by Johan van Diest. Enclosing the whole was an elaborate rail of wrought iron. Wade's gift is broadly based on the wooden altarpieces of Wren's London churches but translated into marble and has a more evidently Palladian influence, as you might expect from one who loved this style. The altarpiece did not remain permanently in the abbey, however.

It was later removed and installed in the hall of Grosvenor Villa, Bath, while the wrought-iron communion rail – the work of William Edney of Bristol – was removed during the 1880s and later discovered on the balcony of a house in Lansdown Place West.

It was returned to the abbey through the generosity of the Dowager Lady Noble, who paid for it to be restored and erected as a screen across the north transept incorporating the arms of Lady Noble and General Wade. Another part of the screen can be seen in St Alphege's Roman Catholic chapel in Bath, where it forms the communion rail. Wade commissioned Johan van Diest to paint *The Three Wise Men* for the altarpiece, and later employed him at his own expense to paint the portraits of the thirty-one Bath councillors, the town clerk and the recorder for Bath as a token of his gratitude to the men who had honoured him with election to Parliament. Seven portraits have survived and can be seen in the Guildhall.

The corporation in return commissioned Johan van Diest to paint a full-length portrait of Wade, and today it hangs in the Banqueting Rooms at the Guildhall. Wade is in good company beside the portraits of Ralph Allen; William Pitt, 1st Earl of Chatham and one-time Member of Parliament for Bath; the poet and humorist Christopher Anstey; Augusta of Saxe-Gotha, the youngest daughter of Frederick II, the wife of Frederick, Prince of Wales and later the mother of George III; George III himself; Charlotte Sophia, his consort; and James Scott, Duke of Monmouth. Their Royal Highnesses, the Prince and Princess of Wales visited Bath in 1738. In honour of their visit an obelisk was erected by Nash in Queen Square for which the poet Alexander Pope agreed to write an inscription. At a special dinner held on November 2nd 1738 the corporation conferred the freedom of the city upon the Prince, and honorary freedom upon members of the royal suite. Before leaving, the Prince 'cleared the prison of all debtors' and gave 1,000 guineas towards the building of the general hospital.

The most important service the General rendered to the city was the aid he gave in clearing the houses clinging to the north side of the abbey. They were described in the *Notabilia of Bath*, written in 1893 by R. E. M. Peach, as a narrow passage, the houses on one side of which were built against the north side of the Abbey Church and extending from the church to the Orange Grove. Clearance would prevent the church (which had become a common thoroughfare) being used by persons passing to the baths. Wade further persuaded the corporation by a money grant to demolish sixteen houses to make a passageway from the Abbey Churchyard to his new home. The route was thereafter known as Wade's Passage.

The architect who designed Wade's house is unknown, but it is now generally believed he employed Thomas Greenway, a local builder and architect. The evidence for this is that a Mr Greenway was a subscriber to *Vitruvius Britannicus*. Wade was a kind and encouraging patron to other artists, and he may have acted in the same way to Greenway. Taking all this into account, it becomes easy to understand how Wade was attracted to Bath, where lay the imagined remains of the classical architecture he admired.

The front and back of Wade's house were ornate. Years later, in the 19th century, the house was much reduced to widen the street, and

the back of the house, situated in the Abbey Churchyard became the front. Today it is owned by the Landmark Trust and let to visitors. It is also home to a National Trust shop.

When funds were needed to rebuild the Blue Coat School, Wade donated £100. In 1733 he donated 500 guineas to the council to be used for 'some public good and advantage to the city'. Ralph Allen acted as a depository for the sum while the council debated how to use it. At the time, John Wood, the architect, was commissioned to design an additional upper chamber to the Pump Room, the existing one being much too small to accommodate all the noble and fashionable invalids who flocked to it every morning; and when Wood showed the designs to Wade, he agreed that the 500 guineas be set aside for that purpose. This was turned down, however, because the Mayor's son, then renting Shaylor's coffee house, felt the improved Pump Room would draw the customers from his son's business, resulting in a loss of trade. It was then proposed to put the money towards rebuilding St Michael's Church. Allen was not in favour of this as he believed the General intended the gift to go towards the Pump Room. In the end Wade agreed to support the rebuilding of St Michael's with a proviso that some of the pews were reserved for the Bath Corporation. He continued to give handsomely to the corporation from time to time for public entertainments and was one of the first to donate to the fund for building the Mineral Water Hospital.

It is unclear why Wade, who was a latitudinarian in religion (allowing latitude, showing no preference among varying creeds and forms of worship) and a despiser of dogmatic theology, should grant handsome sums of money to the church. His reservations prompted Bishop Newton to write in the preface to his *Dissertation on the Prophecies*, published in 1754, 'What first suggested this design were some conversations formerly with a great General, who was a man of good understanding and some reading, but unhappily had no great regard for revealed religion, and when the prophecies were urged as a proof of revelation, constantly derided them'. Wade's preoccupation at that time was not with religious dogma but with current developments. There were murmurings of another uprising throughout the country, which led the government to think seriously about disarming the lawless clans who were intent on opposing the Hanoverian succession. One man believed he had the answer to the government's problems and duly sent his report to London.

Chapter 6

The State of the Highlands

Simon Fraser, Lord Lovat, the chief of the clan Fraser, was born in 1667, the son of Thomas Beaufort. His one true loyalty was to his clan and his family. During the 1715 rising Fraser stayed resolutely out of the action, whilst busy writing to both sides as usual to try to ingratiate himself. In 1719 he went one stage further with his plotting. When the 1719 rising started he wrote to the leader of the Jacobite Highland forces, the Earl of Seaforth, promising to raise his clan and join him. This was leaked to the government in London, but fortunately Fraser was tipped off that he had been betrayed, and managed to wheedle his way out again. He gave orders to his clan to oppose the rising, and then headed to London. His arrival at court, coupled with the news that Frasers had taken Seaforth's lands, brought him into such favour that King George I agreed to be his son's godfather. Simon spent the next few years in an attempt to consolidate his power.

Simon Fraser claimed he could bring about peace in the Highlands, and in 1724 he wrote a paper addressed to the King – 'A Memorial on the State of the Highlands' – in which he advocated strengthening the legal and armed power of the Highland chiefs in order to keep the peace. The King and his advisers read Lovat's report and agreed there was a lot to recommend it. What concerned them most was that the report revealed a little too much about Simon Fraser, who was described as 'the Fox' and the most devious man in Scotland. It was felt that Fraser was out to make Scotland a more profitable place for himself. He was famous for his violent feuding and his changes of allegiance. In 1715 he had been a supporter of the House of Hanover and at other times supported the Stuart cause. Throughout his life Fraser kept a large number of retainers, all seated at the same table as himself but in a social pecking order – the lower end were given whisky whilst Simon and his guests drank fine clarets. Finally Fraser changed sides once too often and, after the Battle of Culloden in 1746, he was obliged to go into hiding. Eventually he was found in a hollowed-out tree on the island of Morar. Escorted to London to stand trial for treason, he was sentenced to death on March 19th 1747. Fraser's execution took place on April 9th and he was the last man to be beheaded on Tower Hill.

It did not take the government long to find their own man – one whom they felt capable of carrying out the pacification of the Highlands, and who most importantly could be trusted. They turned to General Wade, who had the qualities needed for such an undertaking. He was a skilled negotiator, with engineering abilities from his many years in the army overseeing the building of bridges and roads, including the time he spent on the island of Minorca, where he was involved in building the first roads. There were those who believed he was an Irishman – sending an Englishman into the Highlands was likely to cause trouble. He was also a man known for his diplomatic skills, who, it was said, always listened to both sides. The day after Wade received His Majesty's instructions under the royal sign manual dated July 3rd 1724, he proceeded on his journey north, arriving in Edinburgh some days later.

The Highlands were historically a region of wild clans, forbidding mountains, and glowering skies. The Highlanders were used to the cyclonic storms that swept across the Atlantic, and the bitterly cold winters. There were few who would venture into this, the remotest and wildest part of the kingdom, where they believed the inhabitants were lawless and savage. The Highlands held no fears for a man like Wade, who was used to discomfort and hostility. As he travelled through the most uncivilised parts of the Highlands, he would have seen a land of wild, silent places, wilderness and awe-inspiring mountain ranges set in a sea of purple heather. The roads, where they existed, were dangerous; there were few bridges to ford the fast-flowing streams and rivers. The Highlands may have been lawless but the scenery was truly magnificent. The wild landscape reminded him of the Catalonia – the most mountainous area in Spain. Wade would have observed the Highlands as Daniel Defoe saw them when he toured Northern Scotland around the year 1720.

This is an extract from Defoe's account printed in 1724:

> The rivers and lakes are prodigiously full of salmon; it is hardly credible what the people relate of the quantity of salmon taken in these rivers, especially in the Spey, The Nairn and the Ness. The mountains are so full of deer, harts, roebucks, &c. Here is also a great number of eagles which breed in the woods, and which prey upon the young fawns when they first fall. Some of these eagles are of a mighty kind, such as are not to be seen again in those parts of the world. Here are also the best hawks of all the kinds for sport which are in the kingdom, and which the nobility and gentry of Scotland make great use of. The inhabitants are not so wild and barbarous as, perhaps, they were in those times or as our writers have pretended. We see every day the gentlemen born here, such as the Mackenzies, McLeans, Dundonalds, Gordons, McKays and others who are named among the clans as if they were barbarians, appear at court, and in our camps and armies, as polite, and as finished gentlemen as any from other countries, or even as our own; and if I should say, outdoing our own in many things, especially in arms and gallantry.

Wade was mindful that the Highlanders were a force to be reckoned with and that he had a distasteful job to carry out for the King and for the government, but he was determined to fulfil his commission. As we shall see, he made very few enemies in the ten years he spent disarming the clans and building the military roads and bridges. Wade spent many months travelling in the Highlands, and on his return to London he prepared his report – a report that was so well received by the government that they offered him the task of returning to the Highlands of Scotland to set about disarming the disaffected. General Wade's report was delivered to George I on December 10th 1724:

> In Obedience to your Majesty's Commands and Instructions under your Royal Sign Manuel bearing date the 3rd day of July, Commanding me to go into the Highlands of Scotland, and narrowly to inspect the present situation of the Highlanders, their Customs, Manners and the State of the Country in regard to the Robberies and Depredations, said to be committed in that part of your Majesty's Dominions; As also to make strict and particular enquiry into the effect of the last Law for the Disarming the Highlanders and for securing your Majesty's Loyal and faithful Subjects, represented to be left naked and defenceless by paying

due obedience thereto; and to inform your Majesty of all other particulars contained in the said instructions, and how far the Memorial delivered to your Majesty by Simon Lord Lovat and his remarks thereupon are founded on facts, and the present practices of those people;

And whether the remedies mentioned therein may properly be applied for preventing the several grievances, abuses, and violence's complained of in the said Memorial. Your Majesty had farther been pleased to Command me to make such enquiries and endeavours to get such information, relating to the several particulars above mentioned as may enable me to suggest to your Majesty, such other remedies as may conduce to the Quiet of your Faithful Subjects and the good settlement of that part of the Kingdom.

The Day after I received your Majesty's instructions I proceeded on my Journey, and have travelled through the Highlands of Scotland; And humbly beg leave to lay before your Majesty the following Report, which I have collected as well from my own observations, with all faithfulness and impartiality, as from the best information I could procure during my continuance in that part of the Country.

The Highlands are the Mountainous Parts of Scotland, not defined or described by any precise limits or boundaries of Counties or Shires but are Tracts of Mountains, in extent of Land, more than one half of the Kingdom of Scotland and are for the most part on the Western Ocean, extending from Dumbarton to the North End of the island of Great Britain, near 200 miles in length, and from about 40 to 80 miles in breadth. All the islands on the West and North-West Seas are called Highlands as well from their Mountainous Situation, as from the Habits, Customs, Manners and Language of their inhabitants. The Lowlands are all that part of Scotland on the South of Forth and Clyde, and on the East side of the Kingdom from the Firth of Edinburgh to Caithness near the Orkneys is a Tract of low Country from 4 to 20 miles in Breadth.

The number of Men able to carry Arms in the Highlands (including the inhabitants of the Isles) is by the nearest Computation about 22,000 men, of which number about 10,000 are Vassals to the Superiors well affected to your Majesty's Government; most remaining 12,000 have been engaged in Rebellion against your Majesty, and are ready, whenever encouraged by their Superiors or Chiefs of Clans, to create new troubles and rise in Arms in favour of the Pretender.

Their notions of Virtue and vice are very different from the more civilised part of Mankind. They think it a most sublime virtue to pay a servile and abject obedience to the Commands of their Chieftains, altho' in opposition to their Sovereign and the laws of the Kingdom, and to encourage this, their fidelity, they are treated by their Chiefs with great familiarity, they partake with them in their diversions, and shake them by the hand wherever they meet them.

The virtue next to this, in esteem amongst them, is the love they bear to that particular branch of which they are a part, and in a second degree to the whole Clan, or Name, by assisting each other (right or wrong) against any other Clan with whom they are at variance, and great barbarities are often committed by one to revenge the quarrels of another. They have still a more extensive adherence one to another as Highlanders in opposition to the People who inhabit the Low Countries, whom they hold in the utmost contempt, imaging them inferior to themselves in courage, resolution, and the use of Arms, and accuse them of being proud, avaricious and breakers of their word. They have also a tradition amongst them that the Lowlands were in Ancient times the inheritance of their Ancestors, and therefore believe they have a right to commit depredations whenever it is in their power to put them in execution.

The Highlanders are divided into Tribes or Clans, under Lairds, or Chieftains (as they are called in the Laws of Scotland), each tribe or clan is subdivided into little branches from the main stock who have also Chieftains over them, and from these are still smaller branches of fifty or sixty men, who deduce their origin from them, and on whom they rely as their protectors and defenders. The arms they make use of in War, are, a Musket, a Broad Sword and Target, a Pistol and a Durk or Dagger, hanging by their side, with a Powder Horn and Pouch for their Ammunition. They form themselves into bodies of unequal numbers according to the strength of their Clan or Tribe, which is commanded by their respective Superior or Chieftain. When in sight of the enemy they endeavour to possess themselves of the highest ground, believing they descend on them with greater force

They generally give their fire at a distance; they lay down their arms on the ground and make a vigorous attack with their Broad Swords; but if repulsed, seldom or never rally again. They dread engaging with the Cavalry and seldom venture to descend from the Mountains when apprehensive of being charged by them.

On sudden alarms, or when a Chieftain is in distress, they give notice to their Clans or those in alliance with them, by sending a man with what they call the Fiery Cross, which is a stick in the form of a cross, burnt at the end, which is then carried on to the next Tribe or Clan. They carry with it a written paper directing them where to assemble; upon sight of which they leave their habitation and with great expedition repair to the place of rendezvous, with arms, ammunition and meal for their provision.

I presume also to represent to your Majesty, that the manners and customs of the Highlanders, their way of living, their strong friendships, and adherence to those of their own name, tribe and family, their blind and servile submission to the Commands of their Superiors and Chieftains, and the little regard they have ever paid to the Laws of the Kingdom, both before and since the Union, are truly set forth in Lord Lovat's Memorials and other matters contained in the said paper, which your Majesty was pleased to direct should be put in my hands to peruse and examine.

The imposition mentioned in the Memorial commonly called the Black Meal is levied by the Highlanders on almost all the Low Country bordering thereon. But as it is equally Criminal by the Laws of Scotland to pay this Exaction or to Extort it the inhabitants to avoid the penalty of the Laws, agree with the Robbers, or some of their correspondents in the Lowlands to protect their horses and cattle, who are in effect but their Stewards or Factors, and as long as this payment continues, the depredations cease upon their Lands, otherwise the Collector of this illegal imposition is obliged to make good the loss they have sustained. They give regular receipts for the same safe guard money, and those who refuse to submit to this imposition are sure of being plundered, there being no other way to avoid it but by keeping a constant guard of armed men, which, altho' it is sometimes done, is not only illegal, but a more expensive way of securing their property.

The Clans in the Highlands, the most addicted to Rapine and Plunder, are, the Cameron's on the West of the Shire of Inverness, the Mackenzie's and others in the Shire of Ross who were Vassals to the late Earl of Seaforth, the McDonell's of Keppoch, the Broadalbin Men, and the McGregors on the borders of Argyleshire. They go out in parties from ten to thirty men, traverse large tracts of Mountains till they arrive at the Lowlands where they design to commit depredations, which they choose to do in places distant from the Clans where they inhabit; They drive the stolen cattle in the night time, and in the day remain on the tops of the mountains or in the woods (with which the Highlands abound) and take the first occasion to sell them at the fairs or markets that are annually held in many parts of the Country.

Those who are robbed of their cattle (or persons employed by them) follow them by the tract and often recover them from the Robbers by compounding for a certain sum of money agreed on, but if the pursuers are armed and in numbers superior to the Thieves and happen to seize any of them, they are seldom or never prosecuted, the poorer sort being unable to support the charge of Prosecution.

They are likewise under the apprehension of becoming the object of their revenge, by having their houses and stacks burnt, their cattle stolen or hockt, and their lives at the mercy of the Tribe or Clan to whom the Banditti belong. The richer sort (to keep, as they call it good Neighbourhood) generally compound with the Chieftain of the Tribe or Clan, for double restitution, which he willingly pays to save one of his Clan from Prosecution, and this is repaid by him by a contribution from the Thieves of his Clan, who never refuse the payment of their proportion to save one of their own fraternity. The Composition is seldom paid in money, but in cattle stolen from the opposite side of the Country to make reparation to the person injured.

The Chiefs of some of these Tribes never fail to give countenance to those of their own Clan; and tho' they are taken and committed to prison, by the Plaintiff [who is] better satisfied than if the Criminal was executed, since he must [be] at the charge and trouble of a tedious dilatory and expensive Prosecution; and I was assured by one who annually attended the Assizes at Inverness for four years past, that there had been but one person executed there by the Lords of Justiciary and that (as I remember) for Murder, tho' that place is the Judicature, in Criminal Cases, for the greatest part of the Highlands of Scotland.

There is another practice used in the Highlands, by which the cattle stolen are often recovered, which is, by sending persons to that part of the Country most suspected and making an offer of a reward (which the Highlanders call Tascal-Money) to any who will discover the cattle and the persons who stole them, by the temptation of the reward and promise of secrecy, discoveries were often made and restitution obtained. But to put a stop to a practice they thought an injury to the Tribe, the whole Clan of the Camerons (and other since by their example) bound themselves by Oath never to take Tascal-Money, nor to inform one against the other. This they take upon a drawn Durk or Dagger, which they kiss in a solemn manner and the penalty declared to be due to the said oath, is, to be stabbed with the same Dagger. This manner of swearing is much in practice on all other occasions, to bind themselves one to another that they may with more sincerity exercise their villainy, which they imagine less sinful than the

Breach of that oath, since they commit all sorts of crimes with impunity, and are so severely punished if forsworn. An instance of this happened in December 1723, when one of the Clan of the Camerons suspected to have taken Tascal Money, was in the night time called out of his hut from his wife and children and hanged up near his own door. Another of that Tribe was, for the same crime (as they call it) kept a month in the stocks and afterwards privately made away with.

The encouragement and protection given by some of the Chiefs of Clans is reciprocally rewarded by giving them a share of the plunder, which is sometimes one half or two thirds of what is stolen. They exercise an arbitrary and tyrannical power over them. They determine all disputes and differences that happen among their Vassals, and on extraordinary occasions such as the marriage of a daughter, the building of a house, or any other pretence for the support of their Chief, or honour of the name, he levies a tax on the Tribe; to which imposition, if anyone refuse to contribute, he is sure of the severest treatment or at best to be cast out of the Tribe. And it is not be wondered that those who submit to this servile slavery, will, when summoned by their superiors, follow them into Rebellion.

To remedy these inconveniences there was an Act of Parliament, passed in the year 1716 for the more effectual securing the Peace of the Highlands in Scotland, by disarming the Highlanders, which has been so ill executed, that the Clans the most disaffected to your Majesty's Government remain better armed than ever, and consequently more in a capacity not only of committing robberies and depredations, but to be used as tools or instruments to any Foreign Power or Domestic Incendiaries who may attempt to disturb the peace of your Majesty's Reign. By this Act the Collectors for taxes were empowered to pay for the Arms delivered in, as they were valued by persons appointed for that service in the respective Countries, but as the Government was to support the Charge, they did not scruple to appraise them at a much higher rate than their real worth, few or none being delivered up except such as were broken and unfit for Service; And I have been informed that from the time of passing that Act, to the time it was put in execution, great quantities of broken and useless Arms were brought from Holland and delivered up to the persons to receive the same at exorbitant prices.

The Spaniards who landed at Castle Donnan in the year 1719 brought with them a great Number of Arms; They were delivered to the Rebellious Highlanders who are still possessed of them, many of which I have seen in my passage through that Country, and I judge them to be the same from their peculiar make, and the fashion of their locks. These and others now in their possession by a moderate computation are supposed to amount 5 or 6000, besides those in the possession of the Clans who are in your Majesty's interest, provided as they allege, for their own defence.

The Legislature in Scotland before the Union of the Kingdoms have ever considered the Highlands in a different State from the rest of the Nation, and made peculiar Laws for their Government under the severest penalties. The Chieftains of Clans were obliged to send their children or nearest relations to Edinburgh as hostages for the good behaviour of their respective Clans, and in default they might by the Law be put to death.

The Clans and Tribes who lived in a state of anarchy and confusion (as they seem to be in at this present time) were, by the very words of the Act of Parliament to be pursued with Fire and Sword, but as the Execution of the Laws relating to the Highlands was under the care of the Privy Council of Scotland (now no longer subsisting, who by Act of Parliament were obliged to sit the first Day in every Month for that purpose) It often happened that men of great power in the Highlands were of the said Council, who had no other way of rendering themselves considerable than from their numbers of Armed Men, and consequently the less Zealous in putting the Laws of Execution against them. The Independent Companies raised by King William not long after the Revolution reduced the Highlanders into better order than at any time they had been in since the Restoration. They were composed of the Natives of the Country, inured to the fatigue of travelling the Mountains, lying on the Hills, wore the same habit, and spoke the same language; but for want of being put under proper regulations, corruptions were introduced, and some who commanded them, instead of bringing criminals to Justice (as I am informed) often compounded for the theft and for a sum of money set them at liberty. They are said also to have defrauded the Government by keeping not above half their numbers in constant pay; which, as I humbly conceive, might be the reason Your Majesty caused them to be disbanded.

Your Barracks were afterwards built in different parts of the Highlands, and parties of the regular troops under the Command of Highland Officers, with a Company of 30 guides (Established to conduct them through the Mountains) was thought an effectual scheme, as well to prevent the rising of the Highlanders disaffected to your Majesty's Government, as to hinder the depredation on your faithful subjects. It is to be wished that during the Reign of your Majesty and your Successors, no insurrections may ever happen to experience whether the Barracks will effectually answer the end proposed; yet I am humbly of the opinion; that if the number of troops they are built to contain, was constantly quartered in them (whereas there is now in some but 30 men) and proper provisions laid in for their support during the winter season, they might be of some use to prevent the insurrections of the Highlanders; though as I humbly conceive, (having seen them all) that two of the four are not built in as proper situations as they might have been.

As to the Highland Parties, I have already presumed to represent to your Majesty the little use they were of in hindering depredations, and the great sufferings of the soldiers employed in that Service, upon which your Majesty was graciously pleased to countermand them.

I must further beg leave to Report to your Majesty that another great cause of disorders in the Highlands, is the want of proper persons to execute the several offices of Civil Magistrates, especially in the Shires of Ross, Inverness and some other parts of the Highlands. The Party Quarrels and violent animosities amongst the Gentlemen (equally well affected to your Majesty's Government) I humbly conceive to be one great cause of this defect. Those who were in Arms for your Majesty, who raised a spirit in the Shire of Inverness and recovered the Town of that name from the rebels (their main body being then at Perth) complain, that the persons employed as Magistrates over them have little credit or interest in that Country, and that three of the Deputy Sheriffs in those parts were persons actually in Arms against your Majesty at the time of the late Rebellion which (as I am credibly informed) is true. They likewise complain that many of the most considerable Gentlemen are left out in the Commissions of Lord Lieutenants, Deputy Lieutenants, Sheriffs, etc. I take the liberty to observe that the want of acting Justices of the Peace is a great encouragement to the disorders so frequently committed in that part of the Country, there being but one, residing as an acting Justice for the space of above a hundred miles in compass.

Your Majesty's commands requiring me to examine into the State and Condition of the late Earl of Seaforth's Estate, engaged me to go to the Castle of Brahan his Principal Seat, and other parts of the said estate, which for the most part is Highland Country, and extends from Brahan to Kintail on the Western Coast, being 36 miles in length and the most Mountainous part of the Highlands; The whole Isle of Lewis was also a part of the said Earl's Estate. The Tenants before the late rebellion were reputed the richest of any in the Highlands, but now are become poor by neglecting their business and applying themselves wholly to the use of Arms. The rents continue to be levied by one Donald Murchieson a servant of the late Earl's who annually remits (or carries) the same to his Master into France.

The Tenants when in a condition are also said to have sent him free gifts in proportion to their several circumstances but are now a year and a half in arrears of rent. The receipts he gives to the Tenants are, as Deputy Factor to the Commissioners of Forfeited Estates, which pretended power in the year 1721 he extorted from the Factor appointed by the said Commissioners to collect those rents for the use of the public, whom he attacked with above 400 Arm'd Men as he was going to enter upon the said Estate; having with him a body of 30 of your Majesty's Troops. The last year this Murchieson travelled in a public manner to Edinburgh to remit £800 to France for his Master's use, and remained there fourteen days unmolested.

I cannot omit observing to your Majesty; this National tenderness your Subjects of North Britain have one for the other, is great encouragement to the rebels and attainted persons to return home from their banishment.

Before I conclude this Report, I presume to observe to your Majesty the great disadvantages regular troops are under when they engage with those who inhabit Mountainous situations. The Serennes [sic] In France, and Catalans in Spain, have in all times been instances of this truth. The Highlands of Scotland are still more impracticable, from the want of Roads, Bridges, and from excessive rains that almost continually fall in those parts, which by nature and constant use become habitual to the Natives, but very difficulty supported by the Regular Troops. They are unacquainted with the passages by which Mountains are traversed, exposed to frequent Ambuscades, and shots from the tops of hills, which they return without effect, as it happened at the affair of Glenshiels, where the rebels lost but one man in [sic] tho' a considerable number of your Majesty's Troops were killed and wounded.

I have endeavoured to Report to your Majesty as true and impartial an account of the several particulars required by my instructions, as far as I have been able to collect them during my short continuance in the Highlands, and, as your Majesty is pleased to Command me, presume to offer my humble opinion of what I conceive necessary to be done towards establishing order in those parts, and reducing the Highlands to a more due submission to your Majesty's Government.

Proposal

1

That Companies of such Highlanders as are well affected to his Majesty's Government be Established, under proper Regulations and Commanded by Officers speaking the Language of the Country, subject to Martial Law and under inspection and orders of the Governors of Fort-William and Inverness, and the Officer Commanding his Majesty's Forces in those Parts. The expense of these Companies which may in the whole consist of 250 or at most 300 men may be answered by reducing one Man per Troop and Company of the Regular Forces.

2

That the said Companies be employed in Disarming the Highlanders, preventing depredations, bringing Criminals to Justice, and hinder rebels and attainted persons from inhabiting that part of the Kingdom.

3

That a Redoubte or Barracks be erected at Inverness, as well for preventing the Highlanders descending into the Low Country in time of Rebellion, as for the better Quartering his Majesty's Troops, and keeping them in a Body sufficient to prevent or subdue insurrection.

4

That in order to render the Barrack at Killihnimen of more use than I conceive it to be at present (from its being situate at too great a distance from Lake Ness) a Redoubte be built at the West End adjoining to it, which the said Barrack may be able to contain a Battalion of Foot, and a Communication made for their mutual support, the space of ground between one and the other is less than 500 yards. This appears to be more necessary from the situation of the place, which is the most Centrical part of the Highlands, a considerable Pass, equally distant from Fort-William and Inverness, and where a Body of 1000 Men may be drawn together from these Garrisons in twenty-four hours, to suppress any insurrections of the Highlanders.

5

That a small Vessel with Oars and Sails be built on the Lake Ness, sufficient to carry a Party of 60 or 80 Soldiers and Provisions for the Garrison, which will be a means to keep the Communication open between that place and Inverness and be a safe and ready way of sending Parties to the Country bordering on the said Lake, which is Navigable for the largest Vessels. It is 24 miles or more in length, and a mile or more in breadth, the Country being Mountainous on both sides.

6

That the Governors, or such as his Majesty is pleased to appoint to Command at Fort-William, Inverness, or Killihnimen, till the peace of the Highlands is better established, be required to reside at their respective Stations, and to give an Account of what passes in that Country to the Commander in Chief of the Forces in Scotland, and to such other whom his Majesty is pleased to appoint.

7

That inspection be made into the present condition of the Garrisons and Castles in North Britain, and necessary repairs made to secure them from the danger of a sudden surprise, and more especially the Castle of Edinburgh, which remains exposed to the same attempt as was made on it in the year 1715, there being nothing effectually done to it since that time, for the security of that important place, on which depends not only the safety of the City, but of all that part of the Kingdom.

8

That a Regiment of Dragoons be ordered to Quarter in the Low Country between Perth and Inverness (when forage can be provided for their support) which will not only hinder the Highlanders descending into that Country from the apprehensions they are under of engaging with Horse, but may be a means to prevent the landing of small bodies of Troops that may be sent from Foreign parts to invade that part of the Kingdom, or encourage the Highlanders to Rebellion.

9

That for the support of the Civil Government proper persons be nominated for Sheriffs and Deputy Sheriffs in the Highland Counties, and that Justices of the Peace and Constables be established in proper places with small salaries allowed them for the charge they say they are of necessity at in seizing and sending Criminals to distant prisons; and that Quarter Sessions be punctually kept at Killihnimen, Ruthven in Badenoch and Fort-William, and if occasion should require at Bernera near the Coast of the Isle of Skye.

10

That an Act of Parliament be procured effectually to punish the Highlanders inhabiting the most uncivilised parts of the Country, who carry or conceal in their dwellings, or other places, Arms contrary to Law; and as the Penalty of a Fine in the former Act has never been (or from their poverty can never be) levied, it is hoped the Parliament will not scruple to make it Felony or Transportation for the first offence.

11

That an act of Parliament be procured empowering the Heretors and Free-holders in every County to assess themselves yearly, not exceeding a definite sum, to be applied by the Commissioners of the Land Tax and Justices of the Peace for defraying the Charges of apprehending, prosecuting, and Maintaining of Criminals while in Gaol; for, as the Prosecutor is now to defray the Charges it is not to be wondered at that so few of them have been brought to Justice, and so many malefactors escaped with impunity. All which is most humbly Represented and Submitted for Your Majesty's Royal Consideration – London 10th, December 1724 George Wade

King George and the government most certainly did consider Wade's report, and they were not long in coming to their decision. General Wade was appointed commander of the forces in North Britain and on April 29th 1725 the newspapers of the day tell us that the 'Hon. General Wade kissed his Majesty's hand as commander-in-chief of Scotland'. On June 1st 1725 General Wade received his warrant under the royal sign manual giving leave to carry out the pacification of the Highlands. Before leaving London he submitted a further report to His Majesty. He pointed out that the measures so far taken had proved insufficient to reduce the Highlanders to due obedience to the law, and to prevent depredations so frequently committed on the inhabitants of the Low Country, which he said was a great oppression to the well-affected (who were entitled to the protection of the government).

He went on to state that the Highlanders should be disarmed, and that they could (if not timely prevented) prove of dangerous consequence to the peace of the kingdom:

> For, while such a number of men, who are bold, resolute and disaffected, remain in a capacity of doing mischief, they are ready instruments to be employed by any foreign power, who may attempt to invade his Majesty's Dominions or incite his subjects to rebellion.

Wade suggested that an Act of Parliament be procured, empowering His Majesty (or those he was pleased to appoint) to cause the several clans to be summoned one after another to bring in their arms on certain days specified in the said summons, after which whoever was found in arms (except such as were qualified by law) should be transported to serve as soldiers in any British plantations in America, or garrisons beyond the seas. He also suggested including a clause making it lawful for His Majesty's forces to assist the civil magistrate to reduce the clans by force of arms in case they assembled in numbers against the execution of the Act. He said an indemnity clause could be included for any soldiers who should happen to kill or wound any of them, as in the law against riots and tumults. He now presumed to give his opinion of how the scheme for disarming the Highlands could be put into execution:

> That three companies of Highlanders be raised consisting of 60 or 70 men each, commanded by captains. That the six companies consisting of 300 Men be completed and armed by the first of June in order to join the regular troops at Inverness, when they March to their first encampment. Those four battalions of the forces now in Scotland are in readiness to form a camp in the Highlands.

Wade submitted a list of gentlemen well affected to His Majesty's government, who inhabited and had estates in Scotland at Moray, Nairn, Inverness, Ross, Cromarty, Sutherland, Caithness and the Orkneys: 'Lord Seaforth, Macdonalds of Slate, Glengary, Moidart, and Keppoch. Camerons of Lochiel, The Duke of Gordon's followers, Stewart's of Appine, Robertson's of Strowan, Mcintosh's and Farquharsons. McCleans in the Isle of Skye, Chisholms of Strathglas and last the Mcphersons.'

Wade's appointment as commander-in-chief for North Britain was hardly likely to endear him to the Jacobite lairds, but in spite of this he achieved great popularity amongst those one would expect to be his enemies – except Simon Fraser, Lord Lovat, who thought he should have had the general's job. He described Wade as 'that false deceitful Barbarian'. Wade finally left London in June 1725 and arrived in Edinburgh fifteen days later.

The battle Wade faced in the Highlands was a different kind of battle: to win the hearts and minds of the clans and to show them a better way of life; and with Duncan Forbes, the Lord Advocate of Scotland, to leave Scotland to map out its own destiny, policed by its own people. His first task on arriving in the Highlands was to raise forthwith the Highlands Six Independent Companies. The first three were commanded by Grant of Ballindalloch, Lovat, and Campbell of Lochnell. They consisted of 114 men. The other three companies each had seventy-two men and were commanded by Campbell of Skipness, Campbell of Carrick, and Munro of Culcairn. The arrangement and administration necessitated a very busy schedule, involving hours of travelling and negotiating contracts. Wade was anticipating trouble on his arrival, but it came from an unexpected source.

Chapter 7

Wade Arrives in Scotland

A resolution was passed in Parliament at the end of 1724 whereby a malt tax of sixpence a barrel of ale was laid as additional duty on Scotland but was not extended to England. The resentment felt by the Scots exploded in riotous behaviour and a refusal to pay the tax. Pamphlets printed at the time and dispersed throughout the country incited the Scots to rebellion, declaring that England had loaded them with burdens too heavy to bear. Wade's own account states that:

> the inhabitants of Glasgow were still more outrageous, declaring publicly in the street, that they would not submit to a Malt Tax., insulting the Officers of Excise, and threatening to stone them if they attempted to enter their Malt Houses; for which purpose they had piled up heaps of stones at the doors, to show them what they might expect if they proceeded in the execution of that Law.

In preparation for the expected disorders in Glasgow, Wade was awaiting two companies of Delorain's. The five companies from Berwick were temporarily held up by floods resulting from exceptional rainfalls. On the day on which the malt tax was to be introduced in Scotland the mobs assembled in the streets of Glasgow, throwing stones and dirt at the soldiers.

On June 23rd, the excise officers entered the city and met with a blank refusal: the maltsters would not allow them into their stores, and the tax could not be assessed. An ugly situation developed; stones were thrown and the officers thought it prudent to keep out of the way. The Glasgow burghs were represented at this time by Mr Daniel Campbell of Shawfield House in Glasgow. Campbell was out of town at the time, but he was known to be a supporter of the hated tax. Campbell would pay a heavy price for his support when serious rioting broke out at his residence. The mob continued with the outrages all night and part of the following day, looting the Palladian house and gardens. Wade, whose love of architecture was renowned, was greatly moved on seeing the destruction.

The Lord Advocate, Duncan Forbes, thought the incident so grave that he reported it immediately to Their Excellencies, the Lords Justices, who were exercising temporary regency during the King's absence in Hanover. On July 1st Charles Delafaye, their secretary, wrote a letter addressed jointly to the Lord Advocate and the Solicitor General instructing them to have those responsible tried with all possible expedition at Edinburgh. They were to inquire also into the behaviour of the magistrates – especially the provost who had failed to read the proclamation, which under the Riot Act it was his duty to do in such circumstances. On July 10th the Edinburgh paper of the day printed the following account. The troubles in Glasgow were also reported the same day as General Wade's letter in the newspaper of July 10th at Edinburgh.

Edinburgh July 1. Since my last I have inform'd my self more particularly concerning the Tumult that happen'd at Glasgow. When the new Malt Act took Place, the Officers, pursuant thereunto, went to take an Account of Stock in Hand; but as they had declar'd they would not pay one Bawby [a Scottish coin worth an English halfpenny] of the Tax, the said Officers desired the Assistance of some Forces; whereupon two Companies of Delorain's Regiment was order'd into the Town. On the 23rd the Mob began to assemble, which increased the next Day to a great number, when the commanding Officer sent and desir'd the Magistrates of the Town to give him Orders to suppress them; but their Answer was, that they did not think it convenient to make use of his Assistance. The Populace still increasing, they fell upon Mr. Campbell of Shawfield House, and entirely demolish'd it, after having taken everything inside, and drank and destroy'd all the Liquors in his Cellar. After this they were so bold as to attack the Guard, before the Guard House, with Stones, in a violent Manner, notwithstanding all the Entreaties of the Office to be peaceable. Then the Soldiers fired Powder, but it avail'd nothing; so they were oblig'd to retire to the Guard Room, and there they all loaded in good earnest, discharged thro' the Door several Shot, and then sallied out, keeping a constant Fire in Platoons, till some of them dropp'd, and the Streets were clear'd of the rest.

However, in a little Time they return'd, and got to a great Head again with Arms from the Tolbooth, which they had broken open; upon which, the Soldiers, as tis said, by the Advice of the Magistrates, retreated out of Town in very good Order, thro' the

Tron Gate, out of the West Port towards Dumbarton, but were followed by a Body of 300 Rioters, with Arms, for six Miles, who then return'd, having sent two Men on Horseback to Dumbarton, threatening to burn the Town if they admitted the said Companies into it; whereupon the Magistrates, in great Terror, came out and besought the Officer not to enter, which he acquiesced in, and so took to the Castle directly. There were ten of the Rioter's kill'd, and about twelve wounded. Two of the Soldiers being bruised with Stones, fell into the Hands of the Mob, and four others are yet missing. They keep the Alarm Bells ringing, and Drums beating, for the Magistrates have quitted the Town, and left the Mob in Possession, who have plac'd a Guard to keep out the Forces that General Wade has Order'd thither: The Cry was, *No Malt Tax.* The Guards of this City (Edinburgh) are doubled, for fear of the like Doings here.

We have received an Account from GLASGOW, that yesterday about Two in the Afternoon, General Wade, with Troops under his Command marched into that City, with all the Order and Quietness imaginable; his Excellency having that Morning writ a Letter to the Magistrates, as follows,

Gentlemen,

Their Excellencies, **The LORDS JUSTICES**, have been pleased to signify Their high Resentment of the late tumultuous and riotous Proceedings of the Inhabitants of your City, which have been attended with the Circumstances of Rapine and Blood-shed, to the Dishonour of the Government, and in Contempt and Defiance of the Laws of the Kingdom; and they are of the Opinion, That all this might probably have been prevented, if you had acted with Vigilance and Resolution becoming Magistrates.

I am therefore commanded by Their Excellencies to march a Body of His Majesty's Forces into the City of *Glasgow*, in Order to support the Civil Power, in restoring the Peace and Quiet of the City: And being informed, That several of the inhabitants have armed themselves, and keep a Guard in the Town; You are hereby required to cause such Arms to be lodged in some proper Place or Magazine, to prevent any Mischief's that might otherwise happen between the Town's People and His Majesty's Forces.

I am, &c.
GEORGE WADE

Falkirk, 9 July 1725
5 in the Morning

To the Provost and Magistrates of the City of Glasgow.

The Lord Advocate contacted General Wade, newly made commander-in-chief of the forces in Scotland, who was on the point of setting out for the Highlands to see that the clans duly surrendered their arms as required by the Disarming Act. He was instructed to postpone his journey north, and, having collected a force sufficient to restore order, he accompanied the Lord Advocate, Duncan Forbes, to Glasgow. Together they rode into the city on the afternoon of July 9th at the head of a force consisting of one regiment of foot, four troops of the Royal Scottish Dragoons, one troop of the Earl of Stair's Dragoons and the newly formed Independent Company of Highlanders. The ringleaders fled in alarm and the City of Glasgow returned to a more peaceful way of life.

The Lord Advocate procured information of such of the rioters as had not absconded from the town, and issued warrants for apprehending them. They were seized by small parties of the regular troops, and committed to the town gaol, and no further disorders took place. The magistrates were brought before the Lord Advocate, who reprimanded them for their neglect of duty and, with an armed guard, gave orders to take them to Edinburgh. On their return they were greeted by bells ringing and other demonstrations of joy. The outcome of the dispute was that the brewers and maltsters yielded to the malt tax. Donald Campbell, heartbroken at the destruction of his mansion, sold his estate and with the compensation purchased the Isle of Islay.

Wade was determined to delay no longer and proceeded to Inverness at the King's command. Wade was given full authority and, with the sum of £5,000, he sailed at last from Leith on August 1st to start the building programme and to try to make some progress before October, when the first fall of snow was expected to bring about a halt to work on the roads. After four days at sea he landed in Angus and continued his journey overland, arriving at Inverness on August 10th to meet the clans and start the disarming programme.

Wade expected trouble and was fully prepared for it, but he was not to meet much opposition from the clans. Fifty of Seaforth's chieftains came to make their peace, asking to be allowed to hand over their arms to regular troops and not to the Highland Companies. Wade tactfully agreed, and fixed the date for August 28th at Brahan Castle. Seaforth's chiefs encouraged the other clans to come forward and give up their arms.

The King granted Wade the power to receive the submissions of those who repudiated their crimes, and were willing to abandon their allegiance to the Pretender. Among those who came forward and pledged their loyalty to the Crown was Rob Roy Macgregor, otherwise Campbell, who wrote the following letter to Wade dated September 15th 1725:

> The great humanity with which you have constantly acted in the discharge of the trust reposed in you, and your ever having made use of the great powers with which you are vested, as the means of doing good and charitable offices to such as ye found proper subjects of compassion, will, I hope, excuse my importunity in endeavouring to approve myself not absolutely unworthy of that mercy and favour your Excellency has so generously procured from his Majesty for others in my unfortunate circumstances.
>
> I am very sensible nothing can be alleged sufficient to excuse so great a crime as I have been guilty of, that of Rebellion; but I humbly beg leave to lay before your Excellency some particulars in the circumstance of my guilt, which, I hope, will extenuate it in some measure. It was my misfortune, at the time the Rebellion broke out, to be liable to legal diligence and caption, at the Duke of Montrose's instance, for debt alledged due to him. To avoid being flung into prison, as I must certainly have been, had I followed my real inclinations in joining the King's troops at Stirling, I was forced to take party with the adherents of the Pretender; for, the Country being all in arms, it was neither safe, nor indeed possible, for me to stand neuter. I should not, however, plead my being forced into that unnatural Rebellions against his Majesty King George, if I could not at the same time assure your Excellency, that I not only avoided acting offensively against his Majesty's Forces upon all occasions, but on the contrary, sent his Grace the Duke of Atholl all the intelligence I could from time to time, of the strength and situation of the Rebels; which I hope his Grace will do me the justice to acknowledge. As to the debt to the Duke of Montrose, I have discharged it to the utmost farthing. I beg your Excellency would be persuaded, that, had it been in my power, as it was my inclination, I should always have acted for the service of His Majesty King George; and that one reason of my begging the favour of your intercession with His Majesty for the pardon of my life, the earnest desire I have to employ it in his service, whose goodness, justice, and humanity are so conspicuous to all mankind. I am, with all duty and respect, your Excellency's most, &c., Robert Campbell.

Rob Roy Macgregor was a highly proficient swordsman; it was his abilities with the broadsword that made his name. Soon his fame as a warrior spread. He was nicknamed 'Ruadh', which became 'Roy', because of his wild red hair. When many Highland clans were forced to give up their names to those of the pro-English clans, Rob Roy occasionally took on his mother's clan name, Campbell. He stood in high respect in the clan, although he was not its chief. Rob Roy was born in 1671 at Loch Katrine, the third son of a lieutenant colonel. He was given lands at Inversnaid on Loch Lomond, where he built a house. In time he owned large tracts of land along the east bank of the loch, and by 1700 the Macgregors owned all the passes in the Trossachs.

Unfortunately Rob Roy fell foul of the Duke of Montrose, who sent his factor to evict him, his wife Mary and their children from their house and lands. In 1711 Rob Roy persuaded the Duke to advance him £1,000 for investment in herding, but one of his trusted associates disappeared with the money and a warrant was issued for Rob Roy's arrest. The outcome was that he lost his lands, and at the age of forty-three he was branded an outlaw. He was related to the Duke of Argyll, who gave him refuge and actively encouraged him to raid and steal from their common enemy, Montrose. For eight years Rob Roy lived the life of an outlaw, gaining legendary status in the Highlands. Along with as many as 500 supporters he performed repeated raids against Montrose and once again took up the Stuart cause by participating in several Jacobite battles.

He was captured many times but always managed to escape. In 1719 Rob Roy and forty of the Macgregors took part in the Glen Shiel rising, but the Hanoverians prevailed and Rob Roy once again went into hiding before returning again to Balquhidder. In 1715 he again fought on the Jacobite side; however, his benefactor, the Duke of Argyll, had chosen the government side and with mixed allegiances Macgregor was forced to miss the Battle of Sheriffmuir. Even so he was now a marked man with a charge of high treason on his head. Over the next ten years he escaped capture on numerous occasions but in the end was forced to surrender to General Wade, beseeching him to speak on his behalf to the King. Macgregor was charged with treason against the Crown and put in London's infamous Newgate Prison. Like many Highlanders his destiny if found guilty was execution or the lesser sentence of transportation as an indentured servant to Canada or the West Indies.

Rob Roy was indeed very fortunate and received a King's

pardon in 1727. There is reason to believe he was instrumental in helping the government with information. In time he returned to his home in Balquhidder and died peacefully there in December 1734 of natural causes. He was sixty-three years old, although his burialplace in Balquhidder churchyard records his age at death as seventy. His name and exploits have been kept alive by the many books written about his life, notably those by Sir Walter Scott and two English writers, Daniel Defoe and William Wordsworth. It is not known to what extent Wade was able to put forward a plea to the government on Rob Roy's behalf, but his life was saved.

Wade's next task was to set his soldiers to work on building the first of his military roads between Fort William and Kilchiumen, later renamed Fort Augustus. Wade had little experience or guidance, no maps or plans to work from, and it is believed he researched the Roman method of building military roads in Britain and was familiar with the works of Colen Campbell's *Vitruvius Britannicus*.

Gnaeus Julius Agricola was made governor of Britain in the year AD 80. He set about conquering the more remote regions of northern England, Scotland and Wales. When the Romans invaded Scotland they built forts and military roads into the Highlands and it was Agricola, commander of the 20th Legion, then at Chester, who travelled the Roman road into Perthshire. It is through the eyes of his son-in-law, Tacitus, that we see the rugged eastern coast of Scotland, its lochs, rivers and mountains, as Agricola may have recalled them to Tacitus in his later life.

One of Agricola's first acts was to march into North Wales and subdue the troublesome tribe known to the Romans as the Ordovices. He followed this up by an audacious attack on the Isle of Anglesey; although there was no fleet to transport the army across the Menai Straits, Agricola, like other great generals, exploited the advantage of surprise. The new governor had shown his military genius and, later, after establishing forts along the Stanegate in Northumbria he began his advance into Scotland. Tacitus, while describing Agricola's campaigns, fails to mention placenames, so it is only archaeological evidence that has indicated the remains of forts and temporary camps where pottery has been found for the Agricolan period. Tacitus stated that Agricola in his third year of campaigning opened up new nations into the territory of tribes as far as the estuary named Tanaus. Some scholars have thought that the historian meant the Tyne, but the general opinion suggests the Tay is indicated. Miss Anne Robertson Dalrymple, lecturer in archaeology to the Hunterian Museum, stated that a single Agricolan road ran northward from the Forth to the Tay and was flanked by forts.

Three of the forts have been identified: one at Fendoch, at the mouth of the Sma' Glen; the second at Dalginross, at the entrance to Glen Artney; and the third at Bochastle, near Callander, blocking the Pass of Leny. Agricola in the year AD 83 advanced northward into the Highlands and found his way barred by the Caledonian army massed on the slopes of Mons Graupius. This famous battlefield has so far eluded discovery. Perhaps some day archaeologists will at last locate the battlefield where Agricola defeated the Caledonians in a pitched battle, reportedly killing 10,000.

Tacitus has told us of the governor's belief that his countrymen had been much to blame in the virtues of a moderate policy. So he spent large sums on development; he encouraged and helped them to build temples, marketplaces, and houses, praising the eager and admonishing the slothful. He instructed the sons of chieftains in the liberal arts and confronted the British with Gallic learning, so that those who were unfamiliar with the Roman tongue were regarded as lacking in eloquence. Then they were encouraged to adopt the Roman style of dressing and the toga became common. He tried to persuade the British chiefs to give their children a Latin upbringing.

Bath at this time was an important spa but not an important town. It had no military or commercial significance, but the size and quality of its monuments show clearly that people of wealth and influence travelled to it from a wide area of Gaul and Britain. They were for the most part sufferers from rheumatic diseases. For any homesick Roman there was the reassuring sight of the little city as they descended the hills and looked down on the tawny tiled roofs, the glint of glass windows, the high-pillared and pedimented temples, and the hills beyond, and better still the sight and warmth of the baths. Men and women met for the pleasure of washing, to be oiled, sanded, massaged, and bathed, and once refreshed to pay their respects in the temple of the goddess Sulis Minerva.

All roads led to and from Aquae Sulis; the great Roman road, the Fosse, ran from south-west of the province, joining Exeter,

Bath, Lincoln and Leicester. Visitors from all parts of the empire descended on Bath. The hot thermal springs were the wonder of the north, pouring out half a million gallons of hot water at a temperature of 120°F, rising to the surface every day from a depth of about 5,000 feet.

Memorials have been excavated which commemorate visitors from distant parts of the Roman world. Outside the gates of Bath on the road to London, for example, one erected by his trade guild commemorates Julius Vitalis of the 20th Legion, a smith or armourer, native of a Belgic tribe buried by his 'Collegium' aged forty-six years, having served nine years. Succa Petronia, aged three years, four months and nine days, was commemorated by her parents, Romulus and Victoria Sabina. One Lucius Vitellius Tancinus, a Spanish citizen of Caurium, a soldier of the Vettonian Cavalry (heavy-armed Roman auxiliaries with the right of Roman citizenship) died aged forty-five years shortly after his retirement, having served twenty-six years. Others came from Metz and Trier on the Moselle, and Frejus on what is now the French Riviera. There were also, of course, memorials to native-born citizens, such as a Gloucester town councillor and a sculptor from Cirencester.

But they were all Roman citizens, whatever their origin, and they knew and no doubt enjoyed the gracious city beside the Avon as much as those who came centuries later to seek treatment from the waters – not forgetting General Wade.

After Wade's death his dear friend, Ralph Allen, erected a monument to his memory in the grounds of Prior Park. The General is shown in the costume of a Roman soldier.

Today you can still visit the Baths the Romans built and, when you have completed your tour, take lunch on the terrace overlooking the Great Bath, where statues of Vespasian, Agricola and Hadrianus look down from the balustrade. After the Romans left there was a long Dark Age when the baths silted up and the temples and grand villas disappeared. Fortunately in time the baths were restored for the benefit of those in need of treatment.

A major part of the Romans' successful occupation was their road system. A standard Roman road consists of a metalled surface (e.g. gravel or pebbles) on a solid foundation of earth or stone. The agger is a well-drained base in the form of a bank of earth or other layered material dug out from lateral ditches or quarry pits. It can be up to six feet high and fifty feet wide or, at the other extreme, very slight or even non-existent with the road surface

Plan of a Roman Road

How the Road was Built

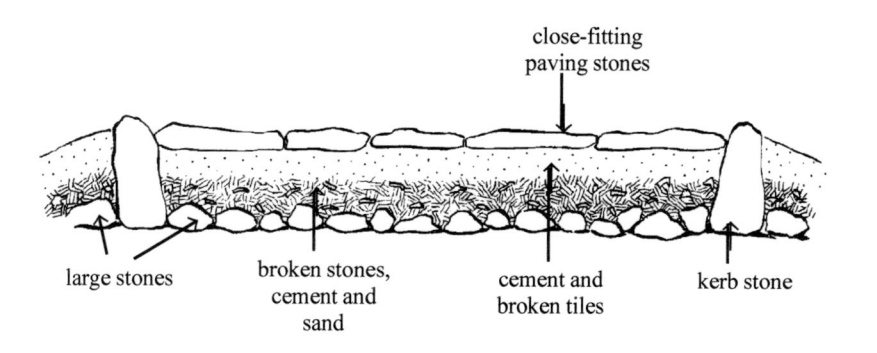

close-fitting paving stones

large stones | broken stones, cement and sand | cement and broken tiles | kerb stone

1) First, the army builders would clear the ground of rocks and trees. They then dug a trench where the road was to go and filled it with big stones.
2) Next, they put in big stones, pebbles, cement and sand, which they packed down to make a firm base.
3) Then they added another layer of cement mixed with broken tiles.
4) On top of that, they then put paving stones to make the surface of the road. These stones were cut so that they fitted together tightly.
5) Kerbstones were put at the sides of the road to hold in the paving stones and to make a channel for the water to run away.

*George Wade in retirement,
(by kind permission of Colnaghi Art Gallery, London).*

ANDREA SOLDI
Florence c. 1703 – London 1771

A Military Gentleman, identified as General Wade
CANVAS: 166.3 × 137 cms.

The subject of this portrait is shown full-length and seated in a gilt rococo armchair, wearing a blue coat and breeches and a gold-trimmed waistcoat. Evidence of his military profession is provided by a dramatic battle scene of charging cavalry in the right background, and by the steel breastplate on the floor to the left of his chair. He points with his right hand to an architectural design for a Palladian-style country house.

The sitter bears a strong resemblance to known portraits of General Wade, such as that by Diest in the National Portrait Gallery or the bust relief by Roubiliac in Westminster Abbey (J. Kerslake, *Early Georgian Portraits*, London, 1977, I, pp. 288-9, I, pls. 824-30). Born in 1673, Wade had a distinguished military career in Flanders, Spain and Minorca, culminating in his appointment as Marshall of the English forces in 1745. He was, however, relieved of his command for failing to halt Bonnie Prince Charlie's advance. He is best remembered for the military roads he built in the Highlands of Scotland after the 1715 Rebellion.

Whereas Diest's portrait (c. 1731) presents Wade as a still vigorous campaigning soldier, by contrast the picture exhibited here shows him in retirement, seated, his breastplate put aside, and his mind turned to gentler pastimes. Wade was a cultivated man interested in music, painting and, especially, architecture. His London house in Old Burlington Street had been designed for him in 1723 by Lord Burlington and was based directly on an elevational design by Palladio (demolished in 1935; illustrated, *Vitruvius Britannicus*, III, pl. 10). The architectural drawing in this portrait is for an unidentified country house on the Palladian model with a central block connected to flanking pavilions by straight and quadrant link walls and the main rooms on the *piano nobile*.

Wade's shield in Bath Abbey.

Wade's monument in Westminster Abbey.

Minorca.

Bath Abbey Church Yard, 1750. George Wade lived in the pillared house on the left.

Wade's London home.

Map of Spain.

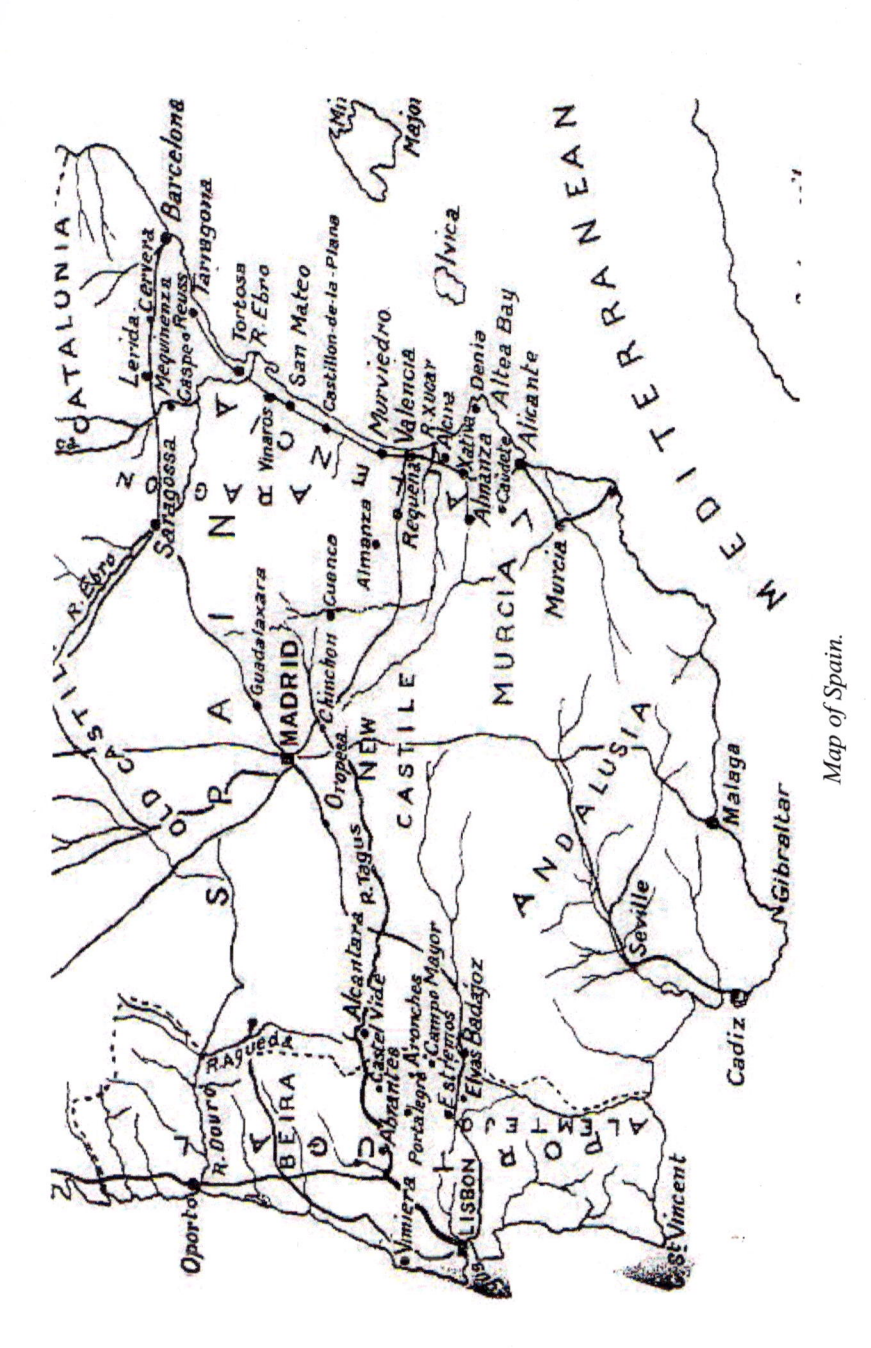

Louis XIV.

Map of the cross-posts established by Ralph Allen, 1721–61.

Ducan Forbes of Culloden.

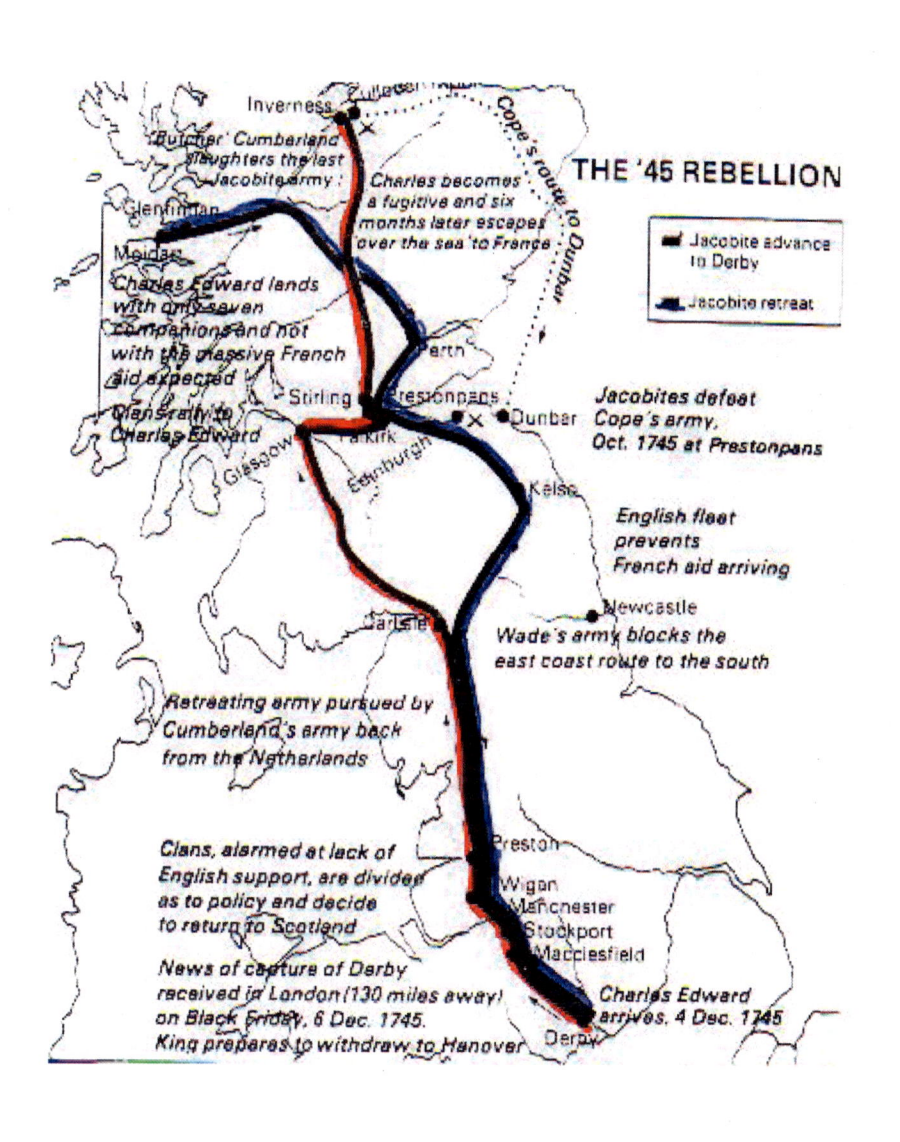

Map of the Rebellion, 1745.

The bridge at Aberfeldy.

Bernera Barracks.

Melgrave, East Bridge.

A Wade bridge just above Laggan.

A Wade road at Glen Cochill.

Weem Hotel.

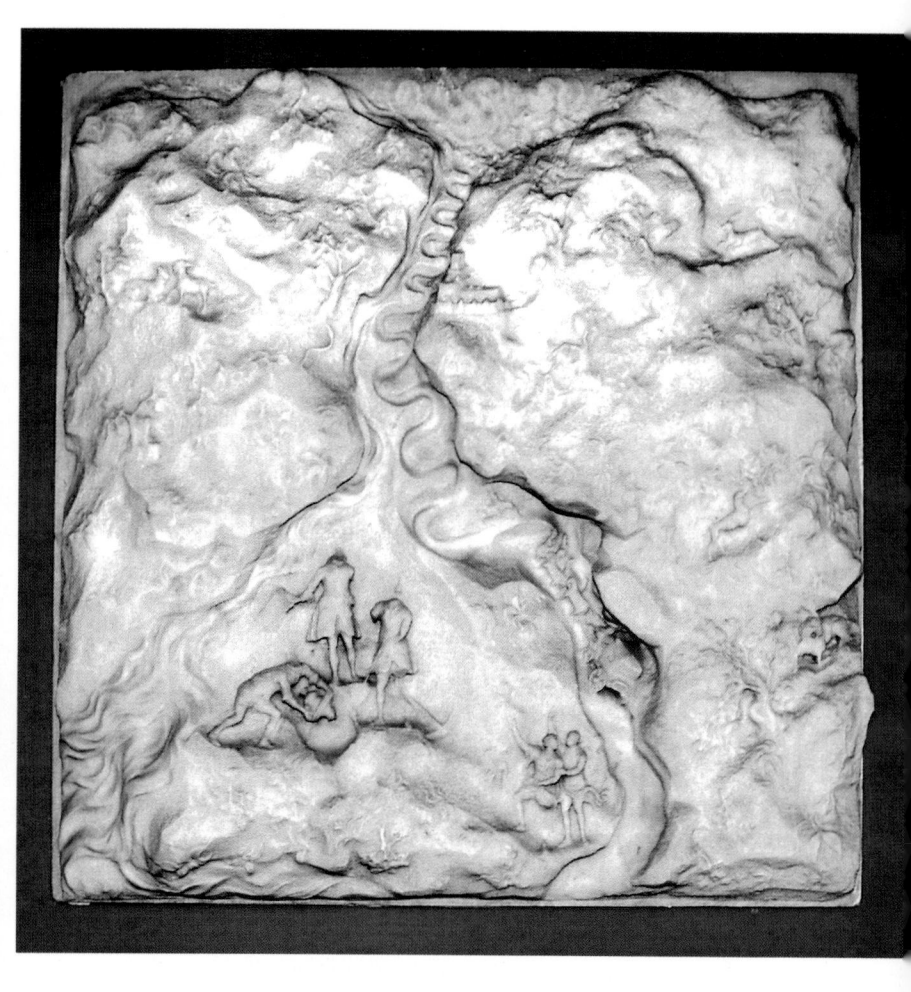

A sculpture on Wade's monument in Prior Park College, Bath, showing a new road in the Highlands

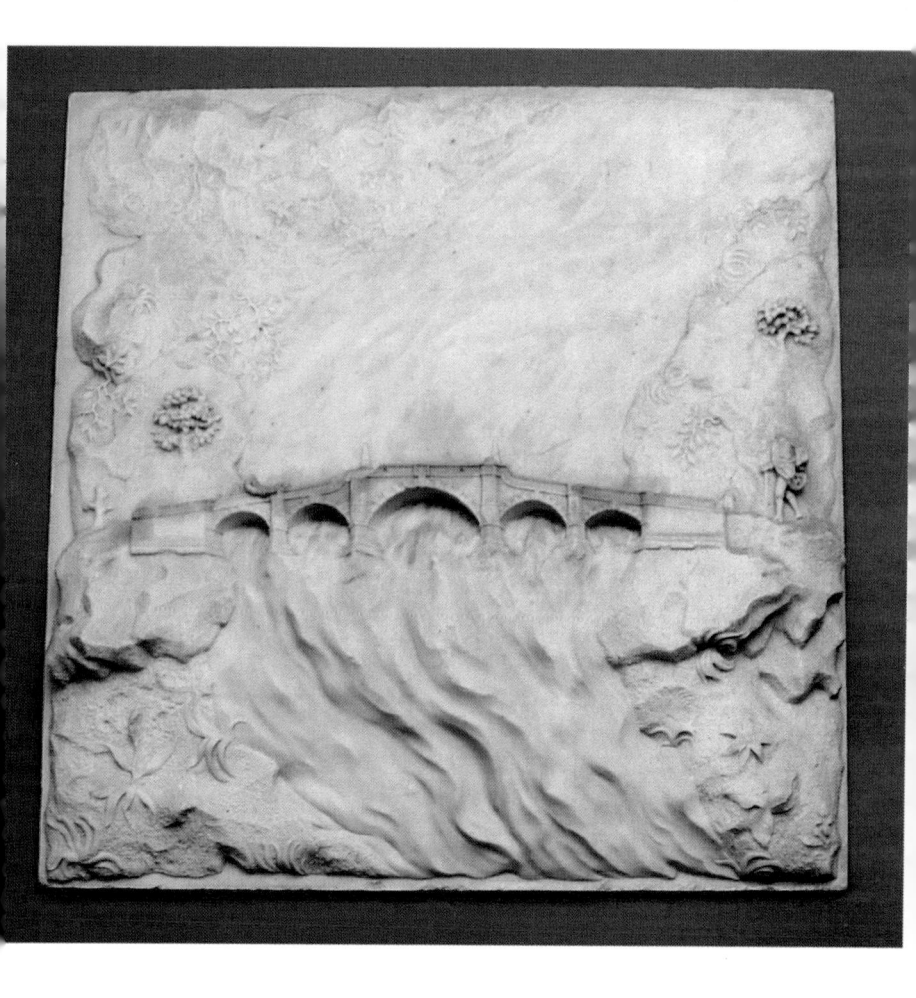

A sculpture on Wade's monument in Prior Park College, Bath, showing the bridge at Aberfeldy.

Wade's house in the Abbey Church Yard, Bath.

Ralph Allen
(by kind permission of the Victoria Art Gallery, Bath).

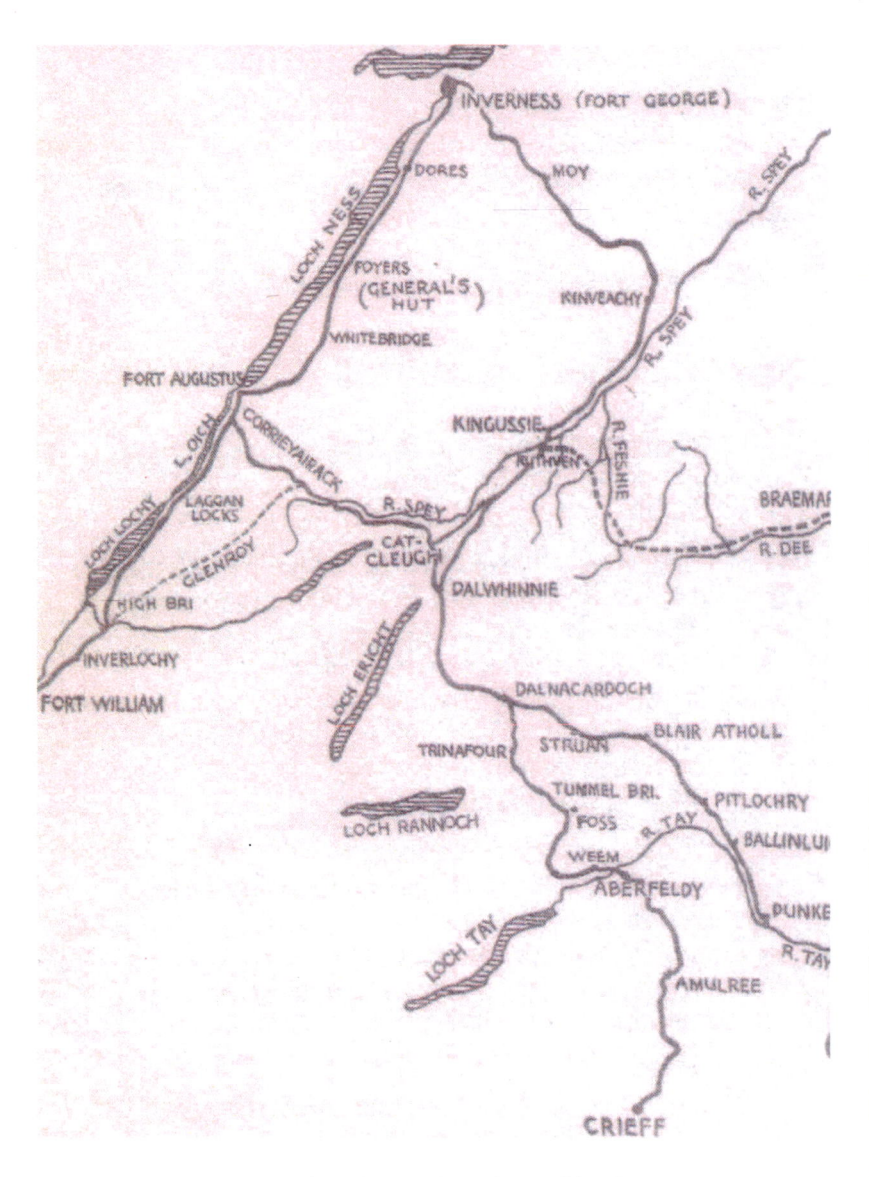

Map of Wade's roads in the Highlands.

laid directly on the ground, and this is especially true on minor roads. Local materials were used where possible, and a layer of large stones, if available, may supplement or replace the agger.

The road surface itself consists of layers of finer material with a total thickness ranging from two inches to two feet. Additional layers are added by resurfacing. The width of the road is up to thirty feet, but more usually around twenty-five, or fifteen to eighteen feet on minor roads. Apart from the scoop ditches, the road might also be flanked by shallow boundary ditches two to four feet wide. These may serve to define an official 'road zone', especially in areas where the surrounding terrain (e.g. woodland) offers the possibility of an ambush. Where a road passed over unstable ground it might be supported on a wooden structure.

Seventeen centuries later, Wade wherever possible followed the Roman precedent, adapting where necessary. Like the Romans, he believed firm foundations were essential and cambered the surface so that water drained off into ditches on each side. His roads followed a straight line wherever possible, going over rather than round high ground, though on occasions the roads ran in line with the forts and barracks. The width of the roads, except in adverse circumstances, was sixteen feet. The tools used were pickaxes, spades, iron crowbars, screw jacks, wheelbarrows, sledgehammers, sways and gunpowder. There was no lack of raw material for road-building. Stones and rocks of all sizes littered the banks and hillsides, and, like the Romans, Wade made use of the materials at hand. First the foundations were dug, and the big stones were broken by gunpowder, if necessary. They were then levered into the bottom of the trench. Smaller stones were packed on top and finally gravel to a depth of a least two feet, to be beaten in with a shovel, wheels and human feet. Kerbstones at the sides held in the paving stones and made a channel for the water to run away. The gravel top surface was usually replaced annually. David Chandler in his book *The Art of Warfare in the Age of Marlborough* wrote that Wade was the first of Britain's great road engineers and the first to build military roads in Scotland after the Romans.

By the time Wade left for London he had built and launched his Highland galley on Loch Ness, as he had proposed (*see Chapter 6*). This was a ship of about thirty tons burden propelled by oars or sails, able to transport fifty or sixty soldiers or twenty tons of provisions. Wade returned to the road being built between Fort

William and Kilchiumen, to congratulate his 'highwaymen', as he jocularly called them, on the progress they had made and to make arrangements for the following year's work.

His 'highwaymen' were professional soldiers, and one of his most remarkable achievements was to obtain from the government an extra payment to every soldier engaged in roadwork. Private soldiers were given an extra sixpence a day, corporals eight pence, sergeants one shilling, and subalterns half a crown. For non-commissioned ranks the extra payment was the same as their daily rate, so roadwork meant double pay. Arrangements were made to return to Scotland in time to start work on April 1st on the next section of the road. It was only possible to carry out road-building from the beginning of April until October, when the inclement weather conditions would force them to leave Scotland.

By the end of his first year in Scotland, Wade had put in a tremendous amount of work. He attended the drilling of the Highland Companies and sent them out on their police duties. He saw the completion of nine miles of his road between Kilchiumen and Fort William. He was unable to continue work on the fort and barracks at Inverness due to lack of contractors in the Highlands, requiring him to obtain the much needed timber from Norway.

A ship with ammunition and ordnance stores was daily expected from London, and ovens were built at Inverness to bake bread for the soldiers; 40,000 biscuits were to be provided for the support of the troops on their marches into the mountains. Wade posted companies of Highlanders at Fort William; Lovat's Company was to guard all the passes from Skye to Inverness, Grant's those from Inverness to Dunkeld, and Campbell's those from Dunkeld to Lorne. The remaining companies were posted at Fort William, Kilchiumen and Ruthven. Wade then set out to disarm the clans at Braemar, Perth, Atholl, Breadalbane, Monteith, Stirling and Dumbarton. In all, Wade collected 2,685 arms, which he dumped in Edinburgh Castle, Fort William and Bernera at Glenelg. He issued 230 licences to carry arms to the foresters, drovers and dealers in cattle, and duly entered their names in a book. By the end of 1725 Wade was able to state that the imposition commonly called black-meal was now no longer paid by the inhabitants bordering on the Highlands.

After a very busy schedule, Wade returned to London for a well-earned rest. There was time to engage in more leisurely pursuits. He was a cultivated man who loved fine furniture, paintings and architecture, and he became one of the governors of the Royal Academy of Music: he had also, however, a mania for gambling, and on occasion for frequenting houses of a rather dangerous character.

Horace Walpole tells a story of one of the General's adventures at a house of this kind:

> Having, with his usual recklessness, brought with him his finest gold snuff-box set with diamonds, Wade found after a time that it was missing. Enraged, he swore no man should leave the room until it was found; and insisted upon an immediate search. A gentleman sat on his right, dressed as an officer, but with clothes much worn. With great humility he had asked and obtained permission four or five times, to go his shilling with the General. The young man with great vehemence declared, upon the honour of a soldier, that he had not the box, nor knew anything of it, but that he would rather die than be searched; he was willing, however, to retire to the next room and defend his honour, or perish in the attempt. Wade, who before this had had his suspicions, was now confirmed in them, and as the sword was referred to, instantly prepared for the attack; but in his confusion, in drawing his sword, he felt the box in a secret pocket.
>
> Stung with remorse at having wounded the honour of a soldier, he said hastily as he left the room: "Sir, I here, with great reason ask your pardon and hope to find it granted by your breakfasting with me, and hereafter ranking me amongst your friends." At breakfast Wade asked the officer, "Why, did you refuse being searched," The young soldier replied that he was a gentleman by birth, and existing on half pay and friendless he had sunk into the most abject poverty, he lived only by what wretched bets he could pick up, and by the scraps of food given him by the waiters out of charity and at the time he had half a fowl with a manchet wrapped in a piece of paper in his pocket and was afraid of being exposed and the thought of it being discovered was ten times more terrible than fighting the room round.
>
> Wade replied, "Enough, dear boy, you have said enough" and after asking the name of the soldier, Wade invited him to dine the next day at 'Sweets' Wade presented him with a Captain's Commission, and a purse of guineas [other references to this episode gave the sum as 100 guineas] to join his Regiment. This exactly explains Wade's character and it does him honour. The poor officer, though evidently fond of fowl, was, it is still more evident, not "chicken-hearted".

During the winter months, Wade was busily engaged with his commitments in London, and before leaving for the West Country he visited Captain Tufnell's Yard in the Old Palace Yard at Westminster, where he had commissioned Samuel Tufnell to design and build a magnificent altarpiece for the Abbey Church at Bath.

The *Taunton Journal* reported on October 1st 1725 that:

> A magnificent Altar Piece is preparing at Captain Tuffnel's Yard, in the Old Palace Yard, Westminster for the Cathedral at Bath, which is the Gift of General Wade to that Corporation, and is computed to be worth 1500 L.

The following May the journal reported that:

> the Abbey is shut up while a fine Altar-Piece is erecting, which was given by General Wade, and 'tis said, cost 1200.L.

On the same day the journal reported from Inverness that Lord Lovat had set out for Bath for the recovery of his health, which he had impaired in the Highlands.

Wade arrived in Edinburgh about the beginning of July 1726, when the *Caledonian Mercury* reported the General reviewing various regiments. He proceeded to the Highlands in the beginning of August, and returned to Edinburgh in the middle of October, where he put in considerable time in examining the fortifications of the castle, and in making arrangements for the building of barracks in the Canongate. He was back in London by the end of November, and was busy with his duties there as Member of Parliament for Bath.

Chapter 8

Back to Bath

At Bath, I'm arrived and I freely declare
I do nothing but wonder, ask questions, and stare:
Here's music, warm bathing, fine dancing, and singing,
With racketing, rioting, gaming and ringing;
Such a bustling and jostling, such hurries are made,
At the pump-room, the ball-rooms, the play, and parade,
You would swear 'twas a fair, or a race, or a show,
With a constant succession of puppets a-row;
All dressed so profusely, you'd think their resort,
Instead of such places, was hourly to Court;
Such a brilliant appearance of plenty and wealth,
That nothing seems wanted – but Virtue and Health.

This verse comes from 'The Register of Folly' taken from *Bath under Beau Nash* by Lewis Melville.

Wade's visits to Bath were always looked upon with pleasure, and once again he enjoyed the round of visiting friends, indulging in the warm spa waters and the gambling houses. Wiltshire's Rooms was a particular favourite but he was a more constant frequenter of Lord and Lady Hawley's, which consisted of a play room, a ballroom and, underneath, a theatre – one of the earliest built in Bath. The rows of seats were placed one upon another until they reached four feet from the ceiling; there was only one box, placed above the door, which held four persons, and the price of admission was half a crown to every part of the house. Thirty pounds was the receipt for a full house, and Her Ladyship was entitled to a third share of the profits. One fourth of the remainder was for the use of scenery and dresses. The standing expense was £2 10s. per night, which included music, attendants, bills and tallow candles; the remainder was divided among twelve performers.

The cost of admission, or lack of interest in the theatre, resulted in the rooms being used by Lord Hawley for gaming tables – gambling at that time being a much greater attraction. Attendance at the theatre was poor, and the players who were paid according to the receipts were unable to live on such a pittance. The play room, which came to be looked on with contempt, was eventually demolished and the site was acquired for the building of the Mineral Water Hospital in 1738. Was Lord Hawley's the low gambling house referred to by Walpole in his memoirs?

Bath was a place where General Wade could stroll without the need of a carriage, and this made a welcome break from long hours of travel. It must be remembered that in those days travelling any distance was not undertaken lightly. The roads were poor and the coaches uncomfortable, while the threat of being held up by highwaymen could not be ignored. A journey from London to Bath took about three days in 1711, and this was reduced to two days in 1740; the new coaches were called flyers.

The increase in speed was largely due to the well-sprung coaches and the stationing of teams of fresh horses along the road, instead of using, as the early coaches had done, the same tired horses for the whole journey and making lengthy stops to rest them. No doubt Wade was able to afford the very best carriage and horses; even so, the hours travelling in all weathers must surely have taken a toll on his health.

There would have been time to call on his friends and meet the numerous pretty ladies who flocked to Bath – such as Mrs Howard, who later became the Duchess of Suffolk, and the beautiful Miss Chudleigh, later the Countess of Bristol. Miss Molly Lepel came to relieve her sufferings from gout, and at once was surrounded by a court of men and women; Lord Sussex, who ended his days in Bath, died a martyr to love – the unfashionable love of his wife. The Bath environment delighted many visitors. Mrs Delany enjoyed her visit so much that she wrote from London on April 22nd 1736 to Swift:

> I think Bath a more comfortable place to live in than London: all entertainments of the place lie in a small compass, and you are at your liberty to partake of them, or let them alone, just as it suits your humour. This town London is grown to such an enormous size

that above half a day must be spent in the street, going from one place to another. I like it every year less and less.

Bath was the only place where Wade could find relief from his infirmities and relax a little in good company. For more peaceful recreation there would be a chance to listen to music. Handel often visited Bath and season tickets to his concerts at Wiltshire's Rooms on The Walks could be obtained for five shillings from Leake's, the bookseller and circulating library at 5 The Walks. A season ticket entitled the purchaser to take home any book, to read the news-sheets of the day and to meet up with like-minded people for interesting discussions or current gossip and scandal. By 1728 Bath Races had become an organised event, and later Wade's nephew, Captain William Wade, delighted his many admirers by riding home an easy winner in the principal race of the day.

Aside from the daily round of amusements, Wade was frequently occupied in the affairs of business, council meetings, and his financial dealings with Ralph Allen. After a shaky start, the cross-posts were now bringing in handsome profits, and Allen was looking at ways to invest his newly found wealth.

In 1726 an important and long-contemplated enterprise got under way: the Avon Navigation Scheme, to open up a navigable river passage between Bath and the great seaport of Bristol, twelve miles away. There were objections, as there always are when progress is feared by interest groups; here it was the local landowners, farmers and colliers. Their concern was the effect it would have on local prices of imported corn, butter, cheese and coal. The most determined were the colliers, who recognised the potential damage that might result from the arrival by water of superior Shropshire coal.

A Bristol merchant, John Hobbs, deserves the credit for putting the scheme into operation. The Bath Corporation transferred the powers of the Act to thirty-two individuals, who undertook to open the navigation 'at the equal cost of each co-partner'. The shareholders included the Duke of Beaufort, General Wade, John Codrington of Wraxall, Ralph Allen, Dr John Lane, Thomas Tyndale, James Hardwick, and John Hobbs of Bristol. A stock company of thirty-two shares was organised in May 1724 and Allen was appointed one of the treasurers.

On December 15th 1727 the first barge moved from Bristol to Bath down the Avon, bringing deal boards, pig lead, Bristol-made window glass, Welsh slates and meal. Bristol Pennant stone could also be shipped up in bulk. This was an important item, for it made the paving of Bath's sidewalks and parades, an essential amenity for long-skirted ladies when good surfaces in the roadways could not be guaranteed. Many years later, in 1825, a correspondent of a Bristol journal asserted that less than £150 each was contributed by the thirty-two original proprietors, and that one share in 1825 had been sold for £4,000. John Hobbs, who was mainly responsible for getting the Avon Navigation Scheme into operation, was rewarded by the Bath Corporation and made a free burgess. Soon there were pleasure boats to be hired, and in May 1728 one of the first to use the new waterway was Princess Amelia, who sailed by wherry to Bristol.

Ralph Allen, never one to miss an opportunity, acquired the quarries on Combe Down and, with the newly opened waterway from Bath to Bristol, he was able to transport his stone to other parts of the country. A railway was built to carry the stone down from the quarries to waiting barges in the Widcombe Basin. In time the railway, no longer required, was demolished. One of John Wood's first commissions in Bath was to build a Palladian manor house in the city for Allen. For some years the work of the Post Office operated from this building. Allen now felt that his local standing called for a dwelling equivalent to the stately homes of the landed aristocracy, and, with this in mind and also to demonstrate the qualities of the freestone, Allen built his mansion, Prior Park, on the slopes of Combe Down. Architecturally it would rank among the great mansions of England. It is justly considered one of the finest Palladian houses designed by John Wood.

Over the next few years, the rich and famous sought to own houses in Bath. William Pitt 'the Elder', MP for Bath, built a house for himself in The Circus, and the Dukes of Beaufort, Monmouth, Kingston and Chandos, Bedford and Marlborough, and Lords Howth, Clive, Sandwich, and Chesterfield all had mansions in Bath.

In 1726 an ode was dedicated to General Wade: 'On Occasion of His Disarming the Highlands' by Leonard Welsted (1688–1747). The ode was a popular literary form at all social levels in the 18th century, from the works of Pope to the news-sheets and the circulating libraries. A popular figure such as Wade was sure to attract the attention of the writers and poets of the day.

Leonard Welsted was an accomplished writer who composed in

a relaxed, light-hearted vein. He was associated with Whig political figures in his later years and would certainly have come into contact with Wade. The ode to General Wade was written in imitation of Horace (Quintus Horatius Flaccus, 65–8 BC) a Roman poet of the Augustan age. It was printed by W. Wilkins in Paternoster Row, price one shilling.

> Some future *Garth*, brave Chief, shall sing,
> Grac'd with a Plume of *Homer*'s Wing,
> Thy Toils by Land, and on the Main;
> The Toils, thou hast not borne in vain!
> In the bleak *Highlands* Trophies won,
> Or underneath th' *Iberian* Sun.
>
> We aim not, valiant *Wade*, to tell,
> On a feebly sounding Shell,
> These, nor the like of Heroic Things!
> The high Demands of injur'd Kings!
> Nor *Popery*'s relentless Rage,
> Murd'ring Childhood, murd'ring Age!
>
> The vengeful *Prussian* in the Field;
> Nor stubborn *Pole*, untaught to yield!
> My Nature, fearful to aspire,
> And the chaste *Nymph*, that rules the Lyre,
> Forbid me in unequal Lays
> To lessen Thine and *George*'s Praise.
>
> What happy Poet, Great *Nassau*,
> Arm'd in Adamant, shall draw?
> Or dauntless *Gallway*'s Acts reveal,
> Mangled all o'er with *Spanish* Steel?
> Or *Stanhope*, in his Life's short Span,
> Thro' Wisdom's Dictates, more than Man?
>
> The Virgin's Griefs, or Lovers' Joys,
> Domestick Cares, and harmless Toys,
> Better suit the *Lestrian* Muse;
> Such Levities for Song I chuse,
> Whether untouch'd by *Cupid*'s Dart,
> Or *Harriot* ling'ring in my Heart.

Leonard Welsted wrote many poems in an attempt to get a position from patronage. He may well have received patronage from General Wade, resulting in a glowing dedication to General Wade, of which this is a shortened version:

> Sir, among the various ends of Poetry, one is to rescue from Oblivion the Actions of great men, and transmit 'em to Posterity with Honour: Happy those Poets, who can thus give, and happy those Men, who receive immortality by them! My own unfitness, *Sir*, for such an attempt, I thought I could not, when I was applying to you, better or more decently express, that in the sense of *Horace*, taken from his Ode to an Illustrious *Roman*, the Darling and Ornament of his Age and Country! Like you, great in War! Like you, respected in Peace.
>
> But this, *Sir*, is the least part of your Praise: Superiority of Genius and understanding has been the lot of many: Many Men, as well as you, have, by the favour of Heaven, been endued with great natural talents, improved by learning: Others also have successfully undergone fatigues and hazards in their Country's Service, and acquired a great name for warlike achievements. The preservation of Kingdoms and Armies has been owing to the skill and courage of other Men: as that of the Confederate Army in *Spain* was, in one remarkable Juncture, to yours. It is not in these views, after my way of considering Men, in which you are to be seen with the greatest advantage: No, *Sir*, You are more a hero in my eyes, when you are less; and make the brightest figure to me, when you are least conspicuous to the multitude: 'Tis then, when I behold your taking into your care the cause of the Widow and Orphan, silent for yourself, importunate in the interests of others, anxious for afflicted merit of innocence.
>
> When I behold you indulging your great Heart in Acts of Beneficence, your only Luxury! Doing all the good in your power, and grieving for what you cannot do; 'Tis then, I most congratulate you on your Felicity, and the virtuous eminence you possess above the most of your species. To this Spirit of Humanity, to your Sincerity, Plainness of Manners, and fine contempt of everything mean and little, to that Dignity of Wisdom, that does not stand in need of cunning and policy, and to your inviolable honour and faithfulness, do you owe, that you are so universally belov'd and esteem'd. Without them, you had been a mere Great Man: But you knew nothing so Great as to do Good: To be unhappy, is the certain road to your friendship; and whoever seeks it, needs bring no bribe but honesty, no recommendation but misfortune; Distress finds access to your heart, like gold to a miser.

Dulce et decorum est pro patria mori:
Mors et fugacem persequitur virum,
Nec parcit inbellis iuventae
Poplitibus timidove tergo.

T. E. Page, in his 1895 edition of the ode, interprets the Latin poem as follows:

> On true manliness – let the boy who means to be a man lead a simple and hardy life as the best training for a soldier's career; in the field, let the enemy fear him and let his courage be inspired by the thought that death is glorious indeed when encountered for his country's cause.

Chapter 9

Wade's Roads in the Highlands

The year 1727 marks the end of the reign of George I. He suffered a stroke while travelling in his coach on the way to Hanover, and died some days later on June 17th 1727. He was buried in the Leineschloss church, Hanover, near the late Electress Sophia. George I had ruled for thirteen years and during that time had tried to secure religious tolerance for his subjects, believing they should be free to attend a church of their own choosing without harassment. He strongly believed in freedom of thought and brought about reforms at the universities of Oxford and Cambridge; the endowment of regius professorships in history was a measure to induce the universities to accept the wider range of subjects already studied in the dissenting academies and at the Inns of Court. George I enjoyed public plays, operas, concerts, masquerades and cards. Apart from the threat from the Jacobites, his reign was on the whole one of peace and prosperity. He responded with restraint to anti-Hanoverian sentiment in Britain. George's lack of prejudice was remarkable, and extended even to his Stuart relatives. According to the diary of Lord Percival in 1716, the King refused to attend a thanksgiving service for the defeat of the late Jacobite rebels: he did not think it fitting that he should render thanks to God for having vanquished his own subjects. Also, it must be remembered, he was the great-grandson of James I of England.

He was judged, however, as cold and dull and he was said to speak very little English. The writer Ragnhild Hatton thoroughly researched the life of George I and stated that his command of English was not as limited as once believed. George was fluent in French, Italian and Dutch, a cultured man and a shrewd and pragmatic ruler. It is not hard to see from this description the respect Wade may have felt for him. Like Wade, George was a brave and wary soldier. He entered the army at the age of fifteen, served in the Dutch and Turkish wars and in 1708 was appointed field marshal of the German Imperial Army in the War of the Spanish Succession against Louis XIV. He also served under the Duke of Marlborough at Oudenarde, where he led the Hanoverian dragoons. A statue for which the King gave a sitting was commissioned for the Rolls House, and now stands at the entrance to the Public Records Office in London.

Once settled back in London from his home in Bath, Wade sat down to write his second report addressed to the newly acceded George II:

> THE REPORT, &C., RELATING TO THE HIGHLANDS, 1727
>
> Your Majesty having been pleased to Command me to repair to the Highlands of Scotland and to proceed in the Execution of the several Orders and Instructions I had before received from his late Majesty of Blessed Memory; Empowering me to put in Execution the Act of Parliament of the eleventh year of his said late Majesty's Reign for disarming the Highlands, and to grant licences to Merchants, Drovers and others to carry Arms for their security and defence; to forward the new Barracks and Fortifications intended to be erected at Killihinmen and Inverness and to cause the necessary repairs to be made for the security of the Castles and other Fortresses in North Britain; to carry on the roads of communication between the Garrisons and Barracks in the Highlands, To protect and secure your Majesty's subjects in the low Country from the Robberies, Depredations and illegal Exactions of the Highlands; To pursue seize and secure such rebels and attainted persons as should refuse to submit to the Laws and pay due obedience to your Majesty's Government, and to perform all other services which might contribute to civilize the Highlanders, preserve the peace and quiet of the Country and render the disaffected incapable of disturbing the tranquillity of your Majesty's happy and auspicious Reign.
> In obedience to these Your Majesty's Commands; I have endeavoured to perform the several services mentioned, in a manner which I humbly hope will meet with your Majesty's approbation.
> But before I proceed to the Particulars, I humbly beg leave to lay before your Majesty the Intelligence I received the beginning of this present year, of some Transactions that were carrying on

in the Highlands in favour of the Pretender.

Soon after the new Alliance was made between the Emperor and the King of Spain, some persons were sent into Scotland to animate the disaffected Clans and prepare them to join a body of Foreign Forces, which they assured them should be landed from Spain on the West Coast of Scotland before Midsummer.

The Principal Persons employed in this Service were, one Sinclair a native of Scotland who for some time past has been a Sea Officer in the service of Spain, and was employed to take a survey of the Sea Coast and to find a proper place for disembarking the said Troops, that were to land in the Western Highlands. Besides this Sinclair, there was another that went by the name of Brown, who has been sent into Scotland before on the like Occasions. [These two may have been the Sinclair and Brown who were arrested in Bath during the troubles in 1715.]

This Brown came to London in February last to concert measures with the Jacobites, and after continuing here some weeks he proceeded to the Highlands where he sent Circular letters to the Chiefs of several Clans reputed to be disaffected to your Majesty's Government, in order to prepare them for the intended invasion.

But as your Majesty will be best able to judge of their proceedings by the following letters, I humbly beg leave to insert the copies of them in the same order as they came into my hands.

Copy of a Letter from a Roman Catholick employed to procure Intelligence; directed to Sir Duncan Campbell, Capt, of one of the Highland Companys

After parting with you I was informed by a very sure hand of the following Particulars Viz.

The Sea Captain that went lately to take a view of proper harbours for landing men is Called Capt. Sinclair. He landed first at Leith, from thence he came to Glasgow – and is now making his way about the West and North Coasts, and will I suppose return by the East Coast. He told my informer, that he reckons Clyde and Dumbarton a fit place of Landing, but he is to take a view of all the good Harbours of Scotland, not knowing where wind or weather may carry the Ships they design for an Invasion. He said that he expected another Ship with further instructions, would land at Leith about the time that he arrived there first himself, which makes my informer suspect, that is the Ship, lately seized there with letters, by the Government Orders. The said Captain Sinclair says that they design to land 4000 men in

Scotland, and 8000 men in England, and that they doubt not but they shall get them Landed, but their greatest difficulty is to carry off their Ships safely again after landing their men. He says further, that they had 46 good transport ships of considerable burthen. The best sailors in Europe ready for this Design before he came off from Spain. Moreover, he says that one Captain Brown came to London and that he is to come down by Land and to be in the Highlands about the end of this Month with instructions and encouragements to such as they reckon their friends in the Highlands. And for that end he is to make a tour among them. He says further, that there is already £20,000 remitted to Edinburgh p. Bill.

My informer assures me, that before the said Captain Sinclair arrived at Leith, there were 400 Broad Swords landed at Leith, all designed for Gentlemen; and that these swords do actually lie privately in some place or places within Edinburgh but in what precise place there he knows not. He is resolved to secure you and your Company as soon as they hear there are men shipped in Spain, without waiting longer for the event of such an invasion, and doubtless the like attempt will be made upon the other Companys.

This letter which I had the honour to lay before his Majesty's Ministers, agreeing with other Intelligence received from abroad relating to an intended invasion in the West of England, as well as in Scotland, I humbly presume induced his Majesty to order Colonel Campbell's Regiment of Dragoons, with Kirk's, Delorains, and Marcartney's Regiments of foot, to march into England in order to form a camp in the West, if it should be found necessary and for the security of the Castles in Scotland, the Garrison Company of Edinburgh and Sterling were raised from 60 to 100 men each and that of Dumbarton to 50, which before consisted of but 15 private men.

The Highland Company Commanded by Captains were made up of sixty to one hundred private men, but those under the Command of Lieutenants were augmented from 30 to 60. These including Officers might on occasion be formed into a Battalion of 525 men; and both the Garrison and Highland Companys were compleat before the 25th March.

There then remained in Scotland two Regiments of Dragoons and four Battalions of Foot who by Additional Troops and Companys, that were soon after ordered to be raised, made up about the same number of men for the service of Scotland, as they consisted of before the march of the Regiments above mentioned.

I presume further to represent to your Majesty that at this juncture I thought it necessary to employ some proper person to observe the Motions of Brown and Sinclair and to give an Account of their proceedings.

The person who seemed to me the fittest for this purpose was R.R: [was this Rob Roy, recently pardoned by the King?] who had then but very lately received his Majesty's pardon. He was an old acquaintance of Brown's and believed by him to continue firm in the interest of the Pretender. He had his Majesty's leave to join Brown and other Jacobites and agreed for a reward of £100 to discover their secrets. Accordingly he gained such confidence with Brown as to be employed as his messenger with letters from him to some of the heads of Clans; as will more fully appear to your Majesty by the following letters.

Letter to me from Sir Duncan Campbell, Captain of one of the Highland Companys.

Edinburgh 2nd May 1727

Sir,

I had the Honour to write to you last on the 15th of March, and then acquainted you with what I had learned from R. R; and having made some further progress in that enquiry, I think it my duty to acquaint you with the Particulars and upon what foot I have now left it.

Sinclair told R: at his coming, That Captain Brown stayed at London to concert matters with their friends in England, and particularly the remitting a sum of money. £20,000 he mentioned to lie ready here for their Service and which he says is now brought here by hands of one Cumming a Merchant in the Parliament Close.

Brown came to this Country in March last, he made some stay here, and from hence he went west. The places he mostly resided at were; My Lord Wigtoun's House at Cumberland, and Stirling of Keir's, two miles west from Stirling. This Gentleman is attainted and at his own House without leave. He came to Rs. House [sic] and resided there some nights, and is now in Galloway.

R. told me that Brown designed one John Stewart of Ardshiel, should receive of him the £3000 he was to give to the Clans immediately, but by Brown's letter to R: of the 6th of April, he seem to have altered that resolution, having probably settled that matter with Lochiel, whom he had an opportunity of seeing at Drummond of Bahadie's House in Dumblain. This Drummond, Graham of Bran, and Keir being the Pretender's chief agents, as R: informs me, in that Country.

R: by my Lieutenant sent me the copy of his instructions from Brown which I enclose, and compared them with the original. Brown's letters to the Clans I myself read under favour of manufacturing the covers a little, and I also enclose copies of them. You'll observe there are no letters for Lochiel, none of the Gordon's none of the McDonel's save Glengary and Keppoch, neither for the McLeods; any of the Duke of Athol's people, nor the Mackenzie's besides the letters which R: showed me he delivered from Brown to Appine.

R: in obedience to Brown's letter of the 6th of April (Copy of which I enclose) is gone to meet with him to receive his second instructions; He will undertake to Brown to deliver his letters, and has engaged so to contrive it, that I shall have an opportunity of seizing him with the original letters, of the Clans to Brown, about him.

Though upon the first notice I had of this matter from R: I was not without suspicion that he might possibly be imposing upon me in the information; Yet having now seen the original letters (whereof I enclose the copies) with my own eyes; wrote in a hand writing like a man of business, on gilt paper neatly folded &c. I think his information genuine, and I think it possible he may give me the opportunity to seize him with the papers as he has promised. I have therefore given him £25 more of the second £50 you allowed me to lay out for this Service, and have renewed my assurances to him, that he will be put in a condition to live, if he goes through with this Service, &c.
  Duncan Campbell

Instructions from Brown to R: R:

You are to deliver the letters given you and likewise to discourse the persons to whom you will give them after this manner.

You are to tell them that both Nobility and Gentry who are for the King's interest in the West of Scotland are for landing in Clyde, and likewise the Gentleman who was sent from the King of Spain to view the West of Scotland is fully convinced that he may save his ships after landing.

You are likewise to tell the Clans, that if they please, there shall be 1000 men landed at Inverlochy for demolishing of the Garrison.

You are likewise to assure them of £3000 to be given them when required to put themselves in better order for the King's service.

You are likewise to advise with them what hands the money

shall be put into; those that are to have it are as follows: The McDonalds, McIntoshe's McPherson's, who are reckoned but one Clan. Stewart of Appine, McLeans, The Cameron's, McDougal's, Laird of Macinven, Chisholm of Strathglass, and Glenmoriston.

You are to advise with Glengary, Appine, Keppoch and McInven, what every Man's share of the money will come to.

You are to assure them; although the arms that were sent already be mismanaged, that there shall be care taken that they shall not want for arms and ammunition.

You may tell them there is a method taken with the rest of the Clans to satisfaction.

You are to advise what methods are to be taken with the Independent Companys for stopping them from joining to come to a Body. If the landing shall be in Clyde, they will do a vast deal of harm to the Braes of Perth and Stirlingshire. They will stop them very much from joining. And you are to return your answer before the 20th of April.

J. Brown

Letter to the Laird of Glengary carried by R: R: from Brown.

Sir,

I had the Honour to be sent over to Scotland by the King's [the Pretender's] *Order to advise his friends that now he is in a condition to serve himself and you. He wants not Men, Shipping, or Money, so that I am ordered in my instructions to send the bearer hereof R:R: to acquaint you of the same and what method is to be taken in doing it, which I hope you will give your opinion frankly as to the place of Landing in Scotland, and likewise what way will be taken with the money which is to be given you in order to put you in a condition to serve your King, for it is ready to be given on Demand.*

I am further ordered by the King in my instructions, that you should take your own prudent way to get My Lord Lovat managed to come into the King's Service, which if he will do, you may assure him of his Pardon from the King, and likewise his patent of Lord Lovat.

I can further assure you that the King has made his peace with the Duke of – and although he does not join himself; see if you can get him brought so far as to let his Clan lie still.

Our Committee here has left to your management Strathglass, Glenmoriston, and any other you will think proper to speak to. Being informed that Sir Hector McLean is in that Country, you are to deliver his letter to him and likewise to discourse him as

you will think most proper. That is all to trouble you at present and I am –
Your humble servant. J. Brown.

Letter from Brown to the Laird of Keppoch, and the same to the Lairds of McIntosh, Glencoe, Clunie, McPherson, McDougal and Sir Hector McClean of Duart.

Sir,
Dear R:
I had the honour to be sent over to Scotland by the King's Order to assure his Friends, that now he is in hopes to be in a Condition to serve himself and you. He wants not Men, Shipping, or Money, so that I am ordered in my Instructions to send the Bearer hereof R:R: to acquaint you of the same, and what Method is to be taken in doing of it, which I hope you will give your opinion freely as to the Place of Landing in Scotland, and likewise what Way shall be taken with the Money which is to be given in order to put you in a Condition to serve your King, for it is ready to be given upon Demand. This is all at present and I am &c.
J. Brown

Letter from Brown to R:R:

Dear R.
Since parting with you I have got information that the Government has got some intelligence of my being in the Country, so that I am advised by the best of the King's Friends in England to keep myself as private as possible and to see nobody. If that other Gentleman you know of is come as far as your House or to the place appointed, let him return as private as possible for fear of Suspicion. As to that Affair I was to employ him in, I have got it done to satisfaction. You may come privately to Mr. Kea's House, where you shall have your second orders from me. I beg that you may come that no Mortal may know of it, I am not to be there myself, but I shall leave it in Writing what you are to do.
Send express to such as you conversed with in the Highlands to keep them as private as possible, and to give no reason to the Government whereby they may have thought that there is anything doing. This is all to trouble you with at present only you may believe that I am afraid that there May be Orders out against you, and three or four more in your Country; if there should be such, I wish you would take a trip to Arran to see your friend Bardowie. J: B:
I am &c J. Brown

Wade's report continues:

I humbly beg leave to assure your Majesty that during this transaction all proper means were used to frustrate the designs of the Jacobites. The several Highland Companys were ordered to assemble in such Stations as might best prevent the Junction of the disaffected Highlanders, as well as to secure themselves from the danger of being disarmed when separated in small party's as was said to be intended in one of the foregoing Letters.

The Oaths of Allegiance to his Majesty were tendered anew to every soldier of those Companys and some of them were discharged whose fidelity was suspected.

Parties were sent into the Country inhabited by the Clans suspected of disaffection and a strict search made after Arms that might have been concealed, but none were discovered except about twenty Muskets that had been hid in a cave ever since the Highlands were disarmed in 1725 and those grown so rusty that they were entirely unfit for Service.

About this time several Letters in Cipher were intercepted in Scotland importing an intended invasion, and some persons seized by Order of his Majesty's Principal Secretaries of State, upon which the above mentioned Brown, Sinclair, and other Emissaries of the Pretender made their escape and had quitted the Country before my arrival in Scotland, nor could I ever learn after the strictest enquiry, that Brown before his departure had paid any part of the £3000 to the Clans as he had promised by the preceding letters.

After my coming to the Highlands, I examined some of the Chiefs of the Clans to whom the above mentioned letters to Brown were directed, who did not absolutely deny that application had been made to them from the said Brown to join the Troops that were expected from Spain, but assured me they had never consented to take up Arms or enter into any Measures that might give disturbance to the Government.

I told them they ought to have acquainted me of these proceedings, and represented to them the folly and danger of listening to the ridiculous proposals of Men whose fortunes were desperate who had nothing of their own to lose and hoped to be gainers by a Change, tho' at the expense of involving their Country in ruin and bloodshed as they had done in the year 1715. That the obligations they had to your Majesty's Royal Father ought ever to be fresh in their memories, whose mercy and clemency had been extended toward them, after having forfeited their lives by engaging in two rebellions against him.

That your Majesty's accession to the Throne was attended with more signal and distinguishing marks of love and affection of your People that was ever known on the like Occasion. That altho' your Majesty's Government was established on the most solid foundation, supported by a considerable body of Regular Forces, and by such Alliances that must render all attempts of the Pretender and his adherents vain and impracticable, yet that your Majesty out of your great goodness and clemency had commanded me to do everything that might contribute to promote the advantage of your Subjects inhabiting the Highlands, however undeserving some of them had been of your Royal favour.

That your Majesty had ordered me to lay out considerable sums of money in making roads through the Mountains for encouraging their Trade and Commerce with the Low Country; And to endeavour by mild and moderate usage to convince them of the happiness they may enjoy by peaceable submitting to your Majesty's Government. Upon which they answered, that they had suffered sufficiently for their past Folly, but were now determined to live peaceably and quietly, and hoped by their future good behaviour to deserve Your Majesty's favour and protection.

During my stay at Edinburgh I signed an order to Sir Duncan Campbell, Captain of the Independent Company whose Station was the Western Highlands, to seize and secure James Sterling of Keir, one of the persons named in the foregoing Letters, who by an Act of Parliament stands attainted of High Treason for the Rebellion of 1715.

He had from that time lived at his house, openly and without disguise, under no apprehensions of being molested by his Country Men who on all occasions are said to have a tender regard one for another, however they may disagree in their opinions and politics. He was seized in September last pursuant to the order and now remains a prisoner in the Castle of Edinburgh till your Majesty's Pleasure be known.

About the same time I gave another order for the seizing the person called Brigadier Macintosh, who had been very active in the Rebellion, he returned lately from abroad and was at that time lurking in the Northern Highlands, but hearing nothing of his being seized, I presume he has quitted the Country.

I think it my Duty also to represent to your Majesty, that there are four other attainted persons who lay concealed the last year in Scotland, and I have reason to believe they still continue there, viz John Steward of Innernitty, Alexander Robertson of Strowan, Sr. David Tripland of Fingask, and John Walkingshaw of Scotstown, whose friends and relations have often solicited me to intercede on their behalf that they might be permitted to make their submissions to your Majesty, in hopes of obtaining your Majesty's Gracious Pardon, as was granted to several others in the same circumstances by your Royal Father in the year 1725.

I humbly beg leave farther to report to your Majesty; that as the disarming the Highlands was happily executed without resistance or bloodshed, so the good effects it has produced already appear beyond what could have been expected in so short a time; for no Arms are now carried in the Highlands but by your Majesty's licence, or by such who are entitled to that privilege by a legal qualification. It is therefore to be hoped that by Prosecuting the same measures, which hitherto have proved so successful, the Highlanders will in a few years forget the use of Arms which in all ages they have esteemed as their greatest pride and glory, insomuch that it was looked on to be a reproach to a Highlander to be seen without his musket, broad sword, pistol and durk. These by a long Custom were esteemed part of their dress and at my first coming to the Highlands were worn by the meanest of the inhabitants, even in their churches, fairs and markets, which looked more like places for a Parade for Soldiers, than assemblies for devotion or other meetings of Civil Societies.

This pernicious practice of wearing Arms was attended with many inconveniences, to themselves, to the inhabitants of the neighbouring Country, and even to the State itself. The Highlanders, who are naturally addicted to revenge, committed frequent murders, which often exasperated the Clans one against another for many generations, and when any person was killed by one of a different name, they imagined no recompense or justice was sufficient but by shedding the blood of one of that Clan who committed the crime, altho' an innocent person who was no way concerned in the fact. By this unjust way of proceeding their animosities were kept up to future times and whole Clans were often engaged one against another, in which great numbers on both sides lost their lives.

The Countries in the Neighbourhood of the Highlands were frequently harassed by Parties of Armed Men who committed depredations on their Cattle and Estates, and obliged them to pay contributions which often amounted to more than their proportion of the Land Tax: But since the surrender of their Arms, these oppressions have ceased; There are no complaints of depredations, no any contributions paid by the inhabitants of the Low Country.

But in my humble opinion the greatest inconveniency that attended the frequent use of Arms in the Highlands, was, their being ready and proper instruments of the Pretender or any foreign power to give disturbance to the Government: For the Superiors and Chiefs of Clans have in all ages assumed an absolute and despotic power over their vassals, who never refuse to follow them, without enquiring into the Justice of their cause, or against whom they are to Act, by which implicit obedience they have frequently been engaged in Rebellions against their Sovereigns, both before and since the Union of the Kingdoms; And I hope your Majesty will pardon my presumption, if I here insert a saying of the Jacobites abroad, as I have been assured from Gentlemen well affected to your Majesty's Government, who in their travels through France and Italy have happened to meet and converse with those people.

They always owned that their greatest hopes were from the Highlands of Scotland, and when it was said that those hopes were in vain, since his Majesty had an Army of 12,000 Regular Forces at Command [the Establishment at that time for Great Britain] their usual answer was, We have also a Standing Army of 12,000 Highlanders, as resolute, as well Armed and as much under Command as the Regular Forces you so much depend on.

The inconveniences arising from the practice of carrying Arms in the Highlands have often been under the consideration of the Privy Council and Parliaments of Scotland before the Union and several rigorous Laws were made to disarm and reduce them to obedience. These have always failed of success; as I humbly conceive from being formed with more severity than Judgment, but I humbly hope the measures your Majesty is now taking will prove an effectual remedy to these evils and will render the Highlands as quiet and peaceable as any other part of your Majesty's Dominions.

I also beg leave to represent to your Majesty; That pursuant to the instruction I received from Your Royal Father for granting Licences under my Hand and Seal, to Merchants, Drovers and others permitting them to carry Arms for the security and defence of their Property; I have sent out in the year 1725, 230 Licences for the whole of the Highlands which were to remain in force for two years and no longer. These Licences expiring in September last were called in and 210 were issued out in your Majesty's name to continue in force for three years, provided the persons possessing the same, during that time, behaved themselves as faithful Subjects of your Majesty, and peaceably and quietly towards the people of the Country.

I presume further to report to your Majesty, that the great road of communication extending from the East to the West Sea, through the middle of the Highlands, has been successfully carried on upon the South side of the Lakes from Inverness to Fort

William, being near 60 miles in length, and is made practicable for the March of Artillery or other Wheel Carriage, as may appear by my having travelled to that Garrison the last summer in a Coach and Six Horses to the great wonder of the inhabitants, who, before this road was made, could not pass on horseback without danger and difficulty.

This work was very troublesome from the interposition of rocks, bogs and mountains; yet was performed by your Majesty's Troops Quartered in those parts without any assistance from the people of the Country. The Non Commission Officers and Soldiers are allowed double pay during the time they are employed in this Service; and if it is your Majesty's pleasure to continue the same allowance out of the Contingencies of the Army as were granted by his late Majesty for the two preceding years, with some addition for erecting stone bridges, where they are wanting.

A Military Way may be made through the Mountains from Inverness Southward as far as Perth, which will open a short and speedy Communication with the Troops Quartered in the Low Country, contribute to civilize the Highlanders, and in my humble opinion will prove the most effectual means to continue them in due obedience to your Majesty's Government. In regard to the Fortifications in Scotland, I humbly presume to represent to your Majesty; that till last year, nothing had been effectually done to secure them from the danger of surprise, to which they have been exposed for many years past; and particularly the Castle of Edinburgh, which, I humbly conceive is a place of the greatest importance to the safety of that part of your Majesty's Dominions.

The Parapet Walls of this Castle were so ruinous that the Soldiers after shutting the Gates had found a way to ascend and descend to and from the Town of Edinburgh whenever they thought fit.

Upon viewing this defect the last Spring, four soldiers were ordered (for the Experiment) to try if they could ascend the Rock and get over the Wall, which they performed with such dexterity; that from the Common Road, they mounted into the Castle in less than five minutes.

The Castle of Dumbarton had lain exposed in the same manner for sometime past, by the fall of a considerable part of the wall on the north side. Upon the representation I made of this to the present Master General of your Majesty's Ordnance, orders were immediately given for repairing those defects, which was accordingly executed before I left Scotland.

The new Fortifications erecting at Inverness, called after Your Majesty's name, Fort George, is situate on a Hill on the South side of the River Ness, near the place where it falls into the East Sea, as Fort William does on the Western Ocean. The Lake Ness and other Lakes extend almost from one of these Forts, to the other in a straight line, through the middle of the Highlands. It is built within half Musket shot of the Bridge of Inverness and consequently commands that Pass which is the only communication between the North and South Highlands for the Space of near 30 English miles as far as Killihinmen, and is therefore in my humble opinion a place of importance for preventing the Northern Highlanders from descending into the Low Country in times of Rebellion.

This fortification is irregular as are all the other Castles and Forts in Scotland, which are generally built upon Eminencies, incapable by their situation to admit regular Works. It is large enough to contain a Barracks for 300 Men, that number being more than sufficient for the defence of a place which in all probability will never be attacked by Artillery. The repairs to the Old Castle, designed to serve as Lodgings for the Officers of the Garrison, were completed in November last; and the new Works were begun the last summer; and if continued may be capable of receiving a Garrison in two years.

The Fort and Barrack proposed to be built at Killihinmen near the West End of the Lake Ness is not yet begun, but materials are providing to go on with the work next spring, as soon as the Season of the Year will admit. This Place being in the centre of the Highlands equally distant from Fort George and Fort William, will, I humbly conceive, be a proper situation for the Residence of a Governor, who, if it is your Majesty's pleasure, may have the Chief Command, not only of the two Forts above mentioned, but of all the Barracks and Independent Companys in the Highlands by which he will be enabled speedily to assembly a body of 1000 men, to march to any part of that Country for preventing or suppressing insurrection; to inspect into everything that may regard your Majesty's Service in that remote part of your Majesty's Kingdom of Great Britain: to curb the insolence of such of the inhabitants, who, depending on the strength of their inaccessible Mountains shall presume to rebel against their Sovereign, and continue to disregard all Laws both human and divine.

I fear I have already presumed to take up too much of your Majesty's time by the length of this Report, and shall only beg leave humbly to offer to your Majesty what I conceive is further necessary to be done in the Highlands for bringing to perfection a Work so essential to the Peace of that part of Your Majesty's Dominions.

Proposal

That the new Fort and Barracks projected to be built at Killihinmen Adjoining to the West End of the Lake Ness, be carried on the next Spring, as soon as the Season of the Year will permit, and proper Store Rooms built Sufficient to contain Provisions for a Battalion of Foot, with Ovens for baking Ammunition Bread or Biscuit for the use of the Garrison or for Detachments that may be sent into the Mountains. And that all due Encouragement be given for erecting a Market Town on the Ground between the Old Barrack and the End of the Lake (a space of about 500 yards in Length and 400 in breadth) which being situate in the Center of the Highlands, will very much contribute to civilise the Highlanders, who by living separate in the Hills, where there are no Towns, are without Examples to induce them to change their Barbarous Customs.

That a small Tower of Stone in the form of a Redoute, capable of containing a Guard of an Officer, and Twenty Soldiers, be built at each end of the Lake Locy, and another at the East end of the Lake Ness, the better to secure the line of Communication between Fort George and Fort William.

That a small Harbour be made at each [end] of the Lake Ness, for the Security of the Highland galley against Violent Storms which are very frequent [in that] Country.

That a Stable for 30 horses to be erected at the Barrack of Ruthven, which being near the middle of the Highlands, and on the Road proposed in the preceding Article; I conceive to be a proper Station for a party of Dragoons to serve as a Convoy for Money or Provisions for the use of the Forces, as well as to retain that part of the Country in Obedience.

All which is most humbly submitted to Your Majesty's Royal Consideration.

Signed George Wade.

It was indeed a very lengthy report and one that left the government in no doubt of what was needed to bring about peace in the Highlands. Wade was soon heading north for his third year in Scotland, to meet the clans who were disaffected and to try to bring them to the peace table. Any chief suspected of Jacobite plotting would see the General's carriage rumble into his country, and the great man emerge to give a little fatherly advice and warning before consuming vast quantities of the offender's claret. Even the fiercest Jacobite of them all, Robertson of Strowan, the chief of the Donnachaidh clan known as the Poet Chief, who was out in rebellion in 1689, 1715 and 1745, succumbed to Wade's charm and adopted him as a close drinking companion.

Robertson became a lifelong friend of Wade, and even composed and recited a poem to him to mark the opening of the Tay Bridge at Aberfeldy. During one of their meetings Robertson confided in Wade that he was having health problems and Wade suggested that he should travel down to Bath for a consultation with Dr Cheyne. Robertson took this advice, and, on returning home, the Rannoch laird cleared out all the women who were in attendance in his house. One can only wonder from what condition Robertson was suffering for such drastic action to be taken. Dr Cheyne was a specialist in gout and its related problems. Wade and Robertson had lived life to the full and not too wisely, and were certainly in need of his services.

In the year 1728 Wade began his great road from Inverness to Dunkeld. The road was to be eighty English measured miles in length and suitable for carriages. Three hundred men were to be employed to work on different parts of the road and it was hoped, with good weather, that it would be well advanced before October.

On August 27th 1728 the *Caledonian Mercury* reported:

> By letters from Inverlochy of the 16th current we learn that his Excellency General Wade has been viewing the lead mine belonging to Alexander Murray, Esq., of Stanhope, in which he is an Adventurer and whereof the following Account; "That among several Edge Veins already discovered, there is one lately found, that in appearance exceeds anything that hitherto has been seen in Great Britain; it is already discovered about two English miles in Length, carrying for most part within a Fathom of the Surface of the Ground very good Ore of an extraordinary breadth, in many places, particularly in one, where the same was measured it was found to be 13 foot broad, mostly solid Ore.

In 1729 Wade was still busy on his Inverness-to-Dunkeld road and by September of that year he was able to report to the Lord Advocate that considerable progress had been made, and that a feast was preparing for his 'highwaymen' of 'four roasting oxen and plenty of bumpers'. After three hours he took his leave and arrived back at the 'hutt' before dark feeling much refreshed, enabling him the next day to make a second survey of the projected road between Dalnacardoch and Crieff in readiness for the work to begin in 1730. Before leaving he erected the standing stone by the side of the road at Dalnacardoch, which can still be seen alongside the modern highway. The following spring he returned with his engineers and, to the amazement of all, he walked over to the standing stone and picked a golden guinea off the top. He explained that he had left it there the year before for safekeeping.

Wade arrived in Edinburgh in July 1730 and, whilst staying at the home of the Earl of Moray, he found the Countess of Moray much troubled by the plight of John Smith, a sentinel in Montague's Regiment who was due to be shot for desertion. The Countess pleaded with him to pardon Smith. Wade intervened and Smith was duly pardoned and given a second chance. Smith once again deserted his regiment, and Wade for a second time took pity on him and pardoned him. Later the Edinburgh news-sheets of the day reported:

> The *Edinburgh Newspaper* printed the following account Thursday next one John Smith of South Britain a sentinel of Montague's is to be shot in the Links of Leith, for desertion. He is an old offender in that way, and is the very person who a few months ago was pardoned by General Wade, at the request of the Rt. Hon The Countess of Moray. He is to be interred in the same coffin then prepared for him. In his last words he acknowledged his having been twice pardoned by General Wade for the like offence; once at Killwhimen, and lately at the Canongate.

In this year Wade's expenditure on the Crieff–Dalnacardoch road amounted to £3,520 8s. This included the cost of ten miles of the Dunkeld–Inverness road, which had not been completed the previous year. The sum was to include the building of bridges where they were thought necessary, employing seven commissioned officers and 348 non-commissioned officers and soldiers.

The new road was to be about twenty-eight measured miles in length, and would cross country which up until that time was scarcely passable by man or horse, and extend over the Corrieyairack Pass – one of the highest in Scotland. Five stone bridges were to be constructed, one over the River Spey consisting of two large arches, 180 feet in length, and four smaller bridges of one arch each and of smaller dimensions.

The Tummel Bridge, with a double arch, would cross the River Tummel a mile west of the house of John Stewart, Esq., of Canagan:

> The bridge is to have an arch of at least forty foot between the landstools or more if the breadth of the river shall require an arch

of a larger dimension. It is to be twelve foot in breadth including the parapet walls, which walls are to be capped with good flag stones. The whole is to be of good materials and well wrought, and to have an access to the same extending so far on both sides of the land, as to render it easily passable for wheel carriage or cannon.

In the following year, 1731, Wade was occupied in making his road from Dalwhinnie to Fort Augustus. Wade was again advanced £3,000 for this work.

The *Gentleman's Magazine* in 1731 gave a good account of the roads then being built in the Highlands:

> We now o'er Mountains easy passage gain, and run with pleasure, where we climbed with pain. Upon the Road for wheel carriages, finished this summer by a detachment from the Regiments quartered near the Highlands of Scotland. It extends from Fort Augustus to Ruthven, by an insensible ascent of six miles to the top of the great mountain Corriarick, on which is a large plain, from whence innumerable rocks and mountains are descried. The descent formerly craggy, steep and boggy, is now firm, smooth and gradual by 17 traverses, the sweeps and angles walled with stones, and the parapets on the lower side, 3 foot high, to secure carriages from the precipice, the trouble and dangers of which were thus expressed. We climb with Danger, and with Pain descend, when shall our toilsome tedious Journey end. But now the road is of fine gravel, and so sloping, that General Wade's coach and six turned every angle, and descended without difficulty. In this road is a bridge of two arches over the rapid and dangerous River Spey, which makes it exceeding convenient for the Country; and merits as many monumental pillars, to distinguish the happy reign to posterity, in which it was affected, as are discovered in the roads of the polite Romans.

In 1732 Wade contemplated building the bridge over the fast-flowing River Tay at Aberfeldy. At that time there was no bridge across the Tay at any point from its source to its mouth. Dunkeld was the obvious place for his Crieff–Dalnacardoch road to ford the river. He engaged William Adam to design the bridge, and in the meantime he sent word to the Duke of Atholl, requesting a meeting with his representative at the proposed crossing point. His Grace was a proud and haughty man and his response to Wade was that generals must come to dukes, not the other way round. The commander-in-chief for North Britain, who was used to being in the company of kings, was not to be intimidated by a local grandee, however big his wig.

So he built the bridge on his Crieff–Dalnacardoch road at Aberfeldy. Sometime later the Duke of Atholl was not too proud to ask Wade for a loan of £12,000. The loan was mentioned in Wade's will to be repaid to his sons, captains John and George Wade.

Throughout the winter of 1732 Wade was once again busily employed with his many interests, and in particular at this time the ever growing problem of the men and women who found themselves in the debtor's prison, and the plight of the sailors pressed into the navy against their will. He was on the committee of the Prison Disciplinary Board, and on his many visits to the Fleet and Marshalsea prisons he witnessed the terrible conditions suffered by those unfortunate enough to find themselves there.

Lord Oglethorpe, a lieutenant colonel in the Queen's Guards and Member of Parliament for Haslemere, was also on the committee of the Prison Board. Oglethorpe was a noted philanthropist, including helping children and defending seamen against impressments. His time visiting the prisons brought him into contact with the idea of creating a colony in the New World.

Oglethorpe gathered around him other celebrated military men from the committee, such as Wade and Admiral Edward Vernon. A charter was proposed for the new colony of Georgia, named in honour of King George II. The grant included all land between the Altamaha and Savannah rivers. The charter specifically prohibited any trustee from making money from the venture. Oglethorpe used his connections to move the Charter for the Colony of Georgia quickly to the King, who signed it on June 9th 1732. The funds to pay for the voyage were raised from the twenty-one members of the committee, and from Parliament. Oglethorpe sailed with the first colonists in January 1733.

Before returning to Scotland, Wade travelled down to Bath for a well-earned rest and to enjoy the company of his brother, who was on a visit from Windsor. Sadly, on February 8th it was reported that Dr William Wade, canon at Windsor Castle, passed away in Bath. Wade spared no expense when the time came to erect a memorial to him in St George's Chapel at Windsor. The inscription on the beautiful marble monument reads:

> Here lies interred the Body of Mr. William Wade who was remarkable for his Benevolence and truly Christian temper. He received his first education at Westminster School from whence he was elected to Trinity College Cambridge of which Society he

afterwards became a Fellow and in the year 1720 was constituted one of the Canons of this Royal Chapel. He had learning and abilities that might have raised him to the Highest Stations in the Church but such was his Modesty and Meekness of his mind that he chose rather to devote himself to the practice of all social virtues in private life. He died in Bath on the 1st day of February in the sixty second year of his age. His most affectionate brother Lieutenant General George Wade erected this monument to his memory.

In his will, William desired his brother to add to his kindness already shown to his children, William and Elizabeth, and appointed him their guardian.

During the summer of 1732, Wade made considerable changes to his road through the Great Glen. Of the required sixty miles, forty were completed, the greatest part being entirely new; the road followed the south side of Loch Ness – a shorter and more convenient way for communication between His Majesty's garrisons. Some 2,000 yards of the said road cut through solid rock. Wade's advance of £3,000 was for enlarging and completing the 'Great Road for Wheel Carriages' between Inverness and Fort William of sixty measured English miles.

Wade left Scotland early that year in time to be present at the proposed reading of the bill put before Parliament on the cost of maintaining a standing army. He spoke frequently on army matters; and when Pulteney complained that the British received far more pay than the French and Germans, according to the *Gentleman's Magazine*, 1732, he replied:

> Those who are acquainted with the Method of maintaining a German Army will not envy them the cheapness of it. What they come short of ours in Pay, they more than makeup for by plundering, and raising contributions upon the Countries where they are quartered. When I was in Italy I dined with one of the German Generals: When I came to his Palace I found the Hall and Avenues full of Country people, some with Wine, and some with Beer, Bread, Fowls, Pigs &c. I could not imagine what all this meant; but when I sat down to table, I found such a variety of dishes, such a variety of wines and so magnificent attendance, and so sumptuous an entertainment every manner of way, which at the time I was told was the General's ordinary way of living, that I was much surprised; and after dinner, over a glass of wine, I took the liberty to I ask the General, for

God's sake, Sir, how are you able to live after this rate; for it would break an English General to live in so splendid a manner; our Pay would not support it. Pay, (says he) why I have none upon this Account from the Government; all this comes from the Country where I am quartered, which they are obliged to furnish me with for nothing; I have 7 miles of Country around allotted to me to Support my Table. Then I found that those Country People about the Hall were come with their Peace Offerings to the General. At this rate, Sir, a German Officer does not stand in need of much pay from the Government; But I hope the Kingdom of England will never be served at such a rate.

The year 1733 was to see the construction of the bridge at Aberfeldy. Wade considered this bridge the crown of his road-building work. It was described in the *House of Commons Journal* on February 7th 1734:

A freestone bridge over the Tay, of five arches, nearly 400 feet in length, the middle arch 60 feet wide, the starlings of oak, and the piers and landbreasts founded on piles shod with iron. The grey chlorite schist, of which stone the bridge is built, was brought from the neighbouring quarries of Farrockhill, the property of the Laird of Bolfracks. Robertson of Strowan supplied the wood.

William Adam, the finest architect in Scotland, designed the bridge. Master masons and carpenters arrived from the northern counties of England, where they were accustomed to works of that nature, and 200 artificers and labourers from the army were employed for an entire year. The preparation of materials took place during the winter season and laying of foundations and construction in the summer. The first stone was laid on April 23rd 1733, and the work reached a foot above pavement level before the end of October. The weather that autumn was particularly bad, with torrential rain, strong winds and violent floods.

Wade inspected the bridge before leaving for London and, in his temporary quarters and feeling dejected, he sat down to write to Duncan Forbes, the best friend he had found in Scotland. Forbes had become liaison officer between the authorities in Scotland and ministers in London. On whatever Scottish business, from the election of a town council to the making of new roads in the Highlands, it was his advice that was sought, and no doubt he was instrumental in Wade's appointment in Scotland.

My dear Lord Advocate, I had expected on my return hither to have the work at the Bridge much more advanced than it was during a fortnight's absence and since my coming hither the weather has been so excessively bad and the floods so violent that little could be done; there is now a prospect of better, and I am pushing it on as fast as possible, the monthly charge past has drained me of all my money and credit; so that the work must be laid aside in a fortnight longer; in which time I am labouring to get it as high as the Pavement and leave the Parapet Wall for another year. I shall continue here till the end of next week and if in that time your affairs shall call you to Edinburgh, I hope you will pass this way. I have had so much plague, vexation, and disappointments that staggers my Philosophy and believe I must have recourse to Culloden's remedy a Bumper: pray give my hearty service to him, as does all our family to you both.

Wade was summoned to London. He left Scotland two days later, leaving the construction in the capable hands of William Caulfield. Caulfield was Wade's right-hand man in road-building; he supervised the building of the Tay Bridge, and became the inspector of roads until 1767. The opening of the bridge is described in Chapter 11.

Very much in the mould of Wade, Caulfield could be trusted to carry out the work in his absence. He was an Irishman by birth and the grandson of Viscount Charlemont. Caulfield, like Wade, often had recourse to 'Culloden Bumpers', for his house was so named after a device which was employed to hoist well-dined guests to their rooms. He was later to become deputy governor of the castle at Inverness. Caulfield is credited with the famous couplet:

> Had you seen these roads before they were made,
> You would lift up your hands and bless General Wade.

Wade was not in Scotland during 1734; for the previous ten years he had travelled repeatedly to Scotland and at the age of sixty-one he may have been in need of a long rest. There was another reason for his absence: as a committee member on the Prison Disciplinary Board he was anxious to hear from Lord Oglethorpe, who was due back from Georgia with news of the settlers.

Chapter 10

State Visit of Tomochichi

The *Aldborough* carrying General Oglethorpe arrived safely at St Helens on the Isle of Wight. On announcing his arrival in a letter addressed to Sir John Philips, General Oglethorpe told him:

> An aged chief named Tomochichi, the mico or king of the Yamacraw, a man of excellent understanding, is so desirous of having the young people taught the English language and religion that, notwithstanding his advanced age, he has come over with me to obtain means and assistant teachers. He has brought with him a young man whom he calls his nephew and next heir, who has learned the Lord's Prayer in the English. I shall leave the Indians at my estate till I go to the city, where I shall have the happiness to wait upon you, and to relate all things to you more fully: over which you will rejoice and wonder.

The *Daily Courant* reported on June 19th 1734:

> On Monday his Majestys ship the Aldborough arrived at Portsmouth from South Carolina, on board of whom is come James Oglethorpe, Esq., Member of Parliament for Haslemere in Surrey; a Gentleman whose singular services to his Country by his indefatigable pains in settling the new Colony of Georgia, will render him ever famous in English History.

After seventy days at sea, Oglethorpe was concerned about Tomochichi and he arranged for the Indian chiefs to stay at his country seat at Westbrook in the village of Godalming, to rest for a few days before their journey to London to meet the trustees of the Georgia Company. Oglethorpe left for London to make arrangements for apartments in Old Palace Yard to be made ready to receive his guests. There was also to be an audience with the King at St James's Palace.

The trustees gathered in Old Palace Yard to hear from Oglethorpe an account of the new colony. They were concerned with his lack of communication and what were perceived as excessive expenditures, and awaited his explanation. Oglethorpe gave them an account of all that had taken place from the time he left the shores of England. He reported:

> After repeated delays, the frigate Anne set sail on the 6th November 1732 from Gravesend sailing down the Thames River into the Straits of Dover, then southward into the English Channel, continuing westward along the southern coast of England and then arriving at the island of Madeira where she took on board five tuns of wine on the 13th January before embarking into the Atlantic Ocean. On March 10th after fifty six days at sea we entered the mouth of the Savannah River, a river in some places broader than the Rhine and abundant with oysters, sturgeon and other fish. The banks were clothed with fresh grass and the music of birds. The voyage had proved entirely successful and only two delicate children had died on the passage.
>
> On April 1st we came ashore at Savannah where we were greeted by Tomochichi the Mico of the Yamacraw and Mary Musgrove, a creek Indian who had been educated in Carolina to learn the ways of the white people. Mary acted as an interpreter for Tomochichi.

Oglethorpe went on to say that he was surprised to be welcomed in his own language, and he bowed and thanked Tomochichi:

> After further instructions, the chief invited us to talk and smoke the pipe of peace, and Oglethorpe described his plans to establish a colony on the bluff, not far from the town of Yamacraw.

Tomochichi could have posed a problem for Oglethorpe if he proved to be hostile. The two leaders agreed there was plenty of room for both the Indians and the English settlers. Tomochichi voiced his fears on allowing the colonists to settle so close: white people had made promises before to the Indians and broken them. Would Oglethorpe keep his word? Tomochichi and Oglethorpe met repeatedly, and soon trust and friendship were established.

During their many conversations, Oglethorpe learnt that Tomochichi was born around the year 1650, and as a boy he had explored forests and meadows and learned how to make arrows.

When he came of age he joined other young Creeks who aspired to become warriors at the Green Corn Festival, as part of the coming-of-age ritual. They drank the sacred black drink to cleanse their bodies and minds, and the people of Coweta came to accept Tomochichi as a grown man. As time passed he became respected for his good judgement and wisdom and was often consulted in matters of politics and law. In time he settled down with Senauki, a young woman of Coweta.

Tomochichi went on to tell Oglethorpe that trade was an important part of life for the Indians in Coweta. They traded with the Cherokee tribe and others for salt, pearls, furs and saddles. Their lives were revolutionised, however, when a white trader arrived. The Creeks were hospitable and welcomed the stranger. They were introduced to things they had never dreamed of: sharp knives, hatchets, hoes, metal pots and pans, mirrors and guns.

Soon the guns and ammunition they received made war easier, and tribal wars broke out over the hunting grounds. Tomochichi told Oglethorpe that he had been among the Creek warriors sent to fight the Spanish-allied Apalachee Indians. After four months of fighting, the Creeks had defeated the Apalachees. Tomochichi had also attended a meeting in Coweta whereby the Creeks signed an alliance with the English settlers in Carolina. The terms of the alliance were quickly broken and some of the English traders were found selling Creeks into slavery. The Creeks had protested to the government of Carolina, who promised to put a stop to it. Their promises did not end the slave trade, however, and the Indians eventually declared war on the English. The war lasted until 1717, when an agreement was negotiated. In the treaty, the Savannah River was named as the Creek-Carolina border. Tomochichi told Oglethorpe that he had decided that life in Coweta no longer suited him, and in 1728 he had left with his wife to establish their own town, Yamacraw, located on the Savannah.

In return it is not unlikely that Oglethorpe told Tomochichi something about his own life: his origins in Godalming, Surrey, where he was born in 1696, the son of wealthy parents; his entry into the army and participation in all the wars surrounding the Spanish succession; and his later entry into Parliament as the Member for Haslemere. He may also have told him of his visits to the debtors' prison and his determination to find a better way of life for the unfortunate prisoners.

Oglethorpe reported to the committee that he had invited Tomochichi, Mico of the Yamacraws, to sail with him on his return to England and how pleased he was when the old Mico gladly accepted the invitation on behalf of himself; his wife, Senauki; his nephew, Toonahowi; Hillispilli, the war captain of the Lower Creeks; and four other chiefs with their attendants and an interpreter. Toonahowi was especially excited, as he had often listened to stories of General Oglethorpe's home in England, and dreamed of the great palaces and the big houses. Oglethorpe also invited Mary Musgrove to accompany them as an interpreter, but Mary was needed at home to care for her parents, who were unwell at the time. Her husband, John, agreed to take her place. Mary was a native of Coweta; her mother belonged to the Wind clan and was the sister of the chief Mico of the Lower Creeks (known as Old Brim to the English). As a young girl she was sent to Charles Town in South Carolina and stayed with an English family. She went to school, learned to speak English and was given the name Mary. In time she met John Musgrove and they moved to Yamacraw.

Crossing the Atlantic in those early days was not undertaken lightly. Tomochichi was indeed a very brave man to attempt the journey at the age of eighty-four. Sailing across the Atlantic in those days was very different from how it is today. Vessels had no stabilisers and the accommodation and the food were very poor. To sail across to Portsmouth with no loss of life was something of a miracle. The trustees expressed their satisfaction with the eminent service Oglethorpe had carried out in the colony, which he left in a flourishing condition. They were looking forward to meeting Tomochichi and the other Indian chiefs. The trustees also told Oglethorpe that a fine ship of 250 tons had been launched at Rotherhithe in June for the service of the trustees for the colony of Georgia, and it had been named *The Oglethorpe* in his honour.

After a period of rest Oglethorpe escorted his visitors to London to meet the trustees. They were completely unprepared for the size and wealth of the city. They had never seen so many people, horses and carriages and such great tall houses. Tomochichi expressed his surprise that short-lived men should erect such long-lived habitations. The wealth and power of London and its environs oppressed Tomochichi when he thought of the helplessness and poverty of his own people.

Wherever they went, great crowds turned out wanting to shake their hands. Tomochichi at eighty-four was still a fine figure, as were all the chiefs. The Indians were naked to the waist with only a cloth wrapped around them like a skirt, and their bodies were painted with tribal markings. Tomochichi was to say later that the English treated them with kindness and every respect was shown to them. After meeting the trustees, the Indians were transferred to comfortable quarters in the apartments in Old Palace Yard.

The *Daily Courant* reported on Thursday August 1st:

> Tomochichi, the King and Senauki his wife with Toonahowi, their son, Hillispilli the war captain and the other Cherokee Indians brought over by Mr. Oglethorpe from Georgia were introduced to his Majesty at Kensington, who received them seated on his throne; when Tomochichi, micho, or king, made the following speech, at the same time presenting several eagle's feathers which are trophies of their country.

> This day I see the majesty of your face, the greatness of your house, and the number of your people. I am come for the good of the whole nation called the Creeks, to renew the peace which was long ago had with the English. I am come over in my old days, although I cannot live to see any advantage to myself. I am come for the good of the children of all the nations in the Upper and Lower Creeks, that they may be instructed in the knowledge of the English. These are the feathers of the eagle which is the swiftest of birds, and who flieth all round our nations. These feathers are a sign of peace in our Land, and have been carried from town to town there; and we have brought them over to leave with you, O great king! Is a sign of everlasting peace? O great king whatsoever words you shall say to me I will tell them faithfully to all the kings of the Creek nations.

To which His Majesty graciously answered:

> I am glad of this opportunity of assuring you of my regard for the people from whom you come, and am extremely well pleased with the assurances you have brought me from them, and accept very gratefully this present as an indication of their good disposition to me and my people. I shall always be ready to cultivate a good correspondence between them and my own subjects, and shall be glad of any occasion to show you a mark of my particular friendship and esteem.

Tomochichi afterwards made the following speech to Her Majesty:

> I am glad to see this day, and to have the opportunity of seeing the Mother of this great people. As our people are joined with your Majesty's, we do humbly hope to find you the common mother and protectress of us and all our children.

The war captain and the other attendants with Tomochichi persisted in wishing to appear at court in their native clothing. Oglethorpe persuaded them to adopt European dress, but their faces were variously painted after the manner of their own country – some half black, others triangular, and others with bearded arrows instead of whiskers.

Tomochichi and Senauki were dressed in scarlet robes trimmed with gold; Senauki wore a dress in the English style. Before leaving Kensington Palace, Tomochichi presented His Majesty with some fine furs and Toonahowi recited the Lord's Prayer and read to the Queen from the English Bible. She was very impressed with Toonahowi, his English and his courage for a boy of fifteen.

It was at this time that the young Indian boy met William (later the Duke of Cumberland), the King's son, who was about the same age. It was said at the time that a firm friendship developed between the two. On returning home Toonahowi asked his uncle if he could name the largest island of their land after his friend, and Cumberland Island still bears the name of the Duke today.

One of the Indian chiefs had fallen ill with smallpox before the visit, and was unable to attend the banquet. Every medical aid and kind attention was invoked on his behalf, but neither the skill of Sir Hans Sloane, the physician, nor the efforts of the nurses could arrest the progress of the terrible disease, and he died three days later. His death weighed heavily upon the spirits of the other Indians, who were reluctant to inter him in a strange land. His burial was a matter of absolute necessity; and here, so far as is known, was the first burial of an American chief on British soil. A grave was prepared in St John's Cemetery, Westminster. The custom of the natives was observed as nearly as circumstances would permit. The corpse, sewn up in two blankets, with two deal boards lashed together with a cord, was carried to the grave on a bier. When the body was lowered into the earth, the clothes of the deceased, a quantity of glass beads and some pieces of silver were thrown into the grave after the manner of the Indians, whose custom it was to bury the effects of the deceased.

Soon after the funeral, Tomochichi became very ill and it was suspected that he too had contracted smallpox. He recovered, however, and travelled to Oglethorpe's country house to recuperate.

From a report in the *Daily Courant* on July 29th:

> Tomo-chi-chi the Indian King, that lately arrived from South Carolina with the Hon. James Oglethorpe Esq., is much indisposed with the small pox, and resting at his apartments in Palace Yard, Westminster, being attended by several Physicians; but being of a favourable kind, there is great hopes of his doing well.

Tomochichi made a miraculous recovery, much to the relief of all. So depressed were the Indians by the loss of one of their chiefs, that in order to divert their attention and afford them an opportunity for quietly regaining their composure, and also for Tomochichi to have time to recuperate, Oglethorpe very kindly took them out to his country seat.

There they remained for nearly two weeks, when, having mourned the dead according to the established usages of their nation, they recovered in great degree from the affliction which had so distressed them. It was a particularly sad time for Senauki, as he was her brother.

The news-sheets of the day reported that the Indians had returned from Godalming and were now in residence at the Georgia Office in Old Palace Yard. Over the next few months a programme of visits was arranged. The King put his coaches at their disposal so that they might ride in comfort. Later that August, the Indian king and queen with their retinue set out for Greenwich and viewed that magnificent hospital and His Majesty's Dockyards at Deptford, which gave them much satisfaction. Later, in the King's coach, they visited Windsor Castle. During their four-month stay in England the Indians saw many wonderful things; they heard the loud church bells ringing over the city from the large 'temples' the English had built for worship.

They were entertained with lavish dinner parties by the trustees. Sir John Percival, one of the trustees and a close friend of Oglethorpe, invited the delegation to his estate. Sir John was impressed by the Indians and spoke often of their intelligence and good manners. Sir John took a particular liking to Toonahowi, the well-mannered Indian boy who could speak the King's English and was truly as amazing as his uncle. Soon Sir John arranged for Tomochichi and Toonahowi to have their portraits painted by William Verelst. He also had an English jacket, called a waistcoat, made for Toonahowi. It was of blue velvet embroidered with silver. He had it made especially for Toonahowi to wear when he met the King and Queen. The portrait of Tomochichi and his nephew hung on the walls at the Georgia Office for many years.

Another visit was to Mr Tombs' china shop in Leadenhall Street, where no doubt they were presented with a gift to take home. In the afternoon the Indians went to the theatre in Goodman's Fields. During their stay they enjoyed a variety of plays, from Shakespearean dramas to comic farces. They expressed much delight with a visit one evening to watch the children having supper at Christ's Hospital. The memories of being visited by Indians would stay in the children's memories for ever. Upon another occasion they visited Eton, where the Indians were accorded every mark of respect by the Reverend Dr George Berriman and the rest of the fellows. At the end of their visit to the schoolroom, Tomochichi begged that the boys might have a holiday when the doctor thought proper, which caused a general huzza.

Oglethorpe made arrangement for his visitors to walk in the Royal Apartments at Hampton Court and the Tower of London. Another time, Tomochichi and his companions were conveyed in the barge of the Archbishop of Canterbury to Putney, where they were most hospitably entertained by Lady Dutry. After dinner, in taking leave of her, the aged Mico expressed his regrets that he was unable in English to convey the thoughts of his heart and tell her how sensibly he was moved by the generous and noble reception she had given him. He also expressed his great gratification in being permitted to see and thank her in person for the assistance she had rendered in peopling the colony of Georgia.

The following day they waited upon the Archbishop of Canterbury at Lambeth. His Venerable Grace received them with the utmost kindness and tenderness, but he expressed fatherly concern regarding their ignorance with respect to Christianity, his strong desire for their instruction, and his sincere gratification at the probability that a door was now opened for the education and evangelisation of their race. Although very weak, His Grace, although pressed to do so, declined to sit during the interview. Tomochichi, perceiving this, with becoming propriety and consideration omitted the reply which he had proposed making and, after craving the blessing of the aged prelate, added that he would not trespass further upon his weakness, but would communicate to his son-in-law, Dr Lynch, what he desired to say.

Later that day at the splendid meal laid on in his honour Tomochichi found time to express the great satisfaction he had experienced in his interview with the Archbishop, and stated that he was deeply moved by the tender consideration which had been accorded to him. He urged the Doctor to consider the necessity for sending teachers to Georgia, so that his people might be educated and their minds enlightened in the doctrines of Christianity. Everyone who came into contact with Tomochichi was impressed with the accuracy of his observations, the pertinences of his inquiries, the maturity of his judgement, the wisdom and liberality of his views and his interest in all things.

Soon it was time to say goodbye to the new friends they had made and return home to tell all the good people of Savannah about the new and wonderful things they had seen and experienced. The *Daily Courant* covered their departure and reported it on Wednesday October 30th:

> The Indian King and Queen along with the Prince, etc., set out from the Georgia Office in the King's coaches for Gravesend, to embark on their return home. During their stay in England, which has been about four months, his Majesty has allowed them £20 a week for their subsistence, and they have been entertained in the most agreeable manner possible. Whatever is curious and worthy of observation in and about the cities of London and Westminster, has been carefully shown them; and nothing wanting among all degrees of men to contribute to their diversion and amusement, and to give them a just idea of English politeness and our respect for them.
>
> In return they expressed themselves heartily attached to the British nation. They had about the value of £400 in presents. Prince William presented the young mico Toonahowi, with a gold watch, with an admonition to call upon Jesus Christ every morning when he looked at it: which he promised. They appeared particularly delighted with seeing his Highness perform his exercise of riding the managed horse, and the Horse Guards pass in review, also the agreeable appearance of the barges, etc., on the Thames on Lord Mayor's Day.

Sailing with the Indians on their homeward journey was Sir Francis

Bathurst, his son and three daughters, along with several servants and fifty-six Saltzburgers newly arrived from Rotterdam.

On his return home, Tomochichi ordered the construction of a school near Savannah where Creek children would be taught to read and write English. Mary Musgrove, who had taught Toonahowi to read and write, became a teacher there.

The death rate in the colony during the first few years was alarmingly high. Pure water was hard to find and the nearby swamps were a breeding ground for disease-bearing insects. The high hopes of these early colonists for a better world left them dispirited and in despair. The only help the colonists received was from the nearby Yamacraw village and the established colony of South Carolina. Some of the settlers began to flee the colony, and others were unwilling to work the fields. An advertisement was placed in the *Virginia Gazette* on Friday, September 10th 1736:

> All sorts of labouring Persons, who are inclined to go to the new settlement of Georgia, on this Continent, may have Twenty Five Shilling's sterling per month, provided they will engage for 6 months after their arrival in the Colony. Any persons who are willing to become inhabitants and freeholders there, are entitled to 50 acres of land, and a town lot, and will be allowed the following encouragement, viz. One years provision; tools, and household stuff of all sorts; necessary arms of all sorts, ironwork, and nails sufficient for building a house of 24ft by 16ft; a cow and calf, a breeding mare, and breeding sow: With several other advantages.
>
> Any persons, who will go to the said Colony, are desired to apply to Mr. Miles Sweney, who is empowered to treat with them; and will put them in a method of getting passages thither, provided they can clear themselves, according to the Laws of this Country. He may be heard of at Mr. Portlock's in Norfolk, or by enquiring at the Printing Office in Williamsburg.

The advert also went on to state that great encouragement would be given to those merchants willing to trade in Georgia. Livestock of any sort was said to sell well, and all would be paid for in sterling and bills of exchange. Pilots were always ready to attend, on firing a gun at Dusucky Sound; Tib's Point, at the mouth of the Savannah River; Jekyll Sound or Pollianna Sound, at the mouth of the Altamaha River; or St Simon's Island.

Eventually life did settle down as more and more settlers continued to brave the Atlantic and arrive with all the skills needed to build a new life.

On October 5th 1739 Tomochichi died at his lodge. He was buried in Savannah with the highest honours, and Oglethorpe was among his distinguished pall-bearers. Nearly 200 years later the stone memorial pyramid which Oglethorpe had ordered was finally placed on the grave.

> In memory of Tomochichi
> The Mico of the Yamacraws
> The companion of Oglethorpe
> And the friend and ally
> Of the Colony of Georgia

During his last few days, Tomochichi exhorted his people never to forget the favours he had received from the King, but to persevere in their friendship with the English. He expressed great tenderness for General Oglethorpe, one of his dearest friends.

Oglethorpe continued to oversee the new colony and, as brigadier general, with a regiment of 600 under him, he was able to maintain an uneasy peace with the Spanish.

Oglethorpe returned from Georgia for the last time in 1743. On his return home, a dispute arose with the trustees, who accused him of using £1,412 of the trust fund for military purposes for which he had already been compensated. Oglethorpe countered that the trustees owed him far more than that amount.

There were other issues that disturbed him, especially the administration of the new colony. In 1743 there were more pressing needs at home, however, with the outbreak of war in Flanders; then in 1745 Charles Edward Stuart landed on the west coast of Scotland in an attempt to raise an army and reclaim the throne of England. Oglethorpe, as a general in the British Army, joined his old friend Wade, newly appointed field marshal and commander-in-chief of His Majesty's forces in North Britain, to halt the advance of the Pretender's army into England.

Chapter 11

Old Scotia

Wade returned to Scotland in 1735; on August 8th he arrived in the little village of Aberfeldy, and along with William Adam the architect he inspected the new bridge over the Tay. The bridge was truly magnificent, consisting of five arches, the middle arch being sixty feet in diameter. The cost of its construction amounted to £4,095. The inspection over, it was time to celebrate with the Highland Companies, who were in camp, and to prepare for the many visitors who were expected next day to celebrate the opening of the bridge.

The following day Wade and his officers dined with the Earl of Breadalbane at Taymouth, and in the afternoon they rode back to the village for the review.

Those present included the Earl of Breadalbane, Lord and Lady Glenorchy, Lord and Lady Hope Chat with Lord Monzie and his lady. Lord Lovat commanded the Highland Companies, who performed their military exercises to the entire satisfaction of the spectators and their commander-in-chief. With the review over, a man rode through the crowds on a white horse. He made for the bridge, dismounted and placed a sheet of paper on the parapet. On the paper was inscribed a poem entitled 'Tay-Bridge to the Passenger'. A reporter made a copy of the verse, and it appeared in the news-sheets of the day:

> Long has Old Scotia Desolation fear'd,
> Pensive, 'till an auspicious Star appear'd:
> But soon as the Celestial Power came down,
> To smile on Labour, and on Sloth to frown;
> Scotia reviving, rais'd her drooping Crown:
> One clos'd her Feuds, and t'other op'd her Womb;
> Rocks inaccessible a Passage knew,

> And Men, too fond of Arms, consent to plow.
> Not less surprising was the daring scheme,
> That fix'd my station in this rapid Stream.
> The North and South rejoice to see me Stand,
> Uniting in my Function, Hand in Hand,
> Commerce and Concord, Life of ev'ry Land!
> But ... who could force rough Nature thus to ply,
> Becalm the Torrents, and teach Rocks to fly?
> What Art, what Temper, and what manly Toil,
> Could smooth the rugged Sons of Abria's Soil?
> Methinks the anxious reader's at a stand,
> Not knowing, George, for George (to bless the Land
> Averse t'obedience) spoke the stern Command.
> And still he seems perplex'd till he is told,
> That Wade was skilful, and that Wade was bold.
> Thus shall his fame, with George's glory rise?
> Till Sun and Moon shall tumble from the Skies.

The poet was Robertson of Strowan, the Poet Chief, and we can see Roberston and Wade as representatives of the two sides in that period of Scottish history, pledged to each other: the romantic Jacobite laird and the down-to-earth Whig soldier and engineer. That the two were great friends is undoubted; they enjoyed each other's company, and were ever ready to avail themselves of 'Culloden's remedy, a Bumper'.

Two inscriptions were placed on the bridge, one in Latin and one in English. The Latin inscription was composed by Dr Friend, headmaster of Westminster School. The inscriptions can still be seen on the bridge at Aberfeldy today.

> At the Command
> Of his Majesty King George
> The 2nd This Bridge was Erected
> In the Year 1733.
> This with the Roads and other
> Military works for securing a
> Safe and Easy Communication
> Between the Highlands and the
> Trading Towns in the low Country
> Was by his Majesty Committed
> To the care of Lieut General

> George Wade Commander
> In Chief of the Forces in Scotland
> Who laid the first Stone
> Of this Bridge on the 23rd of
> April and Finished the Work
> In the Same Year.

The following year materials were being prepared to start work on the next project, the High Bridge over the rapid and dangerous River Spey. A message from Fort William on June 16th 1736 reads as follows:

> Last Friday being the Anniversary of his Majesty's accession to the Throne, our Lieutenant Governor, attended by the Officers of the Garrison, and several other gentlemen were present at the laying of the first stone. The Health's of their Majesties, the Prince and Princess of Wales, the Duke and the Royal family, with many other loyal toasts were drunk, at the instant our great Guns were firing on the happy occasion of the day.
>
> This bridge is to be of three arches, the middle arch fifty foot in diameter, the other two arches of forty foot each; the hills through which the river runs being very high, the causeway, for the better access to the road on each side, will be fourscore feet from the common surface of the water, which is near thirty foot deep The finishing of this work will be complete, safe and easy communication from this Garrison to those of Fort Augustus and Fort George, and likewise all the Military roads, which by his Majesty's command have been carried on through the Highlands under the care of General Wade The Company returned and supped with the Governor, where the above health's were repeated, and the night ended with Bonfires, Illuminations and all other demonstrations of joy.

Wade was away from Edinburgh when the Porteous Riots began in 1736, but he was called upon by Edinburgh residents in support of a condemned man. The riots were a direct result of the execution of one of three men convicted of robbing excise officers at Pittenweem, Fife. Two had escaped the gallows, but the third, Andrew Wilson, was publicly hanged in the Grassmarket in Edinburgh. To the fury of the mob, his body was cut down, and the ensuing riot was such that the hangman had to be placed in protective custody.

The Lord Provost of Edinburgh instructed John Porteous, Captain of the City Guard, to call out the entire guard and to furnish them with powder and shot. The mob began to stone them. The events that followed caused more confusion. Captain Porteous instructed his men to fire above the heads of the crowd, and in doing so they wounded people in the windows of the high tenement buildings opposite. This incited the mob to greater violence and panic set in, resulting in Captain Porteous apparently ordering the guard to shoot into the mob, which led to the deaths of six people. Conflicting reports of the shootings were current after the event.

Porteous was arrested the same afternoon and charged with murder. He was tried at the High Court of Justiciary on July 5th 1736 and condemned to death. Many of the more wealthy citizens signed a petition recommending him to mercy. One lady, Catherine Allardice, wrote the following letter to General Wade imploring him to step in and save poor Captain Porteous. Her spelling was very poor and has been transcribed for easier reading.

> I dare not Dear General Wade but by this time you have heard the fatal sentence of the poor unhappy Captain Porteous how in six weeks time must die if he receives not speedy help from above, by the assistance of men of generosity and mercy such as you really are. It is the opinion of all those of the better sort [that] he has been very badly dealt by, being condemned but by a very slender proof, and tho he was much provoked by the mob and had the Provost and Magistrates order to fire which they now shamefully deny not had he the liberty to prove it tho even in his own defence, but the generous Major Powel will assure you of the truth.
>
> And yet though the Captain had those cruel orders it is proven by Mr. Drummond, Doctor Horton and several other gentlemen [of] undoubted credibility he really did not make use of them, that eyes were fixed on him all the while and have declared upon oath he did not fire, true it is he presented his firelock in hopes to frighten the mob when an unlucky fellow at the same time and just by the Captain fired which led the two witnesses into the fatal mistake that has condemned him. The unfortunate panel both before and after the dismal sentence protested before God and the Judges he was entirely innocent putting all these circumstances together the miserable state he now is in must draw your generous pity on his side.
>
> Therefore dear General Wade continue your usual mercy and plead for him and as our sex are naturally compassionate and being now in the power of the Queen, so generous a pleader as you may easily persuade, considering it is a thing of great

consequence to the whole army which yourself better know than I can inform. The Duke of Buccleugh, Marquess of Lothian, Lord Morton, General Miles all the commissioners and chief Barons are to join their interest with yours in this affair, by your own generous soul I beg again Dear Sir you will do what is in your power to save him. Those that think right go not through this poor short life just for themselves which your good actions how oft consider, and as many just now put a sincere trust in your generous mercy I am sure they will not be disappointed through any neglect of yours let this letter be taken note of amongst the number you will receive from your friends in Scotland on behalf of the unfortunate Captain which will entirely oblige. To dear General Wade from your most affectionate and most obedient humble servant Catherine Allardice.

Wade supported the petition for the reprieve, and Queen Caroline, in the absence of George II, who was on the Continent, granted the petition. This caused great indignation amongst the lower classes of Edinburgh; and on September 7th an armed mob broke into the Tolbooth, where the terrified Porteous was too paralysed with fear to move.

Two men carried him, their hands linked to form a chair. His arms hung loosely around their necks, his head lolled forward on his chest and his feet dangled like the feet of a puppet on strings. The mob at the sight of him screamed, "To the Grassmarket with him! Hang him at the scene of his crimes!" Those looking on were horrified and some fell silent. On arrival at the Grassmarket they hung him from a barber's pole; and so ended the life of poor Captain Porteous.

Charles Erskine, the Solicitor General, appears to have investigated the matter and, from the tenor of his report, it is evident that there was little likelihood of the active participants in the deed being discovered. In the reading of the Porteous Bill in Parliament in 1737, Wade observed that there was one circumstance that proved three things: first, that the original design of the conspirators was to murder Porteous on the Tuesday; secondly, that it was talked of openly; and thirdly, that the citizens and inhabitants of Edinburgh were the murderers. The circumstance was the evidence of a servant, one Colin Alison, who swore that a man came into his master's shop, on the Thursday or Friday before the murder was committed, and informed him that the Tuesday following was the day appointed for revenging innocent blood. Wade observed that the riot deserved the name rather of a well-conducted conspiracy than the proceedings of a mob. He then vindicated Mr Moyle, the commanding officer at Edinburgh, upon the principles of military discipline.

No one was punished except the Mayor, who by an act of 1737 was disqualified from holding office. It would seem that the Mayor had been overcautious in summoning troops to protect the Tolbooth; the indignant authorities in London made him a scapegoat. Rewards were offered for the capture of those responsible for the murder of Captain Porteous, but no one was ever convicted. A fine of £2,000 was levied on the city for his widow, and in time a plaque was erected in the Grassmarket in his memory.

Before returning to London, Wade entertained several military gentlemen at his lodgings in the Canongate; later that day they repaired to the castle for a firework display, after which Major Robertson entertained the garrison to a bonfire. The following Saturday a fire broke out in the General's lodgings by the carelessness of some of the servants, while he was out of the house visiting. His fine wardrobe, carriage, etc. were destroyed at high cost.

Wade left for London on December 17th 1736.

He returned to Scotland in 1738, when he reviewed five regiments of dragoons, with the garrison and the Highland Companies. Three regiments of foot were reviewed on August 11th, another at Stirling on the 18th, at Fort Augustus at the latter end of August, and two more regiments of dragoons on September 26th at Musselburgh. These in all amounted to some 3,000 foot and 600 horse.

There is no record of Wade's being in Scotland during 1739, and it would appear that his work on building the military roads was coming to an end. In 1740 he relinquished his command in Scotland, which passed to Lieutenant General Jasper Clayton.

One of Wade's last acts in Scotland was to review the Black Watch companies. These reviews took place at the Tay Bridge, Ruthven and Fort Augustus in 1740. The soldiers under his command looked upon him as the father of the regiment, and not a martinet to be feared.

He regularly arranged entertainments for his workers and on occasions, such as His Majesty's birthday, he would order an ox feast and liquor. Everything possible was done to make life more bearable for his 'highwaymen'; Wade even provided a doctor. When and wherever it was in his power to save a life, he went out of his way to do so. During his years in Scotland he made a host of friends whom he would keep for the rest of his life.

The General finally left for the south. He was to retain his position as governor of Fort William, Fort Augustus, Fort George, Holy Island and Berwick, and also kept up his interests in the Strontian mines and rental from his many properties in Scotland.

It was said that from the time of Marshal Wade and the Forty-Five, the roads in Scotland were in a better condition than the English roads; and until 1827, when Sir John Loudon McAdam, who invented the system named after him, was appointed surveyor general of all the main metropolitan turnpike roads throughout the country, no first-class roads existed.

In 1757 Armstrong published his county atlas of Scotland, and in the same year Cary issued one for England.

According to *Early Travellers in Scotland*, edited by Dr Hume Brown, 1891:

> In most cases the cross-roads in the former [i.e. Scotland] appear to be more complete than those in England, except in Middlesex and Somerset. In the latter part of the 18th century, the highways in Scotland were tolerably good, which is the greatest comfort a traveller meets with amongst them; they have not inns, but change houses (as they call them) poor cottages, where you must be content to take what you find, perhaps eggs with chicks in them, and some lang cale; at the better sort of them a dish of chaf'd chicken, which they esteem a dainty dish . . .

Roads built during Wade's term in Scotland are as follows:

Fort William–Fort Augustus	1725	30 miles
Fort Augustus–Inverness	1726	31 miles
Inverness–Dunkeld	1727–9	102 miles
Crieff–Dalnacardoch	1730–1	43 miles
Dalwhinnie–Fort Augustus	1732	28 miles
Catcleugh–Ruthven		8 miles

In addition, forty stone bridges were built throughout the Highlands.

When Captain Edward Burt travelled through the Highlands from 1720 until 1737, he wrote to his friend describing the country, its people and their manner of living. In one of those letters he describes the roads then being built in the Highlands. The following passages are extracts from Burt's *Letters from a Gentleman in the North of Scotland*, published in 1754 by R. Hopwood, London.

These new roads were begun in the year 1726, and have continued for eleven years in the prosecution; yet, long as it may be thought, if you were to pass over the whole work (for the borders of it would show you what it was), I make no doubt that number of years would diminish your imagination to a much shorter tract of time, by comparison with the difficulties that attended the execution. But, before I proceed to any particular description of them, I shall inform you how they lie, to the end that you may trace them out upon a map of Scotland; and at first I shall take them as they are made. To enter the mountains, viz One of them begins from Crieff, which is about fourteen miles from Stirling: here the Romans left off their works, of which some part are visible to this day, particularly the camp at Ardoch, where the vestiges of the fortifications are on a moor so barren, that its whole farm has been safe from culture, or other alterations besides weather and time.

The other road enters the hills at Dimheld, in Atholl, which is about ten miles from Perth. The first of them, according to my account, though the last in execution, proceeds through Glenalmond which, for its narrowness, and the height of the mountains, (I remember to have mentioned formerly), and thence it goes to Aberfeldy; there it crosses the River Tay by a bridge of freestone, consisting of five spacious arches (by the way, this military bridge is the only passage over that wild and dangerous river) From thence the road goes on to Dalnachardoch. The other road from Dunkeld proceeds by Blairatholl to the said Dalnachardoch. Here the two roads join in one, and, as in a single road, it leads on to Dalwhinny, where it branches out again into two; of which one proceeds towards the north-west, through Garva Moor, and over the Corriarick Mountain to Fort Augustus, at Killichumen, and the other branch goes due north to the barrack of Ruthven, in Badenoch, and thence, by Delmagary to Inverness. From thence it precedes something to the southward of the west, across the island, to the aforesaid Fort Augustus, and so on to Fort William in Lochaber. The length of all these roads put together is about two hundred and fifty miles.

I have so lately mentioned Glenalmond, in the road from Crieff, northward, that I cannot forbear a digression, though at my first setting out, in relation to a piece of antiquity which happened to be discovered in that vale not many hours before I passed through it in one of my journeys southward. A small part of the way through this glen having marked out by two rows of camp colours, placed at a good distance one from another, whereby to describe the line of the intended breadth and regularity of the road by the eye, there happened to lie directly in the way an exceedingly large stone, and, as it had been made a rule from the beginning, to carry on the roads in straight lines, as far as the way would permit, not only to give them a better air, but to shorten the passenger's journey, it was resolved the stone should be removed, if possible, though otherwise the work might have been carried along on either side of it.

The soldiers, by vast labour, with their levers and jacks, or hand-screws, tumbled it over and over till they got it quite out of the way, although it was of such an enormous size that it might be a matter of great wonder how it could ever be removed by human strength and art, especially to such who have never seen an operation of that kind: and, upon their digging a little way into that part of the ground where the centre of the base had stood, there was found a small cavity, about two feet square, which was guarded from the outward earth at the bottom, top, and sides, by square flat stones. The hollow contained some ashes, scraps of bones, and half-burnt ends of stalks of heath; which last we concluded to be small remnants of a funeral pile. Upon the whole, I think there is no room to doubt but it was the urn of some considerable Roman Officer, and the best of the kind that could be provided in their military circumstances; and that it was seems plainly to appear from its vicinity to the Roman Camp.

The engines that must have been employed to move the vast piece of rock and the unlikeliness it should, or could, have ever been done by natives of the country. But certainly the design was to preserve those remains from the injuries of rains and melting snows, and to prevent their being profaned by the sacrilegious hands of those they call Barbarians, for that reproachful name, you know, they gave to the people of almost all nations but their own. Give me leave to finish this digression, which is grown already longer than I foresaw or intended.

As I returned the same way from the Lowlands, I found an officer, which his party of working soldiers, not far from the stone, and asked him what was become of the urn? To this he answered, that he had intended to preserve it in the condition I left it, till the Commander-in-Chief had seen it, as a curiosity, but that it was not in his power so to do; for soon after the discovery was known to the Highlanders, they assembled from distant parts, and having formed themselves into a body, they carefully gathered up the relics; and marched with them, in solemn processions, to a new place of burial, and there discharged their firearms over the grave, as supposing the deceased had been a military officer.

You will believe the recital of all this ceremony led me to ask the reason of such homage done to the ashes of a person supposed to have been dead almost two thousand years. I did so; and the officer, who was himself a native of the hills, told me that they (the Highlanders) firmly believe that if a dead body should be known to lie above ground, or be disinterred by malice or the accidents to torrents of water, etc., and care was not immediately taken to perform to it the proper rites, then there would arise such storms and tempests as would destroy their corn, blow away their huts, and all other misfortunes would follow till that duty was performed. You may recollect what I told you so long ago, of the great regard the Highlanders have for the remains of their dead; but this notion is entirely Roman.

In the summer seasons, five hundred soldiers from the barracks, and other quarters about the Highlands, were employed in those works in different stations, by detachments from the regiments and Highland companies. The private men are allowed six pence a day, over and above their pay as soldiers: a corporal had eight pence, and a sergeant a shilling; but this extra pay was only for working days, which were often interrupted by violent storms of wind and rain, from the heights and hollows of the mountains.

These parties of men were under the command and direction of proper officers, who were all subalterns and received two shillings and six pence per diem, to defray their extraordinary expense in building huts: making necessary provision for their tables from distant parts; unavoidable though unwelcome visits, and other incidents arising from their wild situation. I should have told you before, that the non-commissioned officers were constant and immediate overseers of the works.

The standard breadth of these roads, as laid down at first projection, is sixteen feet; but in some parts, where there were no expensive difficulties, they are wider. They are carried on in straight lines till some great necessity has turned them out of the way; the rest, run along upon the declivities of hills, you know, must have their circuits, risings, and descents accordingly.

To stop and take a general view of the hills before you from an eminence, in some part where the eye penetrates far within the void spaces, the roads would appear to you in a kind of whimsical disorder; and as those parts of them that appear to you are of a very different colour from the heath that chiefly clothes the country, they may, by that contrast, be traced out to a considerable distance. The old roads, for roads I shall not call them, consisted chiefly of stone moors, bogs, rugged, rapid fords, declivity of hills, entangling woods, and giddy precipices. You will say this is a dreadful catalogue to be read to him that is about to take a Highland Journey. I have not mentioned the valleys, for they are few in number, far divided asunder, and generally the roads through them were easily made. My purpose now is to give you some account of the extraordinary work has been executed; and this I shall do in the order I have ranged as above.

And first, the stony moors. These are mostly tracts of ground of several miles in length, and often very high, with frequent lesser risings and descents, and having for surface a mixture of stones and heath. The stones are fixed to the earth, being very large and unequal and generally are as deep in the ground as they appear above it; and where there are any spaces between the stones, there is a loose spongy sward, perhaps not above five or six inches deep, and incapable to produce anything but heath, and all beneath is hard gravel or rock.

Here the workmen first made room to fix their instruments, and then, by strength, and the help of those two mechanic powers, the screw and the lever, they raised out of their ancient beds those massive bodies, and then filling up the cavities with gravel, set them up, mostly endways, along the sides of the road, as directions in time of deep snows, being some of them, as they now stand, eight or nine feet high. They serve, likewise, as memorials of the skill and labour requisite to the performance of so difficult a work.

In some particular spots, where there was a proper space beside the stones, the workmen dug hollows, and, by undermining, dropped them in, where they lie buried so securely, as never more to retard the traveller's journey; but it was thought a moot point, even where it was successful, whether any time labour was saved by this practice; for those pits, for the most part, required to be made very deep and wide, and it could not be foreseen, without continual boring, whether there might not be rock above the necessary depth, which might be a disappointment after great labour

The roads on these moors are now as smooth as Constitution Hill, and I have galloped on some of them for miles together in great tranquillity; which was heightened by reflection on my former fatigue, when, for a great part of the way, I had been obliged to quit my horse, it being to dangerous or impracticable to ride, and even hazardous to pass on foot.

In the *Bath Chronicle*, June 1744, the following was reported from Edinburgh:

Last week there was the most prodigious Inundation, attended with thunder and lightning in the North that was ever known, insomuch that some houses built low are quite swept away, and two fine Bridges erected by General Wade were destroyed.

Chapter 12

The War of the Austrian Succession

On July 2nd 1739 George Wade was made a full general; the following year, as mentioned in the previous chapter, he was relieved of his command in Scotland, which passed to General Clayton. Throughout 1740 Wade was employed training troops for the war which had broken out with Spain. In 1742 Wade was appointed Lieutenant General of the Ordnance, and in 1743 a privy councillor. On December 14th 1743 the rank of field marshal was bestowed on Wade; this is the highest rank in the British Army and it originated in the reign of George II, who created ten field marshals. The term 'field marshal' reflected the German origins of the Hanoverians: it had long been employed in the Holy Roman Empire, in which the electorate of Hanover was located.

The years from 1716 till about 1740 were, on the whole, peaceful years. That was to change when Charles VI, the Holy Roman Emperor, died in October 1740, leaving his daughter Maria Theresa to inherit the empire. Foreseeing trouble for his daughter, Charles had tried to strengthen her position with the Pragmatic Sanctions – a series of agreements by which Britain, Hanover, Prussia, France and Spain, among others, acknowledged Maria Theresa's right of accession. However, shortly after Charles's death, Frederick II acceded to the Prussian throne and promptly invaded Silesia – one of the imperial dominions. Only England and Hanover stood loyally by their promises. George II urged that Britain should offer immediate assistance, but it was pointed out to him that his forces were already overstretched with the war in Spain, and the regiments posted overseas in Canada and the West Indies. The pros and cons of raising extra men were put before the House in the winter of 1742/3.

There were debates on December 4th and 11th 1742 in Parliament, which continued in January 1743, on the raising of new regiments, and a motion that the newly raised men should be incorporated into the standing regiments. The following extract is from the *Gentleman's Magazine*, December 1742 – January 1743.

General Wade then spoke as follows –
Though I cannot pretend to pursue the Honourable Gentleman through the whole compass of his Argument, nor shall attempt to stand up as his Rival, either in language of Knowledge, or Elegance of language, yet as my Course of life has necessarily furnished me with some observations relating to the Question before us and my present station in the Army, may in some measure, be said to make it my Duty to declare my opinion, I shall lay before the House, a few considerations, with the artless Simplicity of a plain soldier, without engaging in a formal debate or attempting to overthrow the Arguments of others.

It is observed, Sir, that for the greatest part, the farther any Man has advanced in Life, the less confidence he places in speculation, and the more he learns to rest upon experience as the only sure guide in human affairs; and as the transactions in which he is engaged are more important with the greater anxiety he enquires after precedents, and the more timorously does he proceed, when he is obliged to regulate his conduct by conjecture or by deliberation.

This remark, Sir, though it may be just with regard to all states of life, is yet more constantly and certainly applicable to that of the Soldier; because as his profession is more hazardous than any other, he must with more caution guard against miscarriages and errors. The old Soldier, therefore, very rarely ventures beyond the verge of experience, unless in compliance with particular accidents, which does not make any change in his general scheme, or in situations where nothing can preserve him but some new stratagem or unprecedented effort, which are not to be mentioned as part of his original plan of operation, because they are produced always by unforeseen emergencies, and are to be imputed not to choice but to necessity; for in consequence of my first principle an old soldier never willingly involves himself with difficulties, or proceeds in such a manner as that he may not expect success by the regular operations of War.

It will not, therefore be strange, if he who, having served in the Army in the Wars of the Emperor may justly claim the Title of an old soldier, should not easily depart from the methods established in my youth, methods of which their effects have shewn me, that they at least answer the intention for which they were contrived, and which therefore I shall be afraid of rejecting, lest those which it is proposed to substitute in their place, however probable in speculation, should be found defective in practice, and the reasoning, which indeed I cannot answer, should be consulted in the Field where eloquence has very little power.

The Troops formed according to the present Establishment have been found successful in preserving the liberties and they have appeared equally formidable in sieges and in battles, and with strength equally irresistible have pressed forward in the Field, and mounted the Breach. It may be urged, that this vigour, alacrity and success, cannot be proved to have been produced by the number of officers by whom they were commanded; but since, on the contrary, it cannot be shewn that the number of Officers did not contribute to their Victories, I think it not prudent to try the experiment, which, if it should succeed, as it probably may, would produce no great advantage; and if it should fail, and that it fail no man will deny, must bring upon us not only the expense which we are so solicitous to avoid, but disgrace and losses, along with the interruption of our trade, and the slaughter of great numbers of our fellow subjects.

Thus far, Sir, I have proceeded upon a supposition that the balance of the argument is equal on both sides and that nothing could be alleged on one part but experience, or objected to on the other but the want of it; but as I am not called to declare my opinion in a question relating to my profession, a question of great importance to the Public, I should think that I had not discharged my duty to my Country with that fidelity which may justly be exacted from me, if I should omit any observations that my memory may suggest, by which the House may be better enabled to proceed in this enquiry.

I think it therefore proper to declare, that we not only, in the last great War, experienced the usefulness of numerous Officers, but that we have likewise felt the want of them on a single occasion, and that the only greatest advantage which our enemies obtained, was gained over an Army rendered weak by the want of the usual number of Officers. Such were the Forces that were defeated at the fatal Battle of *Almanza*, by which almost all * *Iberia* was recovered from us.

It is indeed natural to imagine, that a greater Number of Officers must promote success, because courage is kindled by example, and it is therefore of use to every man to have his Leader in his

Footnote – * *This Gentleman (then Colonel of a Regiment) at the head of two Battalions repulsed twenty two Squadrons of Enemy, in the Campaign.*

view. Shame at one time, and affection at another, may produce the effects of courage where it is wanted, and those may follow their Commander, who are inclined to desert their duty; for it is seldom known that, while the Officers appear confident, the Soldiers despair, or that they think of retreating but after the example of their Leaders.

Where there are only a few Officers, it is apparent that more is left to chance in which it becomes not a wise man to place any confidence; for if the Officers are killed at the beginning of the action, the Soldiers must become a useless, defenceless herd without an order, without unanimity, and without design; but, by the present method, if an Officer happens to fall, his place is immediately supplied by another, the action goes forward, and the enemy receives no advantage from confusion or delay.

I am therefore of opinion, that in raising Troops for the Expedition now intended, the established method ought to be followed, and that we ought not to hazard success of our attempt, by new regulations, of which no human sagacity can foretell the event.

Tho' it cannot be denied, that some addition might be made to our Companies without any visible or certain inconvenience, yet the augmentation now intended, is too numerous to be so incorporated without some neglect of discipline, as the Officers would be charged with more Men than they could properly superintend.

There is indeed, Sir, another method of incorporation, by adding new Companies to each Regiment; but of this method the advantage would be small, because the number of Captains and inferior Officers must be the same, and the pay of only the Field-Officers would be saved, and this trifling gain would be far overbalanced by the inconveniences which experience has shown to arise from it. There have been Regiments formed of thirteen Companies instead of ten; but it was found, that as the Officers of a Company may be overcharged with Soldiers, a Colonel may likewise have more Companies than he can conveniently inspect, and the ancient regulation was restored, as the least liable to difficulties and objections.

Having thus endeavoured to vindicate the manner in which our new Troops are proposed to be levied, it may be expected that I should now make some observations on the Service in which they are to be employed which I cannot think liable to any unanswerable objection. It is now, Sir, our choice whether we will send the new Regiments abroad or keep them at home; and our choice may easily be determined by comparing the value of our Colonies with that of their Mother Country, if it be not necessary to have an Army here to defend us against insults and invasions. The question about the manner of raising or employing new Regiments is, superfluous, because none ought to be raised, as our old Troops are sufficiently numerous for Foreign Service. But if the security of the Nation requires an Army, would it not be madness to send those Troops to a different Part of the World, in which we can confide most? Would not those who speak with such contempt of an expedition undertaken by Boys, have a better reason for their censure, if only Boys were stationed on our Coasts to repel the Veterans of *France* would not such measures animate our enemies, and invite an Invasion?

It may perhaps be urged farther, that the Troops which are sent into *Columbia* are more likely to succeed in their design, than any Regiments of ancient establishment. The chief danger to be feared in that part of the World, is not from the enemy but the climate, with which young men are most able to contend, though they may not be equally qualified for attempts, in which skill is equally necessary with vigour.

I am convinced, Sir, that this War has hitherto been prosecuted with ardour and fidelity, and that no measures have been taken but such as experience and reason have supported, and therefore affirm, without scruple that if we are not successful, our miscarriages must be imputed to the chance of War, from which no prudence can exempt us.

The learned Gentleman who spoke last, must be acknowledged to have discovered a very special method of reasoning, and to have carried his enquiry as far as speculation without experience can hope to proceed, but has in my opinion admitted a false principle, by which all his argument has been perplexed. He supposes that the advantages must be always in proportion to the money expended in procuring them, and that therefore if five thousand men raised at any given cost will be equal to five thousand, they ought, if they are regulated according to an establishment of double the charge, to be able to encounter ten thousand. But in supposition, Sir, he forgets, that the possibility of loss is to be thrown into the balance against the advantage of the expense saved, and that though the strength of the troops be not increased in proportion to the increase of the cost, yet the additional security against a great loss may justly entitle the most expensive regulation to the preference. Suppose five thousand men to be brought to the field against six thousand, if they can by multiplying their officers at a double expense be enabled to engage successfully a body superior in number, may be justly said to gain all that would have been lost by suffering a defeat.

That we ought not to choose a worse method when we can

discover a better, is indisputably true, but which method is worse or better, can be discovered only by experience. The last war has taught us, that our troops in their present establishment are superior to the forces of *France* But how much they might suffer by any alteration it is not possible to foresee.

Success is gained by courage, and courage is produced by an opinion of superiority; and it may easily be imagined, that our soldiers, who judge of their own Strength only by experience, imagine their own establishment and discipline did not advance to the highest perfection; nor would they expect any other consequence from an alteration of it, but weakness and defeats. It is therefore dangerous to change the model of our Forces, because it is dangerous to depress the spirit of our soldiers.

Tho' it is confessed, Sir, that the *French*, whose officers are still more numerous, have been conquered by our troops, it must be likewise alleged, that they might have yielded us far easier victories had their officers been wanting; for to them are they indebted for their conquests wherever they have been successful, and for their resistance wherever they have been with difficulty defeated; their soldiers are a spiritless herd, and were they not invigorated by the example of their leaders, and restrained by the fear of instant punishment, would fly at the approach of any enemy, without waiting for the attack. I cannot therefore, Sir, but be of opinion, that the necessity of a large number of officers may be learned even from the behaviour of those troops which have been unsuccessful, since it is certain, that tho' they have been often overcome, they have generally resisted with great steadiness, and continued with great order.

If those who are only speculative warriors shall imagine that their arguments are not confuted, I can only repeat what I declared when I first attempted to deliver my sentiments in this debate that I do not pretend to be very skilful in the arts of disputation. I, who claim no other title than that of an old soldier, cannot hope to prevail much by my oratory; it is enough for me that I am confident of confuting those arguments in the field, which I oppose in the Senate

The *Gentleman's Magazine* further reported the debate when it continued in January 1743:

General Wade –

Since the Right Honourable Member has been pleased to insinuate, that by answering a plain Question I may put an End to the Debate,

I am willing to give a Proof of my desire to promote unanimity in our Counsels, and Dispatch in our Affairs, by complying with his Proposal. If I were obliged with a small sum to raise an Army for the Defence of a Kingdom, I should undoubtedly proceed with the utmost frugality; but this noble person's ideas of frugality would, perhaps, be very different from mine; he would think these expences superfluous, which to me would seem indispensably necessary, and though we should both intend the preservation of the Country, we should provide for its security by different methods. He would employ the money in such a manner as might procure the greatest of numbers; I should make my first enquiry after the most skilful Officers, and should imagine myself obliged by my fidelity to the Nation, that entrusted me with its Defence, to procure their assistance, though at a high price.

It is not easy for Persons who have never seen a Battle or a Siege, whatever may be their natural abilities, or however cultivated by reading and contemplation, to conceive the advantage of discipline and regularity which is such, that a small body of Veteran Troops will drive before them multitudes of men, perhaps equally bold and resolute with themselves, if they are unacquainted with the Rules of War, and unprovided with Leaders to direct their Motions. I should therefore, in the case which he has mentioned, prefer discipline to numbers, and rather enter the Field with a few troops well governed and well instructed, than with a confuted multitude unacquainted with their Duty, unable to conduct themselves, and without officers to conduct them.

The question at last was put, that the new raised troops be incorporated into the standing corps; but it fell by 232 votes to 166.

In the end they had no choice, and in 1743 the army was engaged in what was known as the War of the Austrian Succession. The King sailed for the Continent to be in readiness for the troubles brewing and to take command of the Allied Army against the French Army led by Marshal the Duke Adrien de Noailles.

The location was on the right bank of the Main, between Aschaffenburg and Hanau in Germany, on the lower Rhine. George II with an army of Hanoverians, English and Dutch, with contingents from other German allies of Austria attempted to separate the French from their Bavarian allies but was outmanoeuvred and forced to give battle on June 27th 1743. This 40,000-strong army advanced slowly into the Main and Neckar valleys while a French army of 30,000 moved to block its advance. As the two armies approached each other in the valley between Hanau and Aschaffenburg, the skilful Noailles blockaded the Pragmatic Army. With true English sturdiness and Hanoverian stubbornness, George extricated himself from this dangerous situation. The outcome was an allied victory, which led to the French withdrawal across the Rhine. Although of limited strategic importance, the battle is of interest in that it was the last occasion when a British monarch personally commanded his troops in battle. At one stage King George's horse bolted, but he dismounted with the comment that he could trust his own legs not to run away with him. George, with sword in hand, led his English and Hanoverian infantry into the counter-attack. At the end of the day, the allies held the field and Noailles was obliged to retreat.

The *Gentleman's Magazine* reported events on Thursday 16th 1743.

> This Day a desperate Battle was fought between a Body of the Forces commanded by his Majesty in Germany, and another of French commanded by M. Noailles; of which the following short account was published by Authority being sent by the Lord Carteret

> *A Letter to the Duke of Newcastle. Dettingen June 1743*

> His Majesty (God be praised) has this day gained a very considerable battle. The French passed the *Main* as this place with about 25,000 men and have been forced to repass it with considerable Loss. I write this from the Village near the Field of Battle, which the *French* were in possession of; by which means we have secured our Conjunction with the *Hessians* and *Hanoverians*, in number 12,000, which are within two leagues of us, and to intercept whom the *French* made this hazardous attempt, which has failed them. His Majesty was all the time in the heat of the fire; but is in perfect health. The Duke received a shot in the leg which pierced the calf; but the bone is not hurt: He is very well and in high spirits. I must refer the particulars of this great Affair till tomorrow or next Day. General Clayton is killed; and we have taken several General Officers prisoners and many Officers of the *French* King's household in their fine cloaths.

> The Army lies all night under Arms. I am in a cottage with Marshal Neiperig. The Austrians behaved themselves with great

gallantry. The Duke *d'Aremberg* is wounded with a musquet-shot in the breast. This is a good beginning of the Campaign, the Emperor's Auxiliaries having received a very considerable check, and they were the aggressors.

    I am ever, with the greatest truth, and respect, My Lord, Your Grace's Most Humble, and most obedient Servant – Carteret.

P.S. The *Hanoverian* Artillery has had a considerable share in this Victory. The battle began at ten in the morning and lasted to four, when the enemy repassed the *Main* with precipitation.

The victory gained by the English troops seemed novel in England, for there had been no war of any consequence since the days of Marlborough. When the news reached home, the whole country celebrated and the bells were rung throughout the city. Dettingen was on everyone's lips; pamphlets in prose and verse, songs, ballads and epigrams were showered on the public. Handel set about composing a piece of ceremonial music in readiness for the King's return.

    In 1743 Wade was called upon to deal with a mutiny by the Black Watch of a very serious nature. The original Highland Watch had been purely a police force for service in the Highlands, and the men joined on the understanding that they would not be sent abroad. Rumours abounded nevertheless that the government intended to send the regiment to Flanders early in 1743, and the London newspapers contained notices to that effect on March 5th 1743. Orders were issued summoning the Black Watch to London to be reviewed by the King. There was no official suggestion of sending it abroad, but the rank and file were suspicious, and some of the officers knew of the government's intention. The men were told that as soon as the review was over they would return to Scotland, but there is evidence that the spirit of the regiment was 'distrustful'. However, nothing very serious happened till on the march south it met a party of General St Clair's regiment (the Royal Scots) going north to recruit.

    The first battalion of this regiment had just returned from the disgraceful Indian expedition, in which it had suffered cruel losses from disease and in battle. The men of this recruitment party left the Black Watch full of 'apprehension that they were going to be carried to the West Indies', and this fear appears to have been increased by agitators. The Black Watch reached London early in May, and it was then found that the King had sailed for the

Continent on April 27th, and that the regiment would be reviewed by General Wade.

This aroused still more bitter feelings, as the honour of being reviewed by the King in person had been one of the sops most frequently held out by the officer during the march. The review took place on Finchley Common on May 14th, and later in the day there was issued an order which the King had signed before his departure: the Highland Watch was to embark at Gravesend for Ostend on May 20th. The regiment felt that it had been deliberately deceived, and that the terms of service had been broken. The men decided to go back to Scotland, and a rendezvous was fixed on Finchley Common before midnight on May 17th.

A party of 112 men turned up, and although several officers who had got wind of the affair attempted to dissuade them, they marched off northwards, confident that the rest of the regiment would follow. The ringleaders were Corporal Samuel Macpherson, Corporal Malcolm Macpherson, and Private Farquhar Shaw. The men did not consider that they were deserting; they were Highlanders with a high sense of honour, and they felt that they had been cheated and abused.

Immediate measures were taken to follow them and to prevent further desertions, and for these purposes detachments of the Horse and Foot Guards were used. In spite of all precautions, however, forty-four more men got away on May 18th, but some of their officers followed them and eventually persuaded all but eight (seven of whom capitulated later) to return. Meanwhile, troops began to close in on the first party and, on May 21st, 104 of them surrendered near Oundle in Northamptonshire. All these men were taken to London, imprisoned in the Tower, court-martialled, and sentenced to death.

The sentence, however, was carried out only in the case of the ringleaders. The rest of the deserters were sent to serve in various stations abroad. Over the years the Black Watch earned for themselves a reputation as one of the finest fighting forces in the British Isles and was distinguished in practically every campaign. General Wade, who raised the six companies in 1725, would have been justly proud of the fine young men who have earned their regiment such honours. And it is fitting today that one of the monuments to the Black Watch can be seen beside the bridge over the Tay at Aberfeldy – the bridge which is considered to be Wade's greatest achievement.

Verses written by a Highlander the day before he was taken appeared in the *Gentleman's Magazine*, June 1743:

> Ye think our *Highlands* bleak and bare
> O' *Phoebus* bounty ha' na care
> And that, because far north we come
> We're glad to leave our native home.
> But much mist'aen, ye little ken
> Each bonny strath, and verdant glen
> Where violets blow and hawthorn bloom
> Of gardens fine supply the room:
> And *Cowdenknows* and *Yarrow* side
> As much the blithesome *Scotmans's* pride
> Who near these pleasant places dwells,
> As Windsor Castle, or Versailles
>
> *Tis true*, that we are unco' poor,
> Our lords and lairds live on your shore,
> But fare each earns whate'er he gets,
> They're yere ane tykes and turn yere spits,
> While we at hame, wi mickle care,
> Rub thro' our lives wi little gear:
> Yet now and then the piper plays,
> And *Scottish* slaves forget their waes,
> Sing theyr ald sangs, and are as canty
> As English clowns wi aw their plenty.
> Then winder not we're scarce inclin'd
> To be in martial hands confin'd,
> Sent o'er the sea, and far away,
> To make a shew without our . . .
> But if this humour's sae resented,
> Banish us hame, – and we're contented
>
> Take ye a *Robin i' the yard*,
> (And be his case wi ours compar'd
> As lang as ye your crums impart,
> He pecks and sings wi aw his heart,
> And trusting to your kind protection,
> Makes ay your window his election,
> There, wi his plaid athwart his breast,
> He seeks his meat, or takes his rest,

> But if wi' him ye break yere wird
> And seize and cage the little bird,
> Sullen at first he bears his chain,
> 'Till starving quits the greater pain,
> And *Highlanders* like *Robins* be,
> Alive or dead they mun be *free*.

With the Allied Army away fighting in Flanders, the Jacobites were once again plotting to raise an army in the North. Intelligence to and from the Jacobite court found a ready route through the smuggling network along the coasts of Britain. Criminal gangs were attracted by rich rewards for carrying spies, escapees and correspondence. These gangs were powerful enough to take on the authorities. The Hawkhurst Gang, the most notorious of the Kent gangs, alone had about 500 members ready to fight at any one time.

They terrorised the Kent coast during 1735–49 from their headquarters at the Oak and Ivy Inn. The smugglers were known as owlers because they were active at night. The French seaports had large communities of expatriates, most with strong Jacobite ties, who were also engaged in smuggling. It was no wonder that, faced with the threat of another Jacobite uprising, the government grew uneasy and decided to send troops to the areas known to be the haunts of smugglers.

Wade sent a detachment of his regiment down to Kent in order to arrest those thought to be aiding and abetting the Jacobites, and on April 29th 1744 the news-sheets reported that a party of General Wade's Horse conducted to Rochester Gaol the noted Tom Jolly, an old smuggler and one of the Hawkhurst Gang, which had been concerned in running most of the tea on the Kent coast: he was taken in bed the night before at Dartford in Kent.

The *Bath Chronicle* reported:

> Horace Walpole writes that Wade is to have command of the Army, as it is supposed, on the King's not going abroad. The King decided to send Wade, newly appointed Field Marshal to take his place as Commander-in-Chief of the Army in Flanders where he was to share Command of the Allied forces with the Duc d' Aremberg and Count Maurice of Nassau against Marshal Saxe.

The *Bath Journal,* June 5th 1744, reported:

> The Confederate Army, consisting of the English, Hanoverian, Austrian and Dutch Troops, under the command of Marshal Wade, the Duke d'Aremberg, and Count Maurice of Nassau, began to march from their camp at Asche towards Oudenarde. The French army consists of between 90 and 100.000 men; but they are neither so good troops, nor so well armed and clothed as the Allies. We are assured that General Wade has received positive orders to cross the River Scheld and act offensively; the French having made such large draughts from their army as to leave him a match for them there; so that we may at every Post expect news of importance from both places.

The *Bath Journal*, August 3rd 1744, reported from Brussels:

> The whole Confederate Army passed the Scheld last Friday; it is near 70,000 strong, all fine troops and in high spirits: It directs its march towards the lines of the French. The soldiers have taken four days provision along with them. If the lines can be attacked, we shall do it. We are superior in number to the enemy by upwards of 20,000 men, and expect 6000 more. If there is no possibility of attacking the French Lines, we may probably lay Siege to Maubeuge: This week will decide the matter. If the Duke of Aremberg has, as 'tis said, *Carte Blanch;*, As Count Saxe has, the entrenchments will be attacked and probably forced.

The *Bath Journal*, August 6th 1744, reported:

> Brussels, a large and noble City of the Low Countries, subject to the Queen of Hungary, stands 190 miles east of London. The Court has received as express from Duke d'Aremberg with the result of a Grand Council of War, at which the Duke proposed, 'That Divine Providence having so manifestly blessed the Arms of the Queen Maria Theresa, and the Passage of the Rhine having obliged the French to desist from their operations in Flanders, and to fly to the succour of Alsace, to prevent what they were threatened with on that side, he thought that it would tend to the Good of the common cause to detach from the Army of the Allies a Body of 20,000 men towards the Moselle, in order to make a diversion there in favour of Prince Charles: That the thing appeared so much the more feasible to him, as the French had not above 45,000 men in the Low-Countries, exclusive of the Garrisons,' The Duke added in his report, that General Wade had without reserve

declared, 'That he could not give consent thereto,' and that all the other Generals had acquiesced in his Sentiments.

The *Bath Journal*, August 20th 1744, reported from The Hague:

> We are assured that Field Marshal Wade, and the rest of his Britannick Majesty's Generals, has received repeated orders to act in every thing in Concert with the Queen's Troops and her Auxiliaries, and to manage matters so that a resolution may be taken to march up directly to Count Saxe, and force him to a Battle. The advices from Flanders mention nothing but skirmishes of no consequence, the Confederate Army still lying in the same Camp. Although Field Marshal Wade wanted to take the offensive, the Austrian commander General D'Aremberg, did not have sufficient money to pay his troops.

Serving in Flanders at that time was the 3rd Foot, the regiment of Lieutenant General Thomas Howard. There was another regiment at whose head was a Major General Howard. To avoid confusion, Wade, then commanding the British forces, appears to have sanctioned the two regiments being known informally by the colour of their respective facings, and the Buff Howards and the Green Howards came into being.

Wade, now suffering from asthma, had been observed coughing up blood and now he applied for leave to return to England. The Field Marshal had provided a convenient scapegoat for the allies' dismal showing: in fairness to Wade, who was now aged over seventy and in poor health, his performance had been hampered by obstructive colleagues as well as the Continental commanders he was trying to keep together in the alliance. The Austrians also faced a renewed threat from Prussia in the east. So with nothing accomplished, when much might have been achieved, the allies in Flanders went into winter quarters and Wade resigned in frustration.

There were regular complaints about him to his superiors in London, and many of Wade's letters are replies to these complaints. They also show Wade's concern for the welfare of his troops, their horses, and particularly his desire to avoid needless sickness or casualties. In accepting Wade's resignation, the Secretary of State, Lord Harrington, assured him that George II expressed 'the most perfect satisfaction in his services'. The King demonstrated his continuing confidence in Wade by appointing him commander-in-chief in England.

There was much discontent in England over the futility of the Flanders Campaign in 1744. The Duke of Cumberland was appointed to replace Wade, and duly arrived in Flanders on April 21st 1745. Despite advice from the Austrian commander, Field Marshal Konigsegg, to be cautious, he was determined to take the offensive. Unfortunately he seriously underestimated the strength of the French against the Allied Army.

On May 21st the battle took place five miles south-east of Tournai, Belgium where the Allied Army was attempting to break the French siege of Tournai. The British and Hanoverian infantry advanced deep into the French position, driving all before them, but to their left the Dutch and Austrians did not make any progress in their assaults against the villages of Fontenoy and Antoing. Saxe was therefore able to deploy his rallied French Guards and Swiss Guards against the left flank of the British and Hanoverian column, while his six battalions of Irish troops (known as the Wild Geese), along with the French Guards, attacked from the right. The British and the Hanoverians were weak from a twelve-hour lack of food and drink.

Cumberland and Konigsegg acted with the utmost bravery; but it became clear that, with Fontenoy still in the hands of the French, retreat was inevitable. Slowly the depleted British and Hanoverian regiments relinquished the field. The casualties were high: 7,500 of the Allied Army were killed or injured. Amongst the injured was one of Wade's sons, Captain John Wade of the King's Own Regiment of Dragoons. The result was a hard-won victory for the French, who went on to capture Tournai and other fortresses in the Austrian Netherlands.

Wade returned home a very sick man, and travelled down to Bath for the recovery of his health. During his stay he contributed the sum of £500 to the Bath Corporation, towards making the Shambles more attractive; several houses were to be pulled down 'in order to render that laudable design more effectual'. On returning to London, Wade carried with him an address by the Mayor, aldermen and citizens of Bath to be presented to King George:

The Following Address of the Mayor, Aldermen and Citizens of Bath

> To his Majesty by Field Marshal Wade, one of their representatives in Parliament, and Robert Henley, Esq., their Recorder, being introduced by the Right Honourable the Earl Waldegrave, one of

the Lords of his Majesty's Bed-Chamber in Waiting: Which address his Majesty was pleased to receive very graciously. Given under our Common Seal this Twenty-third day of September, in the Nineteenth Year of your Majesty's Reign.

May it please your Majesty – We your Majesty's most dutiful and loyal Subjects, the Mayor, Aldermen and Citizens of your Majesty's ancient City of Bath, beg leave, in the most humble and sincere manner, to congratulate your Majesty upon your safe return to these your British Dominions, and to express the just sense we have of your Majesty's concern for the liberties of Europe, in pursuing with such pains, wisdom and steadiness, that great point, the Election of an Emperor; an event of the utmost importance, and which we have at length seen happily accomplished. We beg leave likewise to express our joy on the success of your Majesty's Arms in North-America, in the acquisition of Cape Breton; a place of the utmost consequence to the trade and navigation of Great Britain, and the loss of which most considered as a wound given to France in its very vitals. While your Majesty is thus invariably pursuing the interests of the People, we cannot but with equal astonishment and abhorrence reflect upon the unnatural rebellion now raised and carried on in your Majesty's Dominions; which outrageous and audacious attempt we are persuaded can end in nothing but the destruction of those who are partakers in it:

And in evincing to the World how absolutely and securely your Majesty reigns in the hearts and affections of your People in general, the Patriot, the Man of Property, and Religion, influenced by the strongest of Motives, Duty and Interest, must join with the utmost Ardour upon all occasion to support your Majesty's person and the present establishment: And we beg leave to assure Majesty, that your dutiful and loyal subjects of this very ancient city will on any emergency appear among the first to hazard our lives and fortunes in so glorious an enterprise.

Chapter 13

The Road to Culloden

On the outbreak of the Jacobite rising in Scotland in 1745, Wade headed the military committee responsible for deciding the government's response to the crisis. It was agreed that Wade should march north with thirteen battalions of foot, including a large contingent of foreign troops.

The *Bath Journal*, Monday October 5th 1745, reported the news from London:

> On Thursday last, Field Marshal Wade kissed his Majesty's hand at Kensington on his taking leave in order to set out for the North.

Soon the citizens of Bath were eagerly reading the news-sheets in the coffee shops and the circulating libraries. How surprised they must have been to read that Wade was to head an army of 10,000 to quell the new Jacobite Rebellion! The *Bath Journal*, only a few months earlier, had reported that Wade had given up his command of the forces in Flanders and returned home a very sick man. It was said he was slow in his actions and muddled in his thinking. However, once again he had been called upon to take on a new command: to turn back Charles Edward Stuart in his attempt to overthrow the Hanoverian Dynasty.

Over the coming months the *Bath Journal* and the *Gentleman's Magazine* reported the news from Whitehall and the Scottish and English news-sheets of the day.

Charles Edward Stuart (1720–88), also known as Charles III, Bonnie Prince Charlie, or the Young Pretender, landed off the west coast of Scotland on the Hebridean island of Eriskay, accompanied only by a small band of companions known as the 'Seven Men of Moidart'. At first the Highland chiefs were reluctant to join him, particularly as he had no French army to back him up. Eventually, however, the clans rallied round, and soon some 1,500 men assembled. The Highland army marched across Scotland, growing in size as it went, and it reached Perth early in September. Here the Prince was joined by Lord George Murray. By September 17th the Jacobite Army entered Edinburgh and Prince Charles took up residence in the Palace of Holyrood. Apart from a few minor skirmishes, the Hanoverian army avoided any major conflict, expecting the revolt to be a feint, as on earlier occasions.

On September 19th the Hanoverian army under Sir John Cope encamped at Prestonpans, five miles east of Edinburgh, to wait for reinforcements from the south. On September 21st they were taken by surprise when the Jacobite Army under the command of Lord George Murray attacked them: in fifteen minutes the battle was over and the victor was Murray. When Prince Charles arrived on the battlefield, he was horrified and sickened by what he saw – soldiers trapped and massacred in cold blood. Horrific injuries had been inflicted on the fallen by the Highlanders using their broadswords and billhooks. The casualties were said to be about 300 dead and 400 to 500 wounded; about 1,500 prisoners were taken.

Prince Charles was even more incensed on knowing that his men refused to bury the enemy dead. It speaks well of the Prince that he cared about those who fought against him, and was prepared to find the money to fund the burial of the fallen. His army also made demands, however, and many of them were published in local newspapers.

The *Bath Chronicle*, September 24th 1745, reported the news from Edinburgh:

> The rebels have demanded from this City 6000 pairs of shoes, 1000 tents, and a proportional number of water cantines, and 2000 targets, for which payment are promised when the present troubles have ceased. Sunday there was no sermon in the churches, the Ministers being generally out of town. Yesterday the Lord Provost visited the Officers who were made prisoners belonging to General Cope's Army. Of the rebels killed, Capt. Robert Stuart of Ardshiels Battalion, Capt. Archibald MacDonald of Kippoch's, Lieut. Allan Cameron of Lindeora, and Ensign James Cameron of Lockheil's Regiment.

This is a copy of a letter from Prince Charles to the town of Glasgow, signed Prince C. R. Lecky, September 23rd 1745.

> I need not inform you of my being come hither, nor of my view in coming, that is already sufficiently known. All those who love their Country, and the true interest of Britain, ought to wish for my success, and do what they can to promote it. It would be a needless repetition to tell you, that all the privileges of your Town are included in my Declaration; and what I have promised I never will depart from. I hope this is your way of thinking; and therefore expect your compliance with my demand, a sum of money not exceeding 15,000.1. Sterling (besides what is due to the Government) and whatever Arms can be found in your City, is all at present I require. The terms proposed are very reasonable, and what I promise to make good. I choose to make these demands; but if not complied with, I shall take measures, and you shall be answerable to the consequence.

The *Bath Journal*, October 7th 1745, printed an extract of a letter from a gentleman in Dundee to his friend in Newcastle:

> The young Chevalier is now in our neighbourhood, and far too well attended. The Government and King want not friends amongst us. The whole army under the Pretender removed Wednesday for Dundee and are daily growing in their numbers. Lord Ogilvie is now at Montrose, has committed great outrages in this Country, and threatening also to visit Dundee. I cannot say what the number of arm'd rebels may amount to; some say 4, others 5, and still others 7000. They speak confidently of their expecting 10 or 15 thousand French and Irish, and say our Country is all their own; and pretend grounds for great assistance the moment they cross the borders.
>
> The Prince is dressed in fine tartan, red velvet breeches, and blue velvet bonnet, with gold lace round it, and a large jewel with St. Andrew appended; he wears also a green ribbon, is above six foot, walks well and straight, and speaks the English or Broad Scots well. I think I durst have ventur'd with two regiments of Horse, and as many Foot, to have sent them to the Mountains. One of their Officers told me many of them did not so much as understand the ordinary use of Arms; and that most of them had not yet been under Arms twenty days. They also have offered to serve wherever his Majesty shall require, and desire to be call'd the King's Royal Hunters. On Thursday last the Nobility, Clergy and Gentry of Lancashire assembled at the Town Hall in Preston

and with the greatest unanimity enter'd into an Association to raise immediately a Body of 3000 Men, for the Security of his Majesty's person and Government.

The *Bath Journal*, October 14th 1745, reported:

Whitehall Oct. 8. By letters received this day from Berwick, of the 5th instant, the main body of the Rebels were, on the 4th, still at Duddington, and those left in Edinburgh, continued where they had taken post in order to cut off all Communication with the Castle. There are likewise advices from Glasgow, that the Town had received a second letter from the Pretender's Son, demanding the sum of 15,000 *l*. Which letter was accompanied with threats of Military Execution, if the demand was not complied with? The Town under this necessity prevailed upon the party of the Rebels, who had been sent to require the above contribution, to less it to 5500 Pounds which, sum they were obliged to pay immediately.

London October 8th 1745 Last Friday 37 Transports sailed from the Nore for Holland, in order to bring over the Horse, which are marching from the Allied Army in Flanders towards England. We hear that the Forces that are coming from Holland have orders to sail directly to Hull, where they are to join the Forces in the North.

We hear that Sir George Wynne, Sir Charles Wynne, Sir Watkin Williams Wynne, and Sir Robert Grosvenor, Barts, and Philip Warburton, Esq., have entered into an Association for raising, arming and clothing, at their own expense, a body of 500 men, for the Defence of his Majesty and the Kingdom, against all Foreign and Domestic Foes.

The Guards have now Orders not to decamp in Hyde Park; but the soldiers who lived at a distance from the Town are ordered to come to their quarters in the City and Liberty of Westminster, and all the suburbs round the City of London.

Similar reports supporting the King and the government were coming from other parts of the country and on October 14th 1745 the *Bath Journal* published from the *London Evening Post* an ode remembering the bad times:

> Ye true British Subjects, whose Loyalty dares
> To face the Pretender, and all the Pope's snares
> Exert all you might in sound Liberty's Cause,
> And Stand by the Nation, and Stand by the Laws

Shall Popery and Rome her Tenets Dispense,
Devoid of all reason, devoid of all Sense?
Shall the Minion of France, and the Dupe of old Rome
Dispose of our Rights, both Abroad and at Home?

Shall the Sons of OLD ENGLAND commence petty slaves?
Be govern'd by Rebels and Jacobite Knaves?
Shall Friars and Monks recover their Land?
And the Host pass in Triumph thro' City and Strand?

If Priest-ridden Tools would your senses deceive,
Be cautious to hearken, be slow to believe?
They'll tell you fine stories, to tickle your Ears,
And gild their designs, to dispel all your fears.

Possest of your Rights, they will lead you a Dance,
And England must then be a Province of France;
French Laws and French Customs, and despotick power,
Like Vultures will prey, and like Vultures devour.

Cape Breton we've conquer'd, Cape Breton we'll keep,
Nor suffer our Foes to cajole us asleep;
And Jemmy's Adherents, we'll bring to the block,
The Nation's united as firm as a Rock.

It was reported from Bristol on October 12th 1745:

That the Right Worshipful William Barnes Esq., Mayor, Mr. Justice Foster, Recorder, and the Worshipful Aldermen, together with the rest of the Corporation of this City, attended by a great number of the principal inhabitants, assembled at the Guildhall, when his Grace the Duke of Newcastle's letter was publicly read, authorising the Magistrates (as from his Majesty) to call the City to Arms, and to martial them into Troops or Companies, at their discretion; as also for them to appoint proper Officers to the respective Corps.

After this was read, an association was entered into for the support of the Common Cause, when the Mayor subscribed 10,000 pounds in the name of the Chamber, and the Master of the Society and Company of Merchants, 500 pounds in the name of the whole Society; which was followed by a generous subscription of the whole Bench of Magistrates, some of whom subscribed 500 pound a-piece, and others 300, 200, and 100 pounds. This generous and loyal spirit was seconded by many of the Gentlemen in the Hall. By the spirit that at present appears among us, we may be bold to say not a City in England is more firmly attached to his Majesty and Government than that of Bristol, which it is believed will raise near 100.000 pounds the first stroke, for the support of the Common Cause. Tis said that 40,000 pounds will be subscribed by one particular Body of Men in this City.

On October 14th 1745 it was reported that:

Field Marshal Wade, Commander in Chief North Britain, set out for Scotland with a large retinue, from his house in Burlington Street, for Doncaster, in Yorkshire, to take upon him the command of the Army assembling there.

No doubt the sale of the *Bath Journal* soared over the coming weeks as it reported the large volume of news coming in covering the rebellion. There was reporting and misreporting, and this chapter sets out to cover, from the contemporary newspapers, Prince Charles's movements as he gathered around him those faithful to the Stuart cause.

The *London Gazette* printed an extract of a letter from Ferrybridge, dated October 21st 1745:

The Regiments of Wade's Horse and St. George's Irish Dragoons passed through Ferrybridge last week and are now at York, who are really complete stout men, and make a fine appearance. The Duke of Montagu's Regiment is now at Wakefield. I am informed also of two Regiments being at Leeds; and this morning the body under Field-Marshal Wade decamp'd from a place called Wheatley-Hills, a mile and a half south-east of Doncaster, and arrived this afternoon at the south-end of Ferrybridge and pitched their tents upon the east and west of the road, contiguous to the Town, being in number 11,000 and on Tuesday morning to march forward. Yorkshire appears now to be the seat of the war. I believe we have now in it 16,000 complete forces, which when they come to join these in the North, and take the Field, will form an Army of 25,000. The Royal Scotch Regiment of Foot is now at Pontefract, and joins in Camp to-night. There was one of the soldiers had a thousand stripes given him at Pontefract for drinking the Pretender's health, and for saying that half the Regiment would run away and join him, if they were sent to engage; he was almost cut to pieces, none shewing him any mercy.

The *Bath Journal*, October 23rd 1745, reported the news from London:

> Yesterday a Draught of 216 Gunners, Bombardiers and Matrosses was made from Woolwich, and sent away with a large train of Artillery for the Forts and Castles in the West of England. The same day they began to pitch the tents in Hyde-Park for the Foot-Guards and Horse Grenadier Guards; and the Camp is ordered to be completed by Friday next. We also hear from York, that his Grace the Lord Arch-Bishop of that place has put on a Lay Military Habit, in order to spirit forward the Execution of what his Grace has so bravely and pathetically recommended in his Speech upon the Association there. The gentlemen of the County of York have already subscribed 90,000 1. for arming, cloathing and paying 4000 men in defence of his Majesty's person and Government, and their own Religion, Liberties, and Properties and have resolved to augment that sum, if there should be an occasion. A great number of Gentlemen volunteers have also engaged to serve at their own charge; among which 1000 horses are expected to be brought into the Field.

The *London Evening Post* reported the news from Whitehall on October 26th 1745:

> Letters from Berwick of the 22nd instant, that some of the transports bound from Holland to Newcastle, had appeared off that place, and that a Boat with a pilot had gone out and conducted them in. These had on board eight Companies belonging to different Regiments, and there were some more Transports with about 25 Companies at Holy-Isand. General Handasyd ordered the eight Companies to land and enter Berwick, to reinforce that Garrison, and the five Companies to remain at Holy-Island till further orders.
>   There is intelligence likewise, that 2000 of the Rebels, with eight pieces of Cannon, had on Monday last marched by Duddington from Edinburgh, and were gone as was said Southward: Those in Mussleburgh, and the other villages adjacent to Edinburgh, were drawing together in order to take the same route as on Tuesday Morning last; and that they were enquiring which were the best roads to Westmoreland.
>   It was likewise reported, that 200 Rebels had mutinied, of whom 100 had marched off, and left their Army; and that several Waggons with wounded men were come into Edinburgh by the Western Port, and it was said there had been action betwixt some of them and the

Garrison at Stirling Castle; but that they expected, as next Day, at Berwick, a more distinct and certain account of those Particulars.

The punsters of the day are of the Opinion, that though we could not *Cope* with the Rebellion at first, we shall make a Shift to *Wade* through it at last.

The *Bath Journal*, October 28th 1745, printed a letter from Hull:

Marshal Wade, with the forces under his command at Darlington on the 26th inst, the troops from Flanders were arrived at Newcastle, Berwick and Holy Island, except five companies of Colonel Ligioner's, and three of Brigadier Price's, the baggage of the whole, and one ship with horses, which were still missing. Letters mention that the Pretender's eldest son had his Quarters at the Duke of Buccleugh's House: that the rebels were 8,000 effective men and that they had brought all their baggage out of Edinburgh to that camp; and that they rob and destroy all around them. There was likewise a report of a French ship having arrived at Aberbrothnock with bombs, mortars, and heavy cannon, with cannoniers and bombardiers.

The *Daily Advertiser*, October 26th 1745, reported:

The following prayer is said to have been used by Mr. Mac Vickers, a Minister at Edinburgh, who had been forbid by the Pretender to pray for his Majesty King George, viz 'O Lord, bless the King, thou knowest I mean King George; establish his Throne in Righteousnes, fix the Crown firm on his Head. And as for the Stranger that is come among us, to seek an earthly Crown, take him to thy self, and give him a Crown of Glory'.

The *General Evening Post*, October 26th 1745, reported:

The following is an account of what Money the rebels have received, viz. from Perth 1,000 pounds, from Glasgow 5,400, pounds, 15,000 pounds at 2s. 6d. per pound, on House Rents in Edinburgh; by goods sold from Leith Custom House 7,000 pounds in all 28,000 pounds.

Bonfire Night on November 5th 1745 was celebrated with more than the usual enthusiasm in the towns and countryside. The *Bath Chronicle* carried reports of those celebrating the occasion:

In London on the Tuesday being the anniversary of the gunpowder plot in 1603, the morning was ushered in with the ringing of bells, and the evening concluded with Bonfires and Illuminations the greatest that has been known in the memory of man. In Several places, the populace expressed their abhorrence of Popery, exhibited mock scenery, in burning the Pope, Pretender, &c

In Bath the same was observed here in an extraordinary manner; not only by the Quality and Gentry, but by the inhabitants in general, who endeavoured, with the greatest cheerfulness, to out vie each other in loyalty. In short, we have had no such rejoicing for many years. Being the birthday of King George the morning was ushered in by the Ringing of bells; The Gentlemen &c. that day wore Cockades of an Orange colour; as did the Ladies Favours, with the following Motto, viz. King George, and the *Protestant Succession.*

When evening approached the inhabitants in general illuminated their windows with candles; Fire works were likewise exhibited in several parts of the City; and all was done, without the least disturbance or disorder, which is much to be admired, and the concourse of people in the streets was very great.

The Corporation assembled in the Evening at the Guildhall; as did the Gentry at Mrs Wiltshire's, where there was a ball, which was conducted with the utmost decency and good order: After that they repaired to Mr. Simpson's to partake of an elegant entertainment which was provided: And the night concluded, among all degrees of People, in drinking his Majesty's and the Royal Family's, and many other loyal health's; and success to General Wade, (our representative in Parliament) against the rebels; That the rebellion may soon be extinguished and that peace and unanimity may reign among all his Majesty's subjects and that Trade may again revive, and be brought into its proper Channel &c.

The *Bath Journal*, November 8th, carried the following report of the celebrations taking place in the surrounding villages:

Tuesday last being the fifth of November among other rejoicings for past Deliverance, and as an instance of Loyalty to the present Happy Establishment, was presented here a Mock Pretender; who, amidst his Alamode Superstitious Dress, was branded on the back with this inscription, the Devil, the Pope, or the Pretender. He held in his right hand, a sword, and faggot, and in his left the following declaration.

> At my Command you will, I hope
> Obey my Orders, and the Pope;
> For if you do my Laws reject,
> Behold the Fate you must expect,
> This Sword and Dagger in my Hand
> Of Hereticks shall purge the land.
> And if you don't observe me well,
> I'll send you ev'ry soul to hell,
> And by St. Dominic I swear
> That neither Old nor Young I'll spare.
> *Signed Charles Grey*
>
> Go. . . . vain pretending spurious Brat,
> Thou boast of Pow'r It ne'er come at
> Go. . . . Bully France or Rome with lies,
> Their Popish Fopp'ries we despise,
> Whilst God unholds his fav'rite Land,
> We ne'er will stoop to their command,
> But still in spite of thee, we'll sing,
> May GOD preserve Great George, our King!
> *Sign'd Protestants.*

At last (not to imitate the cruelty of our enemies) he was not committed to the bonfire, but honourably beheaded – The evening concluded with drinking several Loyal Healths, &c. Tho' our Joys were not a little damp'd on account of a melancholy accident which happen'd to a young man of the Town, occasion'd by a pistol bursting in his hand, which unhappily tore off two of his fingers.

This item was extracted from a letter at Marshfield dated November 8th 1745 on the same day the Worshipful Mayor, the Aldermen, and others of the Corporation, met at the Guildhall, and opened a subscription, and an Association, for the Defence of the King and Country, in this time of open and extreme dangers; to which a great many inhabitants liberally contributed. Ralph Allen raised a company of volunteers, one hundred strong it was said, and paid for their clothing, equipment and drilling. Beau Nash equally keen in showing his loyalty, obtained twenty pieces of artillery from Commodore Knowles in Bristol who had sent them to Bath, where they were placed in the Orange Grove.

Their presence possibly gave the citizens of Bath a sense of security and helped to soothe apprehensions then running rife throughout the country. Eyes and ears were on the alert for any suspicious persons in town, and it was reported that:

> A 'Scotch Gentleman' was seen in the city and believed to come from the rebel army and up to no good, it was hoped that the rascally Banditti may soon be Waded (i.e. dealt with as General Wade did during the 1715 uprising).

Happily neither men nor guns were needed in Bath against the Jacobites. The guns, known afterwards as Mr Nash's cannon, were, however, found very useful for firing when a royal birthday came round, or when an illustrious visitor arrived.

In the *Bath Chronicle* of November 15th there were reports of men signing up to defend the country against the rebel army:

> Upwards of 150 men from several parishes in the County of Surrey appeared in St. James's Park, and were enlisted into his Majestys service. As more men came forward to enlist, none were refused over five feet, five inches. There was also advices from Cornwall, that the Tinners have nearly completed two regiments for his Majestys service, and that as many more of those brave fellows are ready to enter, as their superiors shall think proper to encourage. His Majesty promised once the conflict was over the men would not be forced to stay in the army. It was reported from Alnwick that there is a fifty thousand weight of biscuit ordered for the Army, also 15.000 men, in high spirits, and longing for nothing more ardently than to attack the rebels as reported in the St. James Evening Post.

> From Whitehall – The *Gazette*. November 2nd 1745. An account of the progress of the rebels published by authority, being read with more than ordinary attention, we have copied them from the Gazette, without the intervention of other matter.

> Advices from Berwick of the 25th at night that the carriages which the rebels had demanded from different places, all came into Edinburgh upon the 22nd and 23rd, but were immediately dismissed; and the people belonging to them were told, they should have some notice before their march to get them ready again. Upon the 22nd they had a general review between Leith and Edinburgh. Upon the 26th Glenbucket's and the Atholl men marched to Musselburgh, gave out they were to stay there till further orders. The rebels seemed to be packing up their baggage

upon that day, and their cannon, consisting of seven pieces, were sent eastward. A detachment of 600 of their men was stationed at Alloway at a narrow passage upon the Firth, where they were erecting a battery to secure the passage and building flat-bottomed boats for bringing over their arms, &c. landed at Montrose and Stonehaven. The 'Ludlow' and 'Fox' Men of War were in the road at Leith. It was reported that the rebels had great differences amongst themselves.

They had a small camp upon the plain between Inverness and Dalkeith. Lord Loudon was at Inverness with a good number of men, and had by those accounts been join'd by the Sutherland people, the Monroes, &c. The Campbell's of Argylshire, were said to be in arms for the King, and encamp'd at Inverary. Other letters mention, that John Campbell, Esq., Lieut Col to Lord Loudon's Highland regiment, had, with the three companies thereof, attacked disarm'd and dispers'd 700 of the Macleans, who were upon their march to join the rebels near Edinburgh expecting those from Ireland, which is one day's march behind.

General Wade proposed halting at Newcastle a day or two, and then marching towards Edinburgh. The seven battalions from Flanders were all safely arriv'd at Newcastle and Berwick, together with the seven companies of Brackel's Dutch regiment, which had been in Holland. The following week the *Gazette* reported from *Whitehall* by letters from the North October 31st and November 4th.

There is an account that the rebels continue to seize on all ye horses, forage and provision, they can find between Berwick and Edinburgh, in order to distress his Majesty's troops on their march. Their counsels are too various and fluctuating, that they frequently contradict and countermand the order of the preceding day; they plunder the country and raise all the ready money they can lay their hands on from the collectors of the customs and excise, in the distribution of which to their chiefs and superiors, a few or none are contented with their proportion, and consequently there are great jealousies and ill blood amongst them. Marshal Wade proposed to March towards Berwick yesterday or today.

On Saturday the 26th, of last month, the main body of the rebels having almost entirely evacuated Edinburgh and Leith, pitched their tents to the west of Inverask Church: They had seven or eight pieces of Cannon pointed south-west of their camp: Their sick and some of the baggage were sent westward.

They had ordered 100 light wagons, and a number of baskets for carrying on horseback, to be made; and from the Gentlemen and Farmers of the Shire of East Lothian, had got between six and seven hundred of their best working horses. They have taken possession of a place on the Forth called Hagen's Nook, some miles below Stirling, and had placed a battery on both sides of the Forth at that place, to keep off the Men of War's boats that might hinder their crossing: One of these batteries consisted of six, the other of five pieces of Cannon.

On November 8th it was reported that the following pardon was offered to the rebels by Field Marshal Wade:

Whereas it hath represented to his Majesty, that several of his subjects inhabiting the Highlands of Scotland, and others, have been seduced by menaces and threatening of their chiefs and superiors, to take up arms, and enter into a most unnatural rebellion; his Majesty hath authorised me to assure all such, who shall return to their habitation, on or before the 12th day of November next, and become faithful to his Majesty and his Government, that they shall be objects of his Majesty's clemency; but if, after this his most gracious intention being signified, they shall continue in their rebellion, they will be proceeded against with rigour suitable to the nature of their crime. This pardon was given at the camp at Newcastle upon Tyne this 30th Day of October 1745.

The *Bath Journal* reported:

We are informed by private letters from Scotland, that when General Wade's declarations of granting fourteen days for the rebels to return to their allegiance were known in their camp, many of them were inclined to accept of it; upon which a strong guard was immediately ordered, to prevent any from deserting.

Newcastle prepared itself for a full-scale invasion, and set about repairing and mounting guns. There was a massive concentration of English, Dutch and German soldiers in the town. In his entry for November 8th 1745, shortly after the rebels had entered English territory, the historian John Sykes states:

Prince Maurice of Nassau, accompanied by Field Marshal Wade, and a great number of officers, reviewed the troops that were encamped on Newcastle Moor, where the army was drawn up in battle array, consisting of two grand lines, each three deep, and near two miles long.

Newcastle residents were ordered to deliver anything that could be used as a weapon to the Mayor's house.

Fires were lit around the outside of the town walls, and kept burning, to prevent a surprise attack. Evidently, the town was worried. A Jacobite spy called Nixon was captured, and he told his interrogators that Prince Charles planned to take Tynemouth Castle, where there was a great store of cannon and ammunition, and from there he intended to attack Newcastle from the east. On learning of the scale of the town's defences, however, the Prince decided to invade England down the west side, via Carlisle. Again Newcastle was spared a bloody confrontation with their old foe from the north.

It was reported in the *Evening News* that a gentleman who had recently left Edinburgh arrived at Newcastle and reported that all travellers were obliged to wear cockades for safety:

> You may walk Edinburgh thro' without seeing a person belonging to the town: All the shops are shut up, there being no such thing as traffic, unless making of shoes for the Highlanders, who do not stay in the town, but keep watch, and lie about the walls: Such as wear no Cockades are stripped, and the whole Country is impoverished, the rebels sparing neither Cattle, Grain or Utensils.

The Gazette continued to report from Whitehall on the progress of the rebels:

> The freshest intelligence from Scotland mentions the arrival of four ships in all, in the north ports of that Kingdom, with arms, &c. for the use of the rebels, viz, one at Montrose, two at Stonehaven and the fourth at Dunotyr: That the cargo of the first was carried south in eighty five carts; and two others in more than a hundred, drawn each by two horses. That they brought some brass cannon, and one piece of five inch bore, with some Gunners and Officers:
>
> That the small arms of the first cargo were carried part to Dunkeld and part to Perth, being intended for the Atholl men and McDonalds, and all the rest gone towards Edinburgh. That half of Lord Ogilvy's Men have deserted; and that a party of rebels were employed in forcing them to return, and Lord Strathmore's men to join them, threatening to burn their houses in case of refusal, whereupon many of the Country people were gone out of the way.
>
> That the rebels had small parties in the Passes upon the road to

Inverness, who searched all passengers, and about 40 men at Perth to guard the Officers, who are prisoners there: That the rebels who remained encamped at Dalkeith the 31st past, had received 1000 recruits, being the most part Atholl Men, with some few of the Gordons: Several are wounded and some carried chests of arms which were distributed amongst these recruits, upon their coming to the south side of the Forth. Late at night, on the 31st, about 400 of their men came to Dalkeith camp from Alowa, and brought with them six pieces of brass cannon, much the same size with those they had taken at Preston. That they had with them above 100 carts loaded partly with chests, and partly with biscuit and 12 or 16 French Engineers.

An extract of a letter from Glasgow was printed in *Scotch Affairs*:

On Thursday night the 'Happy Jenner' came up the River Forth, with orders to destroy the two batteries of the Rebels; but could not execute her orders for want of water; but she designs to enter between 3 and 4000 hogshead of tobacco newly arrived from Virginia.

The *London Gazette*, November 9th, at Whitehall, printed a letter from Berwick which had been written on the 3rd:

There are accounts that upon the 27th past a party of rebels had been at Glasgow to demand the old subsidy for the tobacco brought in seven ships, and just landed at Greenock, which amounted to 10,000 Sterling. That upon the 31st past two hundred small carts, in which were six field pieces, ammunition, small arms, &c. lately landed at Montrose, and which came over at Hagen's Nook, passed by on the west side of Edinburgh, and went to Dalkeith attended by two considerable bodies of the rebels: That the Pretenders son left Edinburgh about six that evening, and came the length of Pinkie, about four miles to the east of that City, with those of the rebels called the life-guards, and lay there that night. That all their baggage, six pieces of six pounders, and one field piece, were to be sent off that night or the next day to Dalkeith, and their whole army to follow at the same time:

That about one o'clock upon the 1st inst. The Pretender's son proceeded to Dalkeith, from which place a considerable body of Highlanders who called themselves the advanced guard, marched that evening to Pennycook, and another to Loan Head, both of which places are at a small distance from Dalkeith, upon the road leading westward to Peebles, Moffat, Carlisle, &c. those advanced parties gave out their entire army was to follow the next day: That the Pretender's son was to set out from Dalkeith upon the 3rd and that they were to march thro' Annandale to Carlisle: That the better to disguise their motions; billets for quarters had been sent to Musselburgh, Fisheraw, Inverask, Prestonpans, Tranet and Haddington, and other villages upon the east road to Berwick, whilst considerable numbers were to march by night to the westward: That they had along with them above a hundred and fifty carts and wagons full of baggage, besides great numbers of baggage horses, and that they gave out that their intention was to proceed into England, to endeavour to slip by the troops under Marshal Wade, and to get into Lancashire.

Lancashire was now on high alert, and in desperation the Mayor and gentlemen of Manchester wrote to General Wade for advice on what measures to take to deal with the rebels should they enter the town.

Wade replied from the camp at Newcastle:

To the Mayor and Gentlemen,
    I have just now received the favour of your letter of November 5th with the enclosed intelligence from Dumfries for which I am much obliged to you, although I had received the same word by word from Carlisle. I never doubted your showing commendable zeal you have done upon this occasion and I think you have acted very prudently in the resolution you have taken to ship off guns and other warlike stores should the rebels approach you for if their main body should venture to march into Lancashire it will be impossible in your present situation to repel them by force. But if they by quick marches should enter your Country I propose to march to your relief by the first way that is practicable for the Artillery to pass, which they tell us is from part of Yorkshire.
    All the advice I can give you is that if you have any armed forces as most other Counties have to make use of it by dividing it into small parties who may fire from every hedge and to keep the Rebels from separating from their main body to pillage and plunder which I think will embarrass them more than any other method that can be expected from County Regiments. And it is my humble opinion that the further the Rebels penetrate into England the more certain will be their destruction, tho' Particulars may suffer from their bold attempt.
    I am Mr. Mayor and Gentlemen your most humble servant George Wade at Newcastle Nov 6th, 1745.

Further reports from Newcastle on November 15th suggest that the Prince was introducing the Italian practice of poisoning there:

> For last Saturday or Sunday morning a Highland Boy, of about 14 or 15 years of age, came to Berwick, and being carried before General Handafyd, was asked several questions, when he pretended to have been one of Lord Loudan's Highlanders at the Battle of Preston, and that he was taken Prisoner by the Rebels, and being ill used by them he made his escape and got there; but he seem'd so cunning and evasive, that nothing could be made of him, upon which he was dismissed, with a charge to be taken care of. Soon after a Serjeant of Lord Loudan's Highlanders told him he was a young rogue, and did not belong to their Corps, and threatened him in his own language to have him hanged immediately if he did not confess; whereupon he own'd, that he was sent with a bottle of poison, and directed to introduce himself, if he could, into the Governor's kitchen, and there take the opportunity of sprinkling the contents upon some of their favourite dishes, and so poison the Governor and the Officers. He has been closely confined ever since. P.S. I saw a letter this day confirming the above, with the additional circumstances, of a woman being employed the same way, to poison the water where their horses drink.

The *Gentleman's Magazine*, November 15th, published a letter of November 12th from Mr Thomas Pattenson:

> The Mayor of Carlisle brings advice that on Saturday night the 9th inst that the City was surrounded by about 9000 Highlanders; that at three o'clock that afternoon he, the mayor, had received a message from them, to provide billets for 13,000 men, and to be ready that night, which he refused: that the next day, at three in the afternoon, he received a message in writing from the person styling himself Prince Charles, and subscribed Charles P.R. in the following words. Charles Prince of Wales, Regent of the Kingdoms of England, Scotland, France and Ireland, and the Dominions thereunto belonging, to the Mayor of Carlisle dated November 10th, at two in the afternoon.
> Being come to recover the King our father's just rights, for which we are arrived with all his authority, we are sorry to find that you should prepare to obstruct our passage: We therefore, to avoid the effusion of English Blood, hereby require you to open your gates, and let us enter, as we desire, in a peaceable manner; which if you do, we shall take care to preserve you from any insult,

the King our father's declarations and our own: But if you shall refuse us entrance, we are fully resolved to force it by such means as providence has put in to our hands, and then it will not perhaps be in our power to prevent the dreadful consequences which usually attend a town's being taken by default. Consider seriously of this, and let me have your answer within the space of two hours, for we shall take any further delay as a peremptory refusal, and take our measures accordingly.

The Pretended Prince, the Duke of Perth, with several other gentlemen, lay within a mile or two of the city. An attack was made on Carlisle but was rebuffed by the garrison throwing Granados at them and that the rebels had broke ground about 300 yards from the citadel, and at Spring Gardens, near the horse race ground, that they had been obliged to fetch provisions from as far as Hacket, about five mile from Carlisle.

A letter of November 15th from Marshal Wade was reported in the *Bath Chronicle*:

Mentions that upon the news received by him of the resolution of the rebels to return from Brampton, in order to make an attempt upon Carlisle, it had been determined by a Council via Hexham towards Carlisle to aid the City. In the meantime the Highland Army set about preparing batteries and scaling ladders and with the forces in place attacked Carlisle and the City surrendered. An account that a person sent from the Governor of Carlisle to Marshal Wade, reported, that it was agreed that the town should be delivered up to the rebels, but did not know the conditions. The Governor was determined to defend the Castle to the last extremity, and had prepared everything for that purpose. It was supposed that he will be able to hold out for eight days. We have since heard that on the 15th inst at noon the City of Carlisle surrendered at Ten o'clock that morning.

The following report from Whitehall was dated November 18th:

On Thursday last Carlisle was taken, and laid under a contribution 2000 l. They have given us a specimen of their barbarous politicks, by obliging the Country people both Men and Women, to march before them, carrying their scaling ladders to the Walls, by which means the inhabitants are deterred from firing, lest they should kill more friends than enemies. Yesterday the Army under Marshal Wade marched for Carlisle, and by their route are to be there on the 20th inst. They are to a man in high spirits, and are determined to destroy the villains that thus harass them in this severe season; so in a few days you will hear of a battle or the rebels flying before them.

His army, already affected by dysentery and low morale, were now faced with heavy falls of snow; the ground was so hard they could not pitch their tents: bad roads and with inadequate rations, starving, cold and marching for twelve hours in the day, they eventually reached Hexham on the 16th in a snowstorm of unequalled severity where Wade received the news that Carlisle had fallen to the rebels. Next morning some of his soldiers weakened by lack of food were found frozen to death.

The *Bath Journal* reported Wade's movements at Hexham:

Being adviced of the arrival there, on the 17th at midnight of the Army under his command, in order to the relief of Carlisle, and to give battle to the rebels; but that having received advice, as well of the surrender of that city and castle on the 15th as of the advance of the rebels to Penrith, and finding the roads thro' with a great quantity of snow that had fallen, in a manner to be impassable, it had been resolved by a council of war, to march the army back immediately to Newcastle.

Thomas Grosvenor addressed a letter to George Trevelyan, Esq. at Leahill in Devon dated at Pontefract, November 25th 1745:

Sir – You may be assured that the rebellion is a great prejudice to trade here as well as with you, but I think not to the degree you mention it is with you. We should think it monstrous to give 10s for a £20 bill, tho' premiums run pretty high. We have been greatly alarmed here with the Pretender's coming forward since the surrender of Carlisle, and it has been confidently said that a part of the rebels came on as far as Penrith and Kendall to bespeak quarters. But that they are returned to Kelso and the Borders. However, it has occasioned several people to remove their quarters and best effects to more distant places. But I hope that General Wade, who has a fine army, will stop their career and in a few days either demolish 'em or disperse 'em.

Mr. Blackett, it is said, is indefatigable at Newcastle, in consulting and providing for the safety of the town. It is well fortified and provided within with soldiers for its defence.

Postscript, we have expresses daily passing thro' the town to Lord Malton and Sir Rowland Winn, one whereof this morning imports that General Wade is making towards us, for the more convenient joining by Ligonier, as Edinburgh and the Borders are pretty well lined with the King's troops, to stop the return of the rebels, who, from reports and the nature of their situation begin to dwindle away very fast. Had they come forward they would have met with a warm reception in this county, we being all fast friends to the present Government.

Although the impassable state of the roads had prevented Wade from marching westward, Prince Charles continued his victorious march southward. A fresh army of 8,000 men, commanded by the Duke of Cumberland, was marching across Staffordshire. The Highlanders, under the able leadership of Lord George Murray, out-marched and outmanoeuvred Cumberland, and reached Derby on December 4th. The rebel army was now within reach of London, 125 miles away.

Chapter 14

The December Campaign

Wade's army, largely composed of European mercenaries, marched towards Carlisle in a vain attempt to prevent its fall. They were depleted by sickness and defeated by the bitter weather, and without firing a shot or drawing a sword they struggled back to Newcastle. The Jacobite Army took Penrith on November 22nd, then Preston and Manchester, where they were received with enthusiasm but were unable to muster many recruits. The speed of the advance was impressive – the army covering twenty miles a day.

The *Gentleman's Magazine* reported letters sent to Whitehall from Lancashire, Cheshire and Staffordshire, on November 30th:

> Being accounts that about 200 rebels had that day come to a pass three miles from Manchester, leading to Knutsford, and had made a sort of bridge over the river, by filling it with trees they had felled, and advanced to Altrincham: That afternoon they gave out that they had enlisted great numbers of men at Manchester to which place they returned. They had 16 pieces of Cannon and a great number of covered wagons, and near 100 horses laden. By the 3rd a party of rebels are at Ashbourn. They have taken all the horses they could lay their hands on though a witness stated they were in a very jaded condition. Amongst the rebels were many old men and boys of 15 and 16 years of age, all without shoes or stockings. It was reported from Mansfield that the rebels were upon their march from Ashbourn to Derby. By one that saw them we hear, they appeared to be a good deal fatigued, their yesterday's march having been a great one. At four in the morning the Pretender's son entered Derby with 450 horse, and 2.300 foot. The rest, with the artillery and baggage, were then at Ashbourn and did not arrive until later that afternoon.

Less than a month after entering England, the Prince reached Derby on December 4th. Lord George Murray had misled the Duke of Cumberland by leading a small force west, as if to link up with the Jacobites from Wales and Bristol. As Cumberland moved to prevent this, the Prince outflanked him in the east and reached Derby. There was little support for the Stuarts amongst the townspeople, but there was consternation in London when the news arrived that the Jacobites were now only 125 miles away. It was possible that the Prince might outmanoeuvre Cumberland, whose forces were grouped around Lichfield, Coventry and Newcastle-under-Lyne, at the same time as Sir Watkin Williams Wynn was marching from Wales with supporters for the Prince. The Duke of Beaufort was preparing in the west.

On December 5th the news reached London that Derby had fallen to the rebels. There was consternation bordering on panic. The next morning was called 'Black Monday', as the Chevalier de Johnstone, aide-de-camp to Lord George Murray, remarked with satisfaction. There was a run on the bank, the potential effects of which it is said to have escaped only by the expedient of refusing to pay in any coin other than sixpences. George II had the royal yacht made ready to take him to the Continent, should the Prince reach London. Many of the well-to-do went to earth with their silver and valuables. The panic subsided on hearing that the Jacobites were retreating from Derby and heading north on the advice of Lord George Murray, who advised returning to Scotland and waiting for the spring before launching a new invasion. The failure resulted from the lack of support from south of the Border, combined with the desertion of some of the Scots, and the failure of support from the French. The Jacobites now had the disadvantage of facing Wade's army, a formidable force to the rear, and Cumberland with 8,000 men.

Early in December the Allied Army appears to have passed through Tadcaster or, what seems more likely, to have taken either the road from Leeds through Harewood to Ripon or the North Road through Wetherby to Borrowbridge, where the forces arrived early in December en route for Newcastle. Wade dispatched a flying column under General Oglethorpe from Wetherby via Leeds and Bradford in order to intercept, if possible, the Prince's northward retreat. An old woman, Betty Jackson, who died at Holbeck near Leeds in 1828, aged 106, used to relate that when she was a young woman she accompanied the packhorses with rations to Marshal Wade's army, lying about Tadcaster. The army on arriving at Leeds were billeted upon the able inhabitants, and it is said that the General was the guest of the Wades at Kirkstall Grange.

Again many of the inhabitants took the precaution of hiding their plate and other valuables; but, as no slaughter followed, all survived to dig up their treasures again. From the absence of old trees in the vicinity, it is supposed that the soldiers used all the timber they could find for firewood. Wade's encampment is commemorated in the names Wade Lane, Camp Road, etc., and it is celebrated as the last tented field in actual war in England.

On December 6th and 7th, General Wade's army was encamped at Ferrybridge in Yorkshire. In the near vicinity was the village of Barwick-in-Elmet, which, being close to the Great North Road, was called upon to assist the army in two ways: conveying stores and billeting passing troops. The parish accounts record charges for carrying straw, going with the artillery and baggage from Wetherby to Borrowbridge, Ferrybridge and Pontefract. There are a number of entries which indicate that the Great North Road was busy with military personnel. It was normal for the parish to give each soldier 2d. to see them on their way. Over the following weeks sick soldiers were carried from Barwick to Aberford and the parish continued to assist the wounded and disbanded soldiers over the months ahead.

The accounts show that the armies of the time lacked the facilities for caring for the lame and wounded and that largely they were discharged and had to fend for themselves. From the records of the parish it is possible to tell when General Wade's army was moving north and then south. Barwick-in-Elmet, like so many villages near the route of the marching army was able to give support and comfort to soldiers, and particularly to several Dutch soldiers, far from home and in need of help.

An account from the London news-sheets, dated December 12th, reports:

> Last Sunday night Marshal Wade with his whole army marched from Doncaster and Ferrybridge towards Lancashire, in order to cut off the retreat of the Rebels. There were reports of up to 500 Highlanders deserting from the Pretender's army. On December 10th, Coventry reported the rebels were back at Ashbourn, and

went to Leek that night. They have taken all the horses they could lay their hands upon, and have plundered and done great damage. They had 15 pieces of cannon and one mortar. From Leek the rebels marched to Macclesfield and were said to be 1000 strong. From advices from Lancashire on the 12th December the rebels had quitted Manchester and with great precipitation, on the near approach of his Royal Highness the Duke, who, with his horse, and the Foot that were mounted, had by two forced marches got near up to them; so that it is expected the next accounts will bring advice that his Royal Highness has made himself master of their baggage.

Further intelligence came in from Derby on December 10th:

The rebels are gone from this place, and we have heard this morning that they are at Macclesfield and Congleton; but they shift so often, that there is no certain account where the main body lies. General Wade is at Doncaster, and stays there till he hears whether the rebels go for Wales, or return to Scotland; his men are encamped on Ferrybridge Moor: This is the best account we hear of him. The rebels plundered everybody of their guns and pistols; and some sorry fellows who enlisted with them gave an account to them of the Gentlemen's horses and guns, which they took away. The rebels marched out of Leek on Sunday morning; it was believed for Macclesfield and Congleton: They are 6000 in number; such a set of thieves and robbers, as eyes never beheld in the World! They are eaten up with vermin, and all manner of uncleanliness. They have done a great deal of damage here and raised a considerable sum of money, &c: great part of the excise on ale, malt, leather, candles, soap &c. was collected by them; if they refused, a sword and pistol was clasped to their breast; a great many good horses were taken in and about the Country without asking questions; most of the Gentlemen who had paid their subscriptions for the present Government paid their subscriptions to the Pretender; if refused, their houses were threatened to be burnt or plundered by the Officers: Upon a pretence of searching for arms and horses, they looked into all places for valuable things, as money, &c. and frequently took the same.

It is unfair to judge the condition the rebels found themselves in. They had spent many weeks on the road from one town to the next without proper washing facilities or funds to buy the necessary clothing. The English army fared little better, and during

December the committee at the Guildhall in London, by orders of the Duke of Cumberland and Field Marshal Wade, applied for a subscription to supply the following:

> 12,000 pair of breeches, 12,000 woollen caps, 10,000 pair of knitted woollen gloves, and 9000 pair of woollen spaterdashes, to be forthwith provided for the use of the army. It was also resolved that 5000 l. part of the subscription money be set apart for the rewarding of maimed or wounded soldiers, and 300.1 appointed as Marshal Wade shall direct for the recovery of the sick, in augmentation of the allowance granted by the Crown.

The rebels who supported the Prince to regain his throne were left to their own devices, and when the conflict finally came to an end many would face the death sentence.

The news-sheets of the day continued reporting the whereabouts and number of the rebel army. It was reported they were in Macclesfield, and then at Leek, and some said they had taken the road to Stockport; it was reported the army was making for Wales. Reporting, misreporting and abundance of rumour on both sides turned the campaign into a military game of blind man's buff – a game Wade was no longer in a fit state to play. Now suffering badly from asthma, Wade realised he could no longer continue to command his army. The army was not prepared for a winter campaign and Wade's second-in-command, Lord Tyrawley, complained that Wade was 'muddleheaded' and would not give him his map. There were problems with supply of bread, coal, carriages and straw, all for want of the public supporting them with funds. Such problems were now too much for the Field Marshal. The weeks spent commanding his army on the move trying to outwit the Prince in the most atrocious weather conditions were demoralising even for fit, young soldiers; for a man of seventy-two, in failing health, it was far worse. His command passed to General Henry Hawley, who was ruthless and rough-tongued, and a notorious disciplinarian. Brutal even by contemporary standards, he did not hesitate to hang or execute his men for desertion or cowardice, and he earned for himself the nickname Hangman Hawley.

On taking leave of his regiment, Wade said his farewells to his son, Captain George Wade; his nephew, Captain William Wade; and Captain James Wolfe, later the hero at Quebec. Wade must have wondered how many of his family and dear friends he would see again; and, deeply depressed at what he saw as a dereliction of duty, he made his way home down the Great North Road to face censure from those who had put so much faith in him. After a distinguished career facing the enemy abroad, he was not willingly leaving his army to face a rebel force at home.

He knew the clansmen of old; he admired their fighting skills, their efficiency with the claymore and broadsword, and their ability to withstand even the coldest winter among the hills, wrapped in their thick plaids.

The *Bath Chronicle* reported that on January 2nd His Excellency, Field Marshal Wade arrived at his house in Burlington Street.

Wade returned home a discredited leader. At his best he was not a military genius – not a Marlborough or Wellington. Under four successive monarchs he had won his way to the highest honours in the army. He was brave and wary, generous and methodical; his merits were more solid than brilliant, but until his error at Newcastle they gained the confidence of the troops he led and the government he served. Even in his darkest hour, however, the King continued to hold him in high esteem.

Wade was once again the subject of a verse, but on this occasion a Scottish song was to bring humiliation:

> Horse, foot, and dragoons, from lost Flanders they call,
> With Hessians and Danes, and the devil and all,
> The hunters and rangers, led by Oglethorpe,
> And the church, at the bum of the Bishop of York.
> And, pray, who so fit to lead forth this parade,
> As the babe of Tangier, my old grandmother Wade?
> Whose cunning's so quick, but whose motion's so slow,
> That the rebels march'd on, whilst he stuck in the snow!

Here is another satire written at the time:

> Cope could not cope,
> Nor Wade wade through the snow,
> Nor Hawley haul his cannon to the foe.

Like 'Rule Britannia', the national anthem of Great Britain, 'God Save the King/Queen' was composed by Thomas Augustine Arne

(1710–78). It was first sung in 1745 during the Jacobite invasion of England. It was performed after the staging of Ben Jonson's play *The Alchemist* at the Theatre Royal in London. The invasion constituted a serious threat to the monarchy at that time and this explains why the words of the national anthem have the form of a prayer of petition for the safety and well-being of the monarch. The invasion also explains the following anti-Scottish words in the fourth verse. The lines were omitted when the song was adopted as the British national anthem.

> God save Great George our King,
> Long live our noble King,
> God save the King.
> Send him victorious,
> Happy and Glorious,
> Long to reign over us,
> God save the King.
>
> O Lord our God arise,
> Scatter his enemies,
> And make them fall:
> Confound their politics,
> Frustrate their knavish tricks,
> On him our hopes we fix,
> God save us all.
>
> The choicest gifts in store,
> On him be pleas'd to pour,
> Long may he reign!
> May he defend our laws,
> And ever give us cause,
> To sing with heart and voice
> God save the King.
>
> Lord grant that Marshal Wade
> May by thy mighty aid
> Victory bring.
> May he sedition hush,
> And like a torrent rush,
> Rebellious Scots to crush,
> God save the King.

Over the next few months, the news-sheets of the day continued reporting the happenings in Scotland, and in January 1746 reports came in that the army under General Hawley had been defeated by the Jacobites at the Battle of Falkirk. In less than an hour, Hawley and all of his forces were driven from the field. Between 500 and 600 of his troops were killed or wounded, and several hundred were taken prisoner. The losses on the Jacobite side were reported as only fifty killed and seventy wounded.

There was also a report in the *London News* on February 10th 1746:

> Near on 200 soldiers who were in the Battle of Preston Pans, under Sir John Cope, landed at Tower Wharf from Scotland: The poor men were in a most miserable shocked condition; some without arms and legs and others with their noses cut off, and eyes put out, besides hacked and mauled in many parts of the body, after the most terrible manner.

A Whig historian writing at the time stated:

> The soldiers threw down their arms and surrendered prisoners, but the enemy would grant no quarter. Charles Edward Stuart arriving on the battlefield witnessed the spectacle with horror. He pleaded with his troops to make them prisoners and spare them; exclaiming 'they are my father's subjects'.

Inverness fell to the Jacobites in February 1746, and then began nearly two months of successful campaigning in the Highlands. Unfortunately for the rebel army, however, the tide now turned against them. The Allied Army followed the Jacobites as they withdrew into the Highlands. During the night of April 15th the rebels mounted an abortive attack on the government camp, and then withdrew to Culloden Moor, five miles east of Inverness. The following morning Cumberland's army advanced with the intention of inflicting a decisive defeat on the enemy. The Duke of Cumberland had fifteen infantry battalions, four regiments of dragoons, Scottish volunteer units and sixteen guns – a total of 9,000. The Jacobite Army had twenty-one infantry battalions, 400 cavalry and twelve guns – a total of 5,400. Cumberland's army lost fifty killed and 239 wounded, while the Jacobites lost 1,000 killed and 558 taken prisoner. All their guns were captured. The rebel army at Culloden received a mortal blow and the military power of the clans was broken. The Jacobite cause and the attempt to put Charles Edward Stuart on the throne died in twenty minutes on the battlefield at Culloden, never to recover. Thousands would pay the price for supporting the Prince. And the man in whose name they fought deserted the field and eventually made his way into exile to end his days as 'The King over the Water'.

Twice in half a century the Highland clans had rebelled and now it was the government's duty to take such measures of precaution and punishment as would prevent a third rising. They did so, but within the limits of prudence they were merciful. The result is that no battle has been fought on British soil since Culloden. If Cumberland was harsh in killing prisoners, he was no more severe in punishment than was normal for the time. Had Prince Charles been successful in his conquest of England, the same could be said of the Jacobites; their orders at Penrith on December 20th were to 'give the English no quarter'.

There were reports of terrible atrocities committed by Cumberland and his army; some Jacobites were murdered in cold blood. One report stated that seventeen officers confined in Culloden House, recovering from their wounds, were taken out and shot. The killing fields of Falkirk and Prestonpans were still fresh in the minds of many, and this provides a possible reason for the excessive cruelty meted out. General Hawley needed no such excuse and openly encouraged his men on the battlefield to bayonet any Jacobite still alive. One officer who refused was Brevet Major James Wolfe (later to achieve fame upon the Heights of Abraham in Quebec, Canada). He was ordered to kill Charles Fraser the younger of Inverlochy as he lay wounded on the ground. Wolfe refused, but a private soldier carried out the execution in his place.

Had the Battle of Culloden been fought under the command of General Wade, who was known for compassion towards his fellow man, it is probable that more lives would have been saved and the wounded cared for. From the years Wade spent in Scotland, he had learned to respect the Highlanders and would not have rejoiced in their downfall or the terrible fate that awaited them. One cannot imagine Wade authorising the hacking to death of prisoners who had surrendered, or the summary execution of wounded men. It was not in the nature of the man. On hearing these reports, Wade must have been heartbroken at the savagery of the government troops.

In volumes published in 1928 and 1929, the Scottish History Society gives the following data:

> In all 3471 prisoners were taken. Of these 936 were transported, 120 were hanged, 40 of them deserters from the English Army. Another 222 were banished from the Kingdom; 1,287 were exchanged or released as prisoners of war; 88 died in prison; 58 escaped; and 76 received a conditional pardon. That left 684 who appear in the returns under the heading 'method of disposal not known'. Four Peers were arrested, taken to London and put on trial; they were Kilmarnock, Derwentwater, Lovat and Balmerino. All four received the death sentence.

Simon Fraser, Lord Lovat, had changed sides once too often and, on hearing that the rebel army had been defeated, he went on the run. He was captured by Captain Fergusson, and brought to London where he was lodged in the Tower awaiting his trial. On March 9th 1747 he was put on trial in Westminster Hall, and he was convicted on March 18th. Lovat conducted himself with great dignity throughout, and when sentenced to be executed on April 9th he showed remarkable courage. Whilst waiting for the fateful day to arrive, he arranged to have a fine suit of clothes made, and found enough time for Hogarth to paint his portrait.

Lovat was taken to Tower Hill and beheaded – the last person to be publicly executed in Britain. In a final ironic twist of fate, one of the wooden stands set up for the Londoners to watch the execution collapsed, resulting in several deaths. Lovat was not alone when he went to meet his Maker.

It was now time for the government to look into the way the war was conducted and to bring to account those they felt were responsible for letting the Prince get as far as Derby and outwit them. Sir John Cope, Colonel Peregrine Lascelles and Brigadier Fowke went before courts-martial. General Wade, who came in for so much censure, was not on the list. It was considered he did the best that could be expected given the atrocious weather conditions prevalent at the time, and his age and the state of his health were taken into consideration. It was said that Wade was utterly baffled and perplexed by the movements of the rebels; this criticism, it must be said, was also levelled at the Duke of Cumberland. Prince Charles very cleverly outwitted the army until his downfall at Culloden. The Court Martial Bill was reported in full in the *London Gazette*. Those on the board were George Wade, Cadogan, John Foliat, Richmond, Lenox, Aubigny and John Guise.

The *Gentleman's Magazine* stated:

> The report made to his majesty by the board of general officers appointed to examine the conduct of Sir John Cope, and Col. Lascelles, from the breaking of the Rebellion, till the action was over at Preston Pans; and likewise into that of Brigadier General Fowke, from the time he took the command of the two regiments at Edinburgh, till the said action was over.

> The several examinations being finished, all parties were dismissed; whereupon we the said Field Martial, and other general officers before named, having duly weighed and considered the several matters laid before us, upon our examination into the conduct, behaviours, and proceedings of Lieut. General John Cope, Colonel Peregrine Lascelles, and the Brigadier Thomas Fowke, contained in the foregoing state thereof, do, in further obedience to your Majesty's said warrant, most humbly report, that having made all enquiry we could after proper persons, who were able to give us information relating to the matters aforesaid, and having examined all such as could be brought before us, there being several others whose duty on your Majesty's service in Scotland would not admit of their leaving to us, and we are unanimously of the opinion that Sir John Cope, made all the proper and necessary preparations for the support of the troops, with as much dispatch as he was able, both in Edinburgh and Stirling.

> That he also made proper applications to the chiefs of the clans that were reputed to be well affected to your Majesty's troops. That he used all possible diligence and expedition before and on his march to Dalwhinney, considering the difficulties and disappointments he met with that his attacking the rebels on the Corryarrick, with any other prospect of success was impracticable.

> That his march to Inverness is justified by the unanimous opinion of the council of war, and the repeated assurances of being joined on the march, and at Inverness by the clans that were well affected to your Majesty and Government; of which he afterwards found himself disappointed, except by 200 Monroes who marched with him from Inverness to Aberdeen. That his going to Aberdeen, and then by sea to Dunbar, was the

only proper measure he had left to take. That Sir John Cope's disposition of his body of troops on the field of action was judicious, and the ground on which they were engaged (according to the plan and description of many officers who were present) appears to have been well chosen.

That he did his duty as an officer, both before, and after the action and his personal behaviour was without reproach; and that the misfortune on the day of action was owing to the shameful behaviour of the private men, and not to any misconduct or misbehaviour of Sir John Cope or any of the officers under his command. As to Colonel Peregrine Lascelles, it does not appear to us, that any misconduct or misbehaviour can be laid to his charge; he having plainly proved that he was at his post before and at the action.

As to Brigadier General Thomas Fowke, we are of the opinion, that his march from Calbridge to Dunbar was right; and the offers he made twice to the Lord Provost of Edinburgh to march into the city with the dragoons for its defence (tho refused) were commendable; and that his behaviour in the action was also without reproach; and that he did not quit the field of action before the troops were entirely broke and dispersed. Upon the whole, we are unanimously of the opinion, that Sir John Cope's behaviour had been unblameable; and there is no ground for accusation against the said Sir John Cope, Colonel Peregrine Lascelles, or Brigadier Fowke. All which is most humbly submitted to your Majesty.

Signed. George Wade, Cadogan, John Foliat, Richmond, Lenox and Aubigny and John Guise.

There were many who spoke up for Sir John Cope, and worthy of special mention is the Lord President of Scotland. Writers of history through the years have given damning evidence against his character. A careful study of the facts have produced a very different story. General Sir Robert Cadell, KCB, in *Sir John Cope and the Rebellion of 1745*, states that a distinguished officer who was made a KB for showing distinguished bravery at the Battle of Dettingen can scarcely be looked upon as a coward.

General Cope also had a great reputation as a gallant. On one of his many visits to Bath, in an attempt to cure his gout, he caught St Anthony's fire (erysipelas) by drinking the waters, and this led Dr William Oliver, physician to the Bath Mineral Water Hospital and inventor of the Bath Oliver biscuit, to inscribe to him some verses, being his advice on catching the disease:

See gentle Cope with love and gout oppress'd
   Alternate torments rattling in his breast,
   Trys as a cure, but tampers still in vain,
   What eases one, augments the other pain.
The charming girl who strives to lend relief,
   Instead of healing heightens all his grief,
He drinks for health, but then for love he sighs;
   Health's in her hand, destruction in her eyes;
She gives us water, but with each touches alas
   The wicked girl electrifies the glass;
To ease the gout we swallow draughts of love,
   And then, like Etna, burst in fires above.
Sip not, dear Knight, the daughter's liquid fire,
   But take the healing beverage from the sire,
'Twill ease your gout, for love no cure is known,
   The God of physick could not heal his own.

St Anthony's fire is an eruptive skin disease caused by a toxin (ergot), produced by a mould on cereal plants. A pilgrimage to the shrine of St Anthony was supposed to cure it miraculously. The cure probably resulted from moving to an area where cereals other than rye or barley were a staple food. The mould, which may be found in bread, can contract the arteries and lead to gangrene and death. Sir John Cope, it would appear, contracted the disease from the waters at Bath.

Chapter 15

Wade in Retirement

No City, dear Mother, this City excels
In charming sweet sounds both of fiddles and bells;
I thought, like a fool, that they only would ring
For a wedding, or a judge, or the birth of a King;
But I found 'twas for me that the good natured people
Rung so hard that I thought they would pull down the steeple;
So I took out my purse, as I hate to be shabby,
And paid all the men when they came from the abbey;
Yet some think it strange they should make such a riot
In a place where sick folk would be glad to be quiet:
But I hear 'tis the business of this Corporation
To welcome in all the great men of the nation;
For you know there is nothing diverts or employs
The minds of great people like making a noise;
So with bells they contrive all as much as they can
To tell the arrival of any such man
If a broker, or statesman, a gamester, or peer,
A naturalised Jew, or a Bishop, comes here,
Or an eminent trader in cheese should retire
Just to think of the business the State may require;
With horns and with trumpets, with fiddles and drums,
They'll strive to divert him as soon as he comes;

Christopher Anstey

In September 1747, Wade's return to Bath, as with that of all persons of note, was announced in the newspaper, along with Lord St John, and Tyrawley, Countess Strathmore, Lady Chichester, Richard Nash, Esq., Sir John Strange, Sir Maynard Gearing, Lady

Newgate and others. All were welcomed with the ringing of the abbey bells.

With the last of his military duties behind him Wade was able to devote more time to his constituents in Bath. The *Bath Chronicle* announced on July 6th 1747:

> Field Marshal Wade wrote a handsome letter to the Mayor and Corporation of this City, wherein he mentions his desire of being a representative in Parliament for the said City once again: and it is not doubted but the said worthy gent will be chosen.

Wade was indeed duly elected that day to serve the said constituency. For their second member they chose someone much less distinguished, but one who was well known and popular in Bath – Robert Henley, a lawyer who had just inherited family estates in Hampshire.

Wade thanked the corporation for electing him, and as usual he donated a handsome sum of money for entertainments and improvements. There may have been a visit to Ralph Allen. Allen enjoyed showing friends and visitors round his house and most were probably shown first the Blue Parlour, where they would see a half-length portrait of Allen's great friend and patron in an elegant golden frame.

Allen was a very hospitable host, and among those who were welcomed as house guests was Henry Fielding, who later recreated Allen as Squire Allworthy in *Tom Jones*. Another distinguished guest was Alexander Pope, who always found a warm welcome at Prior Park and the certainty of cultured and amusing company. There was also Philip Dormer Stanhope, 4th Earl of Chesterfield, who had taken a house in Pierrepont Street, primarily because, like so many others, he hoped the waters would ease his gout and dispel the vapours. This did not distract from his love of gambling, strolling along the newly built Parades, and attending the balls at the Assembly Rooms. Chesterfield worked with Allen on the hospital scheme, and it was from Bath that he wrote many of his famous letters to his son, and where in old age he gave utterance to his celebrated *bon-mot*: "Tyrawley and I have been dead these two years, but we don't choose to have it known."

In 1742 Chesterfield wrote to Dr George Cheyne from London to thank him for his book and medical advice. The following letter is typical of many letters from grateful patients benefiting from the treatment they received in Bath:

> Your enquiries and advice concerning my health are very pleasing marks of your remembrance and friendship; which, I assure you, I value as I ought. It is true, I have, during these last three months had frequent returns of my giddiness, languors, and other nervous symptoms, for which I have taken vomits; the first did me good, the others rather disagreed with me. It is the same with my diet; sometimes the lowest agrees, at other times disagrees, with me. In short, after all the attention and observation I am capable of, I can say what does me good and what not. My constitution conforms itself so much to the fashion of the times, that it changes almost daily its friends for its enemies, and its enemies for its friends. Your alkalised mercury, and your burgundy, has proved its two most constant friends. I take them both now, and with more advantage than other medicine. I propose going to the Spa as soon as the season will permit, having really benefited by those waters last year; and I find my shattered tenement admits of but half repairs and requires them annually.
>
> The Corpus Sanum, which you wish me, will never be my lot; but the mens sana, I hope, will be continued to me, and then I shall better bear the infirmities of the body. Hitherto, far from impairing my reason, they have only made me more reasonable, by subduing the tumultuous and troublesome passions. I enjoy my friends and my books as much as ever, and I seek for no other enjoyments; so that I am become a perfect philosopher; but whether malgre moi or no, I will not take upon me to determine, not being sure that we do not owe more of our merit to accidents, than our pride and self-love are willing to ascribe to them.
>
> I read with great pleasure your book, which your bookseller sent me according to your directions. The physical part is extremely good, and the metaphysical part may be so too, for what I know; and I believe it is; for, as I look upon all metaphysics to be guess-work or imagination, I know no imagination likelier to hit upon the right than yours; and I will take your guess against any other meta-physician's whatsoever. That part, which is founded upon knowledge and experience, I look upon as a work of public utility; and for which the present age and their posterity may be obliged to you, if they will be pleased to follow it.
>
> I am, etc –

Dr Cheyne was one of the most famous doctors of his time – a humorous, witty man, well loved by his patients. He lived some years at Bath, where he was an authority on the spleen, gout, and diet. Cheyne later published a new theory of fevers on the mechanical system. Born in Aberdeen in 1671, he went to London in 1702, where he was elected a Fellow of the Royal Society, and in later years set up a practice in Bath. A larger-than-life figure, weighing an amazing thirty-two stones, Cheyne warned 'Folks use their physicians as they do their laundresses; they send their linen to be cleaned in order to be dirtied again.'

Wade donated another generous sum towards the building of the Mineral Water Hospital, and when the foundation stone was laid in 1738 the *London Evening Post* reported:

> Last Thursday, being the Day appointed for the laying of the intended foundation stone of the General Hospital of this City, above twenty trustees and contributors met at the Rummer Tavern, and proceeded from thence to the place appointed for erecting that Hospital, where the first stone was laid, on which was the following inscription: This stone was the first which was laid in the Foundation of the General Hospital at Bath July 6th, A.D. 1738 – God Prosper the Charitable Undertaking. When the ceremony was over, the Gentlemen returned to the 'Rummer', where his Majesty's Health, that of the Prince and Princess of Wales, General Wade, and other benefactors, were drunk, all the demonstration of joy possible shewn on the Occasion, everyone appearing pleased with a Design so excellently well calculated for the Good of Mankind in general, and the Welfare and the Happiness of the Poor, Wretched and Miserable in particular. A handsome present was made to the workmen and the Bells rung on this happy occasion.

Wade was president of the hospital in 1741, and later one of the governors until his death. Ralph Allen was the president in 1742, and during the next fifty years the list of presidents of the hospital was impressive. They included Frederick, Prince of Wales, Earl Spencer, the Archbishop of York, and Lord Palmerston.

Soldiers appear regularly in the early hospital records, particularly when the British Army was engaged in action. Provisions were made for the large numbers who were admitted in the aftermath of 1745 and 1746. The soldiers were required to bring a certificate from their commanding officers, signifying to what corps they belonged, and stating that they would be received back into the same corps when discharged from the hospital. But it was necessary that their cases be described, and the description sent in advance, and they were required to bring with them £3 caution money. A subscription was carried on at the Guildhall in 1746 towards the 'Relief, Support and Encouragement of the Soldiers employed in suppressing the late Rebellion, in consideration shown by the Governors of the said Hospital that they may continue the like Charitable Benevolence to them for the future'.

What kind of treatment might Wade have expected for his gout in the 18th century?

> When the invalid suffered from frequent acute attacks, a course of the waters once a year or twice a year was said to lengthen the period between attacks, and if persevered in to prevent their recurrence. The waters were so powerfully stimulating in their effects that for most people a bath every second day was as much as they could stand. A course of eight to twelve baths was recommended with treatment lasting over six weeks to bring about a marked difference in the patient's health. It was also considered beneficial to drink one glass of the mineral water in the morning before breakfast, and one in the evening. Gout in all its forms greatly benefited from this treatment. After bathing the patient would experience a state of wellbeing, his spirits raised, and the appetite sharpened and secretions augmented. Then he would be carried home wrapped in hot blankets in a sedan chair and this feeling of well-being would last for some considerable time.

Wade had lived life to the full, dined well and enjoyed an excess of alcohol, and a love of the fairer sex. The pleasure and comfort of the warm mineral waters would give him some respite from the pain in his joints and enable him, refreshed, to enjoy all the entertainments Bath had to offer.

From the time of Wade's first visit, Bath had developed from an insignificant to a beautiful Georgian city. He witnessed the building of Queen Square, started back in 1727, and Pierrepont Street was begun in the same year. The Palladian town house built for Ralph Allen in 1727 lies hidden from view and is only seen through a space between the buildings in York Street. After Allen's removal to Prior Park the house was used as the post office. Wade did not live, however, to see the building of the upper town, the Grand Circus or the magnificent Royal Crescent.

During his last stay in Bath there was time to socialise, visit the playhouse, and indulge in gambling. There was a fine ball at

Mr Simpson's and music playing at the Pump Room. There was great excitement on Monday October 5th in the marketplace, when:

> a purse of five guineas will be played for at Sword and Dagger. He that breaks most heads in fair play, to have the purse, the following day will be played for at Backsword in the same place for a purse of three guineas; on the same terms. To begin each day at ten in the morning; and every man to mount the stage ready dressed, or be excluded from playing.

There were the usual visits to the coffee houses for the exchange of news, gossip and opinion, including the topic of the late troubled times, as Wade visited his army friends then resident in the city. Among them were Sir John Cope and General Edward Wolfe at his home in Trim Street. His son, James Wolfe, was present at the Battle of Dettingen in 1743, later followed Wade in his futile campaign of 1745, and served under General Hawley at Culloden. In 1759, as the hero of Quebec, he went ahead of his men to scale the Heights of Abraham, but was wounded in the chest by a musket ball at the moment of victory. He died a hero in the eyes of his men, and his dying words were "Now, God be praised, I die happy." The death of Montcalm in the same battle put an end to the dream of a French empire in America.

For Wade there may have been visits to Corsham Court, the home of his friend, Sir Paul Methuen, or the Burlingtons at Marston Court, both within a short distance of Bath. Just a short walk from his home in the Abbey Church Yard were two of the best-known bookshop-libraries in the country, run by William Leake at 18 The Parades and 5 The Walks, where Wade would be sure to buy a copy of the publication in weekly parts of *Flanders Delineated*, or, 'A View of the Austrian and French Netherlands' noting castles, forts, towns and accounts of remarkable sieges, along with illustrated maps of the several countries dedicated to Field Marshal Wade by an officer of the Allied Army in Flanders. The whole will be comprised in 12 numbers at three pence a copy.' Subscribers were assured that should the numbers exceed 12, then the rest would be given gratis.

Soon it was time for Wade to leave the city he had come to love and journey back to his home in Highgate. During this his last visit in 1747 he contributed another handsome donation of £500 to the cost of building a neat (calf) butchers' market.

During his time in Parliament, Wade had voted assiduously with the administration, missing only one out of fourteen recorded divisions between 1716 and 1746. He spoke frequently on army matters in support of the government; and when Pulteney complained, in January 1732, that the British received far more pay than the French and Germans, he replied:

> It is well known that what the German Army come short of ours in pay they do more than make up by plundering upon the countries where they are quartered.

On March 28th and 30th 1732 he spoke on Sir John Barnard's proposals for reducing the interest on the national debt to 3%, unsuccessfully moving an amendment to substitute 3.5%.

He was capable of taking an independent line on other subjects – for instance, opposing on disciplinary grounds an opposition motion on February 13th 1734 that an officer not above the rank of colonel should not be removed except by court martial or an address of Parliament. He defended the government's proposals for raising new troops. On March 2nd 1741 he spoke against a clause in a press bill providing that volunteers should be entitled to £6 a year for life, arguing that pressed men should share this bounty.

In preparation for his retirement, Wade acquired two acres of land in Southwood Lane, Highgate; and, after demolishing the existing house, he set about building a fine new house. The architect who designed it is unknown; Wade may have engaged a local builder who was versed in the current architectural fashion. Wade retained his house in London designed by Lord Burlington. During his campaign in Flanders he brought back a very large cartoon by Rubens – so large that it would not fit into the rooms in his house. After Wade's death, Walpole referred to the cartoon in a letter to Mrs Montagu in 1748:

> I went to see Marshal Wade's house, which is selling by auction; it is worse contrived on the inside than is conceivable, all to humour the beauty of the front. Lord Chesterfield said, "it is literally true that all the directions he gave my Lord Burlington, was to have a place for a large cartoon (Meleager and Atlanta) of Reubens that he had brought back from Flanders but my Lord found it necessary to have so many correspondent doors, that there was no room at last for the picture; and the Marshal was obliged to sell the picture to my father and it is now at Houghton.

In London there was time to enjoy one of his many pleasures – listening to music. As governor of the Royal Academy of Music, he mixed with all the famous musicians and operatic singers of the day. No doubt he was present when the fine *Te Deum* composed by Handel was played in London to celebrate the victory at Dettingen in 1743. The *Dettingen Te Deum*, and the Dettingen anthem, *The King Shall Rejoice*, combined stately pomp, martial vigour and melancholy in memory of the fallen. Back in 1717 Handel had composed the *Water Music* to serenade George I at a river party on the Thames, and the following year he was appointed music director of the Royal Academy of Music. For a time he travelled on the Continent recruiting singers for the academy, which opened in April 1720.

A great favourite in London at the time were the castrati. They were male singers castrated to prevent their voices breaking. They had truly beautiful voices, which combined the clarity and purity of a boy soprano with the power of the mature male voice. In Italy poor families keen for their sons to make good money in opera would have their sons castrated at around the age of seven or nine years. The first of the great castrato singers to visit England were Valentini and Nicolini, Senesino and Farinelli. As one would imagine they caused a sensation in London and nights at the opera were looked upon with great pleasure, rather like going to a pop concert today.

Wade's last few months were spent at Southwood House. He had been ailing for some time, and died on the afternoon of Monday March 14th 1748. He was carried to Westminster Abbey, where his body rested in the Jerusalem Chamber before burial in the abbey. In 1750 a large monument was erected on the window ledge in the south aisle of the nave. The sculptor, Roubiliac, said it was his favourite work. It shows a medallion portrait head of George with a figure of Fame pushing away Time, who carries a large scythe. The inscription is similar to that on the gravestone except that the stone gives his date of death as 1747 – that is, by the old calendar.

By 1751 the Julian calendar was eleven days out of step. In that year Chesterfield's Act stated that January 1st should be the first day of the year (previously the year commenced on March 25th).

As news spread of his death, numerous newspapers gave accounts of his life, and expressed sadness at his passing. The obituary in the *Bath Chronicle,* March 21st, ran as follows:

> Monday last in the afternoon died, in London, GEORGE WADE, Esq., Field Marshal of his Majesty's Forces, Lieutenant General of the Ordnance, &c who with great ability and integrity had long served his King and Country in the most eminent Stations – He has for many years represented the City of Bath in Parliament, and was ever ready to serve it on all occasions. Some years ago he was at the sole expense of erecting that beautiful Altar Piece in the Abbey Church: and has, from time to time contributed largely to everything that appeared for the Publick Good. His Private Charities were universal; and by his Death, the City of Bath has lost a Worthy Benefactor.
>
> > He was a Man; Take him for all in all
> > I shall not look upon his like again
> > Taken from Hamlet (Shakespeare).

Henry Fielding published the following obituary in the *Jacobite Journal,* No. 16, Saturday, March 19th 1748:

> 1748 Monday died the Right Hon. George Wade Esq. Field Marshal of his Majesty's Forces, Lieutenant General of the Ordnance, &c. who with great ability and integrity had long served his King and Country in the most eminent Stations. G.E. He was besides, in private life, a Gentleman of the highest Honour, Humanity and Generosity, and hath done more good and benevolent actions than this whole Paper can contain.

The *Scots Magazine* carried the following obituary:

> At London, aged 80, George Wade, Esq. a Field-Marshal, Colonel of the third regiment of dragoon-guards, Lieutenant-General of the Ordnance, member for Bath, and one of the Privy Council. His first commission bore the date December 26th, 1690; whence he rose under four succeeding princes, to the highest military honours. In 1704, he was made Adjutant-General with a brevet of Colonel, by Lord Gallway. Five years after, he was honoured with a letter from the Emperor, and a commission of Major General. In 1724 he was appointed Commander in chief in Scotland; and, while in that station, made the roads thro' the Highlands. He commanded the allied army in the Netherlands in 1744, and the army in Yorkshire and Northumberland in the late rebellion. He died worth about £100,000, £80,000 of which, he has left to his two sons, officers in the army, and the remainder to his two daughters.

The Last Will and Testament of George Wade

In the name of God Amen this is the last will and testament of me George Wade, Field Marshal of his Majesty's forces of the parish of Saint James in the County of Middlesex – imprinis – I give and devise to my two natural sons George Wade now a Captain in my Regiment of Dragoon Guards and John Wade a Captain in General Bland's Regiment of Dragoons, all my lands tenements and herediments whatsoever in the County of Middlesex with the appurtenances thereunto belonging as also all monies that shall remain due to me at the time of my death on mortgages of Lands in any part of Great Britain to hold to the said George and John Wade equally and their assigns forever. They pay out the said estate the annuitys following viz: One hundred pounds a year to Mrs. Sarah Guest during her natural life for the performance of which I have given her a Bond. Sixty pounds a year to my mistress Mrs. Elizabeth Jefferies widow and forty pounds a year to Mrs. Wade, widow of my brother during their natural lives to be paid them half yearly. Item – I give to my natural daughter Mrs Jane Erle the sum of fifteen hundred pounds, I give to William Wade only son to my nephew Major Wade one thousand pounds. I give to my mistress Mrs. Elizabeth Jefferies above mentioned five hundred pounds. I give to my worthy friend the Rt. Hon Sir Paul Methuen one hundred pounds. I give to the Rt. Hon Lord Carpenter one hundred pounds. I give to Ralph Allen Esquire of Prior Park near Bath one hundred pounds. I give to John Mason Esquire and to Emilia Mason his wife one hundred pounds each. I give to John Baines esquire one hundred pounds. I give to Jerome Van Diest, painter, one hundred pounds. I give to Lieutenant John Archer of the train of Artillery now in Flanders two hundred pounds. I give to Peter Warren my valet de Chambre one hundred pounds. I give to Lewis Harbut, my butler, fifty pounds. I give to the rest of my servants who shall be in my service at the time of my death one hundred and fifty pounds to be divided among them in such proportions as my executors shall think fit. I give five hundred pounds to erect a· monument to my memory in Westminster Abbey or the Great Church in Bath.

Item, I give all the residue of my estate not herein given or disposed of to George and John Wade mentioned equally if they are both living at the time of my death or the whole to the survivor of them if one should dye during my life as also all moneys which be due to me from the Government or any other persons at the time of my decease. And also all my books, plate, pictures, furniture, equipage and other effects and I do appoint the said

George and John Wade the sole executors of this my last will and testament and hereby revoke all former and other wills made by me in witness whereof I hereunto set my hand and seal this first day of June in the year 1747 in the twentieth year of his Majesty's reign. *GEORGE WADE* signed and sealed and declared to be the last will and testament of the said *GEORGE WADE* in the presence of those subscribing and witnesses and the Testator, Sarah Ince. A Pinnell and John Gainball.

Memorandum – I have made a deed disposition and assignation of the twelve thousand pounds owed to me from his Grace the Duke of Athol to Captain George, and Captain John Wade or the survivor of them bearing the date the Twenty Fifth day of May 1747. *GEORGE WADE*

Very little is known about Wade's private life. From his will we can determine the existence of some of his children:

Jane Erle never married and in her will in 1759 she mentions her sister Emilia, and her two brothers John and George.

Emilia married the Reverend John Mason and after his death the Reverend John Jebb, chaplain to Dr Herring, Archbishop of Canterbury.

Captain John Wade (1720–99), place of birth unknown, educated at Westminster School, served in Major Bland's army, was wounded at Dettingen in 1743, and later worked for the East India Company. He died in London in 1799.

Captain George Wade (1721–99), place of birth unknown, educated at Westminster School, served in his father's regiment as a lieutenant colonel of the 3rd Regiment of Dragoon Guards. He married Sarah Shortridge at Silverton in Devon and died at the Hotwells, Bristol in 1799.

William Wade (1734–1809), often identified as the illegitimate son or nephew of Field Marshal George Wade, was in fact his great-nephew, grandson of his brother, William Wade, canon of St George's Chapel, Windsor. He was educated at Westminster School and later joined the army, becoming a captain in the 73rd Regiment. On December 16th 1760 he married Katherine, the daughter of the prosperous Henry Gore of Leatherhead, at St Anne's, Soho, Westminster; thereafter his newly acquired wealth allowed him to put his military career behind him. In 1769 William was elected master of ceremonies at Bath. Thomas Gainsborough's magnificent portrait depicts a commanding gentleman – mature, tall and handsome. To a later observer he was quite simply 'the immaculate Captain Wade' (*Bath Chronicle,* September 25th 1777). Wade restored some of the respect for the role of master of ceremonies as established by Nash. He also supervised the building in 1771 of the New Assembly Rooms – at £20,000 the town's most expensive 18th-century structure.

In July 1777 Wade resigned as master of ceremonies after being named in the divorce proceeding of Elizabeth Eustatia, née Basset, and John Hooke Campbell the Lord Lyon of Scotland. Wade's attachment to Elizabeth Campbell outlasted the scandal, and, following the death in 1787 of his first wife, Katherine (with whom he had five children), the couple married on June 30th 1787 at St Marylebone, London. On leaving Bath, he became full-time master of ceremonies at Brighton, where he remained until his death at his residence in New Street on March 16th 1809. Gainsborough's portrait of William Wade hangs in the Octagonal Room of the New Assembly Rooms in Bath.

George Wade remembered his dear friend Ralph Allen; another lifelong friend was Paul Methuen, whose great picture collection can be seen at Corsham Court in Wiltshire. There was also a bequest of £200 to Lieutenant John Archer – who may be a member of the family or another of Wade's sons. Wade never married, and although he mentions his mistress, Elizabeth Jefferies, in his will there is no doubt that during his lifetime he had other mistresses, as was common among the military at the time. There was also a bequest to Jerome van Diest, the artist.

The General's grave in Westminster Abbey is in the centre aisle of the nave and shows his carved coat of arms. In 1750 a monument was erected to him in the south aisle of the cloisters in Westminster Abbey. It is said that Roubiliac, the sculptor, considered this monument his best work, and used to come and weep beneath it because it had been placed too high to be appreciated. The *Scots Magazine* for August of that year describes it thus:

> Over the door leading to the cloisters in Westminster Abbey, an elegant monument, to the memory of Field-Marshal Wade is lately finished by Mr. Roubiliac. From the midst of a very curious pedestal, on which is affixed a medal, arises a Doric column of red marble, crowned with an urn. This column is adorned with a trophy composed of an ensign of honour, arms, &c., which figure

of Time, placed on the left side, appears ready to destroy: but is repulsed by another figure on the right, which represents Fame. Several ornaments enrich the base, on which is the following inscription. The inscription is similar to that on the gravestone except that the stone gives his date of death as 1747 according to the old calendar.

> To the memory
> of
> GEORGE WADE
> Field-Marshal of his Majesty's Forces,
> Lieutenant Gen. of the Ordnance,
> Colonel of his Majesty's third regiment of Dragoon Guards,
> Governor of Fort William, Fort Augustus and Fort George,
> and one of his Majesty's most honourable Privy Council.
> He died 14 Mar. 1748, aged 75.

Ralph Allen erected a statue in honour of his dear friend and patron on a natural terrace above Prior Park, named in Roman times Camalodunum. In John Wood's description of Bath in 1765 can be found the following entry:

> The Comb in which this village is situated, sinking into the North side of Camalodunum, extends almost to the summit of that hill, with natural terraces rising above one another, like the stages between the seats of a *Roman* Theatre; and on one of those terraces Mr. Allen, one of the citizens of Bath, hath lately built himself a Seat, consisting of a Mansion House in the center, two Pavilions, and two Wings of Offices: All these are united by low buildings; and while the chief part of the whole line fronts the body of the City, the rest faces the summit of Mar's Hill. The name *Camalodunum*, comes from *Camalos*, or *Camulus* one of the names of the British God of War, and *Dunum,* a hill.

General Wade is shown in the costume of a Roman soldier. The panels surrounding the base of the statue depict, in high relief, the soldiers working the roads, deer in the woods, a coach and six winding up a new road, and a wayfarer crossing the bridge at Aberfeldy. It is thought that van Diest designed the monument, and the carving was carried out by Mathieson. Allen was probably aware that Wade admired the Romans for their prowess and their knowledge of building military roads; the monument was a fitting tribute to his friend. The statue disappeared many years ago, but the panels can still be seen in the hallway at Prior Park. After

Allen's death the estate was sold, and today it is a Roman Catholic college.

A Poem Dedicated to General Wade
by Aaron Hill (1685–1750)

More just they mind, more generous in the muse!
Albanian born, this English theme to choose:
No partial flattery need thy verse invade,
That in the ear of Scotland sounds a Wade.
When ages hence, his last line's lengthener dies
And his lost dust reveals not where it lies,
Still shall his living greatness guard his name,
And his works lift him to immortal fame.
Then shall astonished armies, marching high,
O'er causewayed mountains that invade the sky,
Climb the raised arch, that sweeps its distant throw,
Cross tumbling floods, which roads unheard below,
Gaze, from the cliff's cut edge, through midway air,
And, trembling, wonder at their safety there!
Pierce fenny deep with firm unsinking tread,
And o'er drained deserts wholesome empire spread.
While charged, the soldier dwells on wonders past,
Some chief, more knowing and more touched – at last,
Shall, pointing to the attentive file, explain,
How, many a century since – in George's reign,
Wade's working soul, that graced his prince's throne,
Built these vast monuments – and spared his own.

In Thema
by D. McBane

When therefore, he is dead and gone,
Let this be writ upon his stone:
He never liked the narrow road,
But ran the King's highway to God.

His fame, great as it was in his day, flickers faintly now; from extinction it will be saved by the couplet credited to William Caulfield, which so amused Sir Walter Scott:

> Had you seen these roads before they were made,
> You would lift up your hands and bless General Wade.

In October 1924 Field Marshal Lord Methuen unveiled a mural tablet which had been placed by the Bath Tablet Committee on the house in the Abbey Church Yard for many years occupied by Field Marshal Wade.

The portrait of General Wade was shown in an exhibition by Colnaghi in 1986.

The General is shown full-length and seated in a gilt rococo armchair, wearing a blue coat and breeches and a gold-trimmed waistcoat. Evidence of his military profession is provided by a dramatic battle scene of a charging cavalry in the right of the background, and by the steel breastplate on the floor to the left of his chair. He points with his right hand to an architectural design for a Palladian-style country house.

This portrait by Andrea Soldi (Florence c.1703–London 1771) points to *General* Wade as the sitter, as does that by van Diest in the National Portrait Gallery, or the bust relief by Roubiliac in Westminster Abbey. Whereas Diest's portrait (c.1731) presents Wade as a still-vigorous campaigning soldier, by contrast the picture shows him here in retirement, seated, his breastplate put aside, and his mind turned to gentler pastimes.

Wade was a cultivated man, interested in music, painting and, especially, architecture. His London home in Old Burlington Street was designed for him in 1723 by Lord Burlington, and was based directly on an elevational design by Palladio (illustrated in *Vitruvius Britannicus*, iii, plate 10). The architectural drawing in the Soldi portrait is for an unidentified country house on the Palladian model with a central block connected to flanking pavilions by straight and quadrant link walls and the main rooms on the *piano nobile*.

Chronology

1673	Born Kilvally, Westmeath, Ireland, or Tangiers.
1690	Entered the Army in London, December 26th, in the Earl of Bath's Regiment – Ensign Captain Richard Trevanion's Company, 10th Foot.
1691	With the regiment in the Channel Islands.
1692/3	At the Battle of Steenkerke; promoted to lieutenant.
1694	Promoted to captain lieutenant.
1695	Appointed captain of the grenadier company.
1702	In France with Sir Bevil Grenville (later Lord Bath); in Flanders; served at the sieges of Kaiserwerth, Venloo and Roermond; in action with the French near Nijmegen; At the siege of Liège.
1703	Promoted to major in August at the siege and capture of Huy. Appointed lieutenant colonel.
1704	Volunteered for service in Portugal; staff appointment as adjutant general and brevet colonel in August.
1705	In spring at the siege of Valencia d'Alcantara; after the death of Robert Duncannon, colonelcy of the regiment was bestowed on Wade.
1706	Wounded at the siege of Alcantara; continued to serve on Galway's staff; continued on to Madrid in June.
1707	Wade earned fresh laurels at the fatal Battle of Almanza, April 25th, commanding as brigadier general, then aged thirty-four.
1707/8	Second in command to General James Stanhope, expedition to Minorca, sailing from Barcelona in September.
1710	Remained in Spain and fought at the Battle of Saragossa.
1714	Returned home; promoted major general of the forces in Ireland – a post he did not accept, as he was returned as the MP for Hindon, Wiltshire.

1715	Sent to Bath and Bristol to quell the Jacobite Rebellion, in command of two regiments,
1717	George I bestowed the colonelcy of the 3rd Dragoon Guards on Wade.
1719	Appointed second in command on an expedition to Vigo.
1722	Now forty-nine years old, elected MP for Bath until his death in 1748.
1725	Sent to Scotland to build the roads to the Highlands.
1727	Promoted to lieutenant general.
1732	George II bestowed a sinecure on Wade: the governorship of Berwick and Holy Island.
1733	George II bestowed on Wade the governorship of Fort William, Fort Augustus and Fort George.
1742	Appointed privy councillor and Lieutenant General of the Ordnance.
1743	Promoted to field marshal; made commander-in-chief of the British forces in Flanders.
1744	Wade, now seventy-one years old and in failing health, returned from Flanders.
1745	George II made Wade commander-in-chief of North Britain; sent to turn back Charles Edward Stuart; in December his health broke down and he handed command to the Duke of Cumberland.
1748	Died at home in Southwood Lane, London, on March 3rd; buried in Westminster Abbey; left a fortune of £100,000.

Bibliography

Annals of Bristol in the 18th Century
Atton, Henry, and Holland, Henry H., *The King's Customs*, 1908
Barbeau, A., *Life and Letters at Bath in the 18th Century*
The Barwicker, magazine No. 49, Barwick-in-Elmet Historical Society
Bath Abbey, General Wade's coat of arms, copyright of A. J. Morley
Bath and County Graphic
Boyce, Benjamin, *The Benevolent Man: A Life of Ralph Allen of Bath*
Bryant, Arthur, *Samuel Pepys: The Saviour of the Navy*
Burt, Edmund, *Burt's Letter from a Gentleman in the North of Scotland*, 1754
Chesterfield, Lord, *Letters of Lord Chesterfield*, 1774
Chevening Estate letters from George Wade to Stanhope
Cottrell, Leonard, *Seeing Roman Britain*
Eveleigh, *The Life of Beau Nash*, New York, 1908
Fielding, Henry, *The Jacobite's Journal*
Gardiner, S. R., *History of England*
Gentleman's Magazine, 1731–50
House of Commons Journal, Vol. XXXI (1731), pp. 275–9
Robertson, Barrie, *Jacobite Activities in and around Inverness, 1688–1746*
Jones, Charles C., *Historical Sketch of Tomo-Chi-Chi*, 1868
Kay, F. George, *Royal Mail*
Lair, Jules (ed), *Louise De La Valliere and the Early Life of Louis XIV*
Lockyer, Roger, *Tudor and Stuart Britain, 1471–1714*
McCleod, Donald, *Memoirs of the Life and Gallant Exploits of the Old Highlander*

McIntyre, Alastair (alastair@electricscotland.com), *General Wade's Report to King George* (1724/5)
Meehan, J. F., *More Famous Houses of Bath & District*
Murray, C. de B., *Forbes of Culloden*
The Dictionary of National Biography
The National Archives of Scotland, GD158/2897
The *Daily Courant*, London
The *Bath Journal*, 1744–8
Norton, Rictor 'Tumult in Glasow' – early 18th-century newspaper reports
Peach, R. E., *The Life and Times of Ralph Allen*
Peach, R. E., *Historic Houses in Bath*, 1883
Peach, R. E., *Street-Lore of Bath*
Pooll, A. H. Batten, *A West Country Potpourri*
Publications of the Thoresby Society, Vol. XLVI, 1957
Salmond, J. B., *Wade in Scotland*, 1934
Special Libraries and Archives, The Reading Room, King's College, Aberdeen
Raybould, Major J. L., (webmaster@norfolkbc.fsnet.co.uk)
Sitwell, Edith,
Stevenson, Sandy, 'Tour Scotland' home page (sandystevenson@ thefreesite.com)
Taunton Journal
Thomson, George Malcolm, *The First Churchill,* New York, 1980
Warrand, Duncan, *More Culloden Papers*, Vol. 3, 1725–45
Wood, John, *A Description of Bath*, 1765
Wright, Thomas, *England under the House of Hanover*